MAZ STAR: A MASSIVE INCONVENIENCE

A COMEDY SCI-FI STORY

MAZ STAR ADVENTURES
BOOK 1

KATIE J LEE

MIRAMUS BOOKS

Copyright © 2024 by Katie J Lee

All rights reserved.

No part of this book may be reproduced in any form or by any electronic or mechanical means, including information storage and retrieval systems, without written permission from the author, except for the use of brief quotations in a book review.

Cover art by Alex Milway.

A NOTE FOR AMERICAN READERS

This book is written in UK English. For you, that will mean a lot of extra vowels and some weird spellings, for which I apologise (*apologize*). You might notice some different past participles, slang you don't recognise and some stray Ls scattered about the place. In many cases, there will be an S where you would prefer a Z.

I hope you can forgive this. If in doubt, please assume it's some weird British thing.

For Al

CHAPTER 1
A MASSIVE INCONVENIENCE

WHEN MAZ STAR was abducted by aliens, she'd been on her way back from the Tesco Metro.

As the beam of light lifted her into the sky, as she tried and failed to free herself from its vice-like grip, there was a small part of her brain thinking about the bag of cold stuff that lay abandoned on the pavement.

That ice cream will never make the freezer now, it thought.

Maz would ask someone to grab the bag, but the beam of light had her gripped so fully that it was nearly impossible to open her mouth. Floating towards the gaping maw of the spaceship, seeing the round hatch above, red light bouncing off the edges of the spacecraft's rim, her brain sent another thought.

You forgot Jim's haemorrhoid cream.

It was a relief in a way – to finally remember – even if it was too late now. It had been bothering her all the way around the shop, niggling at the back of her mind; *what had she forgotten?*

Jim had been going on about his sore bum for days,

but then Maz had got distracted by a weird old Scottish woman and a three-for-two dump bin of early Christmas stocking fillers for the kids, and, in the grips of a bargain-bin-based fervour, Jim's piles had fallen clean out of her mind.

Desperate to remember what she was missing, Maz had wandered the shop, casting about in the hope she'd spot whatever it was on the shelves. But, she now realised, she wasn't very likely to see haemorrhoid cream on the crisps aisle.

A part of her brain – the part that seemed to be very good at ignoring the ongoing alien abduction – chuckled to itself.

You big prannet, Marion, it thought.

It wasn't that the alien abduction was unstressful. It most definitely *was* stressful.

In fact, Maz was fairly confident she had soiled herself when the ray of light first started lifting her up (although she couldn't be certain if it was a number one or a number two). It was just that alien abduction was so… unlikely.

Plus, if this was an abduction, it seemed so laughably *rubbish*. As though whoever had organised it had done so with a budget that would break even the most resourceful BBC art department. She may be rising up towards an alien vessel, but the speed was slow enough to make a snail blush. In the last minute, she estimated she had gone up no more than a few centimetres.

This couldn't be the norm, could it? This wasn't a standard abduction? Because if it was, it was a miracle no one had captured the event on film. This sort of thing should be all over the internet. She felt a moment of shame for her fellow man, unable to gather evidence of even this sorry excuse for a close encounter.

If this is an abduction, she thought, it is the most inept one imaginable.

And it was so retro.

It was like the sort of alien abduction you would expect to find in a news report from the 1950s – all flying saucers and gravity beams. She couldn't help suspecting it was all a big wind-up.

She was half-expecting one of her old mates from school to pop their head out from the base of the spacecraft and shout, "Ha! Had you going there, Maz! You should see your face!"

Of course, if that happened, Maz would do her best to pretend to be a good sport, joining in with the laughter, hoping that whatever mess she'd created in her underpants wasn't showing through the crotch seam of her jeans.

So yes, it was definitely stressful, and it was most certainly a massive inconvenience, but on reflection, the abduction probably still only counted as the third most unpleasant thing to have happened to her that day.

At least the light beam was filling her with a mild sense of euphoria. She could almost believe she was being raised up to heaven. And so weightless! It was like being on a bouncy castle, but with just the nice up in the air bit and none of the landing on a pile of bony seven-year-olds bit.

Whichever way you cut it, alien abduction was preferable to the cervical smear test she had finally dragged herself to earlier this morning.

"This may hurt a little," said the nurse, just as Maz fainted.

And it was a positive treat compared to the hour she had endured in the soft play centre at the local fitness centre with her boyfriend Jim's kids.

She had a sudden dark thought: "Oh god, what if they impregnate me?"

The last thing Maz wanted was alien progeny to raise. At the soft player earlier, Inca had found a poo in the ball pit and had brought it over to Maz as a kind of gift. If "gift" could be defined as: *something you give to someone you don't like with the sole intent of making them wish they were dead.*

Because Inca really did wish Maz were dead.

So did Inca's twin, Aztec, for that matter.

They were a pair of poorly named psychopathic preschoolers whose chief desire was to see their dad's girlfriend trip and fall into a food processor. Or break her neck on the toys they left on the stairs when they knew she was carrying the laundry basket down.

No. The twins were bad enough without some flesh-eating, multi-armed monster wanting a portion of chicken nuggets too. Although, there was a chance her alien child wouldn't want the nuggets and might be induced to eat the twins, which would certainly cut down on food bills.

"Ngh," Maz said.

This felt like a big moment. She could make a "Ngh" sound, and while that fell short of her usual vocabulary, it was at least *something.* Maz she took in her options. She couldn't speak, but she could make the, "Ngh," noise, which she now deployed liberally (to little or no effect). She couldn't move, but she could swivel her eyes to see if anyone was gawping up. She looked down, expecting to see a horde of kids from the estate pointing their phones at her, but the housing estate appeared to be empty.

Where were the estate's moped gangs when you needed them? Usually, there were at least four youths out by the bins smoking synthetic weed and sexting. And where was Mrs Morrison poking her head around her net curtains and calling the police on those sexting youths?

It was typical. She felt quite grumpy about the whole thing.

Perhaps I'm low on glucose, she thought.

Maybe that was why she was feeling so testy. Or maybe it was just that she was slowly being sucked up into the sky by an alien spacecraft and, despite it being reasonably early on a Thursday night, no one seemed to be out and about.

Maz supposed she would have to resign herself to her fate. Maybe being a human lab rat for some almond-eyed Little Grey Man wouldn't be so bad. Maybe he'd let her raise her little grey alien babies in peace.

I hope I won't have to lay an egg, or have the baby rip through my stomach, she thought. But even accounting for alien probes and impregnation, it was still preferable to taking the twins to the soft play.

The part of her brain that had previously been thinking about bags of peas and bum ointments had wandered off onto other matters, and – having rummaged around in her recent thoughts about soft plays and egg laying and local youths with mobile phones – it was now attempting to get her attention with a fairly urgent message:

Phones!

Why hadn't she thought of it sooner? Her phone was right there, still grasped in her hand. If she could make a call, perhaps she could raise the alarm. *She could summon help.*

"Ha!" she said triumphantly and then she said it again to celebrate having managed to squeeze a new sound out.

Now then. Who to call?

The fire brigade was probably the most sensible option. They could bring one of their tall ladders and try to reach her before the spaceship hoovered her up into the unknown. They came out for cats, why not for her?

But what would she say?

"Hi there, I'm being sucked into a spaceship. Could you please send assistance?"

She imagined the whole awkward conversation and concluded she would rather be taken aboard an alien spacecraft and have probes inserted than subject herself to the shame of being laughed at by an emergency services operator.

Besides, time was of the essence. Even if she could convince the fire brigade to come, there was a chance the abduction would be over before they arrived.

She thought of her best friend Belinda, who lived just round the corner. Belinda's husband Geoff ran a window and gutter cleaning business. Maybe Geoff could rush out with his long gutter vacuum and try to nudge her out of the sky? Maz was willing to concede that becoming subject to the laws of gravity again after floating fourteen feet in the air might not be the best plan, but on balance, she would trade a broken limb or two for an unprobed existence.

With painstaking effort, she tried to lift her phone up to dial Belinda. She made it to about three inches from her thigh before her hand snapped back to her side. It was no good. She couldn't lift it: the force of the beam of light was too great. Voice dial was the next option. She just needed to regain control of her vocal cords and make it past, "Ngh." Eventually, after a few "Ngh"s and a couple of "Ooh"s and at least one "Hmf"s, she succeeded in forcing out a juddery phrase.

"Oh-hay oogle," she gurgled. "Hall Vlinda."

The phone lay silent as a surly teenager ignoring a request to load the dishwasher. This did not surprise her. The phone had a habit of beeping cheerfully into life to ask her what she wanted any time she was mutely wandering the house, but if she actually attempted a direct command, it gave the digital equivalent of a shrug and a, "Sorry, I didn't catch that," and went back to ignoring her.

She tried again, really giving the consonants her all, and, finally, the phone beeped to let her know it was listening.

"Hall Elinda," said Maz.

"OK, playing 'I Can't Go For That (No Can Do)' by Hall & Oates," replied her phone.

"No!" cried Maz as the drum beat kicked out of her speaker. "Call," Maz managed, "Be-lin-da."

"OK," said the phone. "Turning off Front Light."

"Ngh," said Maz, reverting to her tried and tested phrase.

Hall & Oates were blaring out and, in the near distance, she could see her porch light had gone dim, but Belinda remained uncalled. She gathered all her grit and determination, told her vocal cords to get a grip and tried one more time.

"CALL BELINDA."

"OK. Calling Belinda," said her phone, as though the last obdurate minute hadn't happened.

Maz experienced the dual sensations of triumph and frustration: triumph that she had finally convinced her phone to obey her and frustration that it had taken so long to capitulate.

She managed to tap the speaker button just as the call connected.

"How spooky! I was just thinking about you," said a voice. "You must be psychic."

"Vlinda!" croaked Maz as loudly as she could in the direction of her hand. All around her, the light from the spaceship was growing more intense.

"I've had a hell of a day," piped Belinda's voice through the speaker. "I was late into the shop, and then some idiot clipped my rear bumper, so then I was late to the nursery pick up. Didn't even leave a note, miserable sod, so now I'll have to claim that on the insurance, and that'll be the third time this year already."

"Velinda."

"My premiums are going to go through the roof, and all because some inconsiderate so-and-so doesn't know how to park properly. And then Lloyd asked me to put the red stickers on the out-of-date items. Who does he think I am? The new kid? Honestly, I'm going to have to say something or I'll go mad. I can't be doing with being treated like that any–"

"Velinda! Isten!"

"Are you alright? You sound terrible. You haven't got this cold that's been doing the rounds, have you?

Because if you have, you can stay away until you're better, thank you very much. I can't be doing with getting ill again. I'm only just over the last one. I'm pretty sure you gave me that an' all. And bloody Geoff doesn't lift a finger to help when I'm out of action."

"Gff!" said Maz. "Get Geoff."

"I know, I know. I should make him do more. It's not like I don't have a job, but it's just easier to do it yourself, isn't it?"

"Hel–" began Maz.

"Put that down," yelled Belinda. "Not in mummy's eyes! I'm sorry Maz, I've got to go. I need to murder the threen-ager."

"Geoff," gasped Maz in a last desperate bid to get her friend's attention.

Belinda hung up.

Well, thought Maz, that went as well as I should have expected.

There would be no point in trying to phone her back. If experience was anything to go by, Belinda would be at war with her toddler for the next twenty minutes at least. Maz felt a surge of irritation.

Bloody Belinda.

"Ngh," she said.

Something had changed.

Abruptly, she stopped thinking about Belinda's shortcomings as a friend, and started thinking about how she could feel all the atoms in her brain wobbling.

The sensation travelled down her spine until every inch of her was vibrating. It was pleasurable to begin with, like having a massage everywhere all at once, but soon the feeling went from "gentle massage" to "pins and needles" to "a million small electric shocks". It was like she was epilating her entire body from head to toe, including all the private areas; every hair being plucked one by one. It made her want to scratch and shout.

Maz gave an involuntary shudder – or as much of one as she could with her whole body rendered immobile. And in that moment all the disparate bits of her mind – including the bit that had been wandering aimlessly – seemed to catch up with reality.

She was being abducted by aliens.

No one was going to save her.

Maz hadn't even got her passport and now she was heading for a UFO that could be taking her to live as a slave or a living specimen or something you go and peer at in the zoo. Maybe she'd be farmed for meat or eggs, or she'd be kept as a pet. Maybe they'd make her perform in a circus or stick her in a gold bikini and sit her next to a giant slug. Who knew?

And there were no witnesses. No one would know where she had gone or why she was missing. It wasn't like those tech bros in Silicon Valley were going to mount a search party in the upper atmosphere. She was stranded. Alone.

She thought of all the things she hadn't done in her life – and all those things she *had* done and wished she hadn't. The plans she'd had! She was going to buy an old bus and travel around the country. She was going to visit Venice and flirt with a gondolier. She was going to try to learn to like celery. But now all her dreams were squashed under the weight of a light beam that seemed made entirely from stinging nettles.

The thrumming in her body increased until she wasn't sure if she was even breathing anymore. And along with the pain came a new intensity to the vibrations, increasing until every bit of flesh quivered like jelly on a tumble dryer.

It was now, Maz was willing to concede, almost as bad as the cervical smear test.

Then it got worse.

She had been, she admitted, a little bit disparaging about the ineptness of the abduction. So slow! So laboured! But now things were starting to speed up, the beam lifting her towards the mouth of the ship ever more rapidly, she was ready to admit she had been ungrateful. Turned out she was less impatient to get this over with than she'd realised. Turned out, she'd trade speeding towards a small hole for spending the rest of her life hovering in suspended animation a few metres above some wheelie bins on the Trenchmire Estate in Telford. Turned out, she wasn't ready to die just yet.

Thanks to the rapidly increasing acceleration, she was nearing the top of the beam now. Pressed on all sides, Maz just about managed to glance up to see the hole she would be travelling through.

There was none.

Where the hole should be was what looked like a… well, there was no other way to describe it… Yes, it was definitely a sphincter. Rubbery-looking and ridged with dark flanges that seemed to meet in the centre of the circle.

She was heading at speed for a hole that didn't exist.

What would happen when she reached that dark puckered ring? Finally, after all those minutes of floating surprisingly calmly in space, Maz Star began to panic.

When your life flashes before your eyes, it's meant to be your brain sorting through memories in the hope of finding a solution to imminent death. Why wasn't her subconscious helping out here? That's what was supposed to happen, wasn't it?

But Maz's subconscious had nothing for her. The bit that had been thinking about frozen peas and thrown her the phone call suggestion offered up nothing useful at all. Apparently, her brain had no precedent for what was currently happening. No bright idea flashed before her eyes as she rose high enough to touch the base of the spaceship. No great plan came to her as her cheek began to press into the rectum of the machine. No lightbulb moment occurred as her face entered the puckered lips and the flanges began slowly devouring her.

Maz had just enough time to reflect ruefully on how much of her day had been about bums before she passed out.

CHAPTER 2
SPACE GARAGE

I WHO AM? Thought the human female.

…

Am I who?

…

Gradually, as if trying to manually realign her synapses, the human female slowly gathered her thoughts.

She lay quite still a moment, waiting for her mind to reboot. Her eyes were closed, but only because she hadn't yet remembered that she owned eyes.

She could hear a soft thrumming and feel a gentle vibration along her back – or she would have if she hadn't lost the ability to identify any of her senses or body parts.

Who am I?

From nowhere, a memory floated past her eyelids. She was staring up from a crib at a couple of doting parents. She shook her head: that had never happened.

A new memory: she had grown up in care. That was

more like it. That was a real memory. There were no doting parents.

Bit by bit, the human female's identity reformed. She was Marion – Maz – Star, a disappointed woman who lived on the Trenchmire Estate in Telford.

"Oh well," she said.

Everything felt hazy and yet somehow incredibly simple, as though each thought was forming an orderly queue, patiently waiting for its turn to be thought. It was the most peaceful Maz had ever been.

The next thought reached the front of the queue. Despite her big dreams of becoming a rock star or a museum curator, she was actually a part-time dental nurse. The highlight of her day was popping into the Tesco Metro for some bits.

A thought jumped the queue.

She had left the shopping out.

Then another.

She had forgotten Jim's arse cream.

Something big bubbled to the surface.

She had been abducted by aliens.

In response to that, her mouth came back online. A shout arrived, but failed to form into anything beyond: "Gaaaargh."

Aliens!

She had been abducted by aliens, like… Her rebooting brain failed to find someone famous for being abducted by aliens. There was no one because being abducted by aliens wasn't a thing.

Elvis.

He'd been abducted by aliens hadn't he? Or did he work in a chip shop?

I have to get out of here, she realised.
She remembered she owned eyes. She opened them.
She was in a spaceship.
She sat up.

"I'm in a spaceship," she said out loud, her brain making connection with her tongue.

At least, she assumed it was a spaceship. Her eyes joined the senses gang next and she began to take in her surroundings.

The room had all the hallmarks of a garage, complete with bare floor, metal shelving units, and boxfuls of stuff. All around were piles of what she could only think of as crap.

One pile appeared to be the alien equivalent of doilies, placemats, hats and blankets. There were stacks of things that looked like magazines, books and pamphlets – and those free posters you get by sending a stamped addressed envelope in to the alien equivalent of the BBC. There were shelves stuffed with boxes and a maze of crates and large plastic tubs crammed full with knick-knacks and thingamabobs. A tall unit held what felt to Maz like collection of obsolete media formats, probably the alien version of cassette tapes or VHS. Bunches of once-colourful dried flowers collected dust in broken vases or stuffed into pots and cups.

Nothing was completely recognisable, and yet everything was familiar. Except, that is, for one thing.

The thing she was sitting on.

Were they *towels*?

Maz frowned. Perhaps it was a pile of bed linen. If so, sheets were gossamer thin in space. Perhaps it was cobwebs or layers of pale spun sugar. She shuffled backwards, her legs re-engaging enough to scooch her along the floor away from them. A gust of air rippled through a vent on the wall and the... whatever it was... rippled, too.

Maz swallowed, thinking about the time she'd found a grass snake skin in the recreation ground behind her house.

Was that what this was? A pile of... skin?

Because it really did look like snake skin. Like giant snake skins. In fact, she was sure she could see the ghostly outline of a large lizard-like creature lying on the top of the pile.

And then she was sure.

The aliens were keeping the skins of their enemies in the hold of their spaceship!

"This is not good," she said out loud, her voice echoing round the chamber.

She shuffled backwards – still unable to stand, but desperate to get more distance from the skin stack – and found herself hitting a pile of something that resounded with a loud clatter.

"Shh," she told herself, like a drunk entering a house at 2am. She didn't want to bring the aliens running, or lolloping, or slithering – or whatever god forsaken method of propulsion they used.

She closed her eyes and tried to slow her breathing. *Calm.* She exhaled quietly. *Breathe.* She inhaled. *Scream.*

She opened her eyes. Meditation was way past helping her now. Attempting to cling to sanity was a fruitless exercise. She decided, instead, to give into the full blown nervous breakdown that was keen to take hold. That actually seemed like the more sensible option at this juncture. No point trying to be rational when all around you lay evidence that you were either already well over the cliff of insanity or teetering very close to the edge.

But then something caught her eye, surprising her back towards the land of the rational.

She tilted her head. It was a stack of crockery. And not just any crockery. She reached out and lifted a plate off the top. Princess Diana and Prince Charles stared back. Diana in a blue jacket, lips pressed together in a bloodless hyphen of disappointment; Charles standing behind, grasping her shoulder like the arresting officer in a crime drama.

Below was another painted plate. A couple stared off into the distance, the man smiling with a blaze of white teeth, the woman more dreamy, her red hair held aloft by what could only be weapons-grade hairspray. They resembled a court artist's illustration of a cult leader and his Primary Wife. It took Maz a moment to realise who it was.

Sarah Ferguson and Prince Andrew.

OK, thought Maz, these aliens are seriously deranged.

She began casting about for an exit. There must be one, surely? Even aliens needed health and safety laws, didn't they? She just needed to find the special door and locate some kind of space parachute or escape pod. Then she could flee this nightmare and get back to her life with Jim and the twins on the Trenchmire estate in Telford.

There! Behind a pile of boxes, Maz spotted what had to be a door. It looked pretty easy to open. Like a normal garage door, in fact. And it didn't feel like the ship was moving, either…

A horrible suspicion presented itself.

She had been right all along; it was a wind-up. It had to be. She was being filmed for a Saturday night TV show and was currently the laughingstock of middle-aged Britain. Two gurning light entertainers were presumably on the other side of the door, giving themselves little gleeful cuddles and cackling.

"I'd better win a holiday for this," she said to the air.

Awkwardly, she clambered to her feet and went over to the door. She tried to twist the handle. *Locked*. She gave it a couple of energetic wiggles. It rattled a little but refused to budge.

She moved towards a panel next to it. Now, *this* looked far more like a spaceship door. Apart from the cotton doily pinned to it, that is. The doily took away from the overall effect in Maz's view. In fact, it was so out of place, it made her question her Saturday night TV show theory.

But that wasn't important right now.

She could work out the whys and wherefores later. For now, she just needed to get away from the piles of skin and the commemorative plates and, more importantly, the aliens who collected them.

She searched around the panel for a hidden knob. Perhaps there was a magic button somewhere which opened the door with a swoosh of sci-fi efficiency. Nothing. Next, she tried walking boldly towards it ("boldly" feeling like an important part of the space experience), thinking it might be automatic like a supermarket entrance.

"Ow!"

She rubbed her nose as she banged into the still very much shut door.

The impact detached the doily, which fell away from the panel and fluttered quietly to the floor. Maz stared. The doily had been covering a circular window. A window that apparently held the vast emptiness of space. Except it wasn't empty.

"Oh," said Maz in a monumental moment of realisation.

The stars were almost blinding. A billion trillion pinpricks of light glimmered against a backdrop of deepest black and hazy blue. Galaxies swirled like a stirred psychedelic cappuccino. Even in the depths of the Shropshire countryside, far away from the light pollution of Telford, you didn't get stars like this. Maz felt both lightheaded with fear and euphoric with excitement at the same time.

This was really something.

"It's space," Maz said. "It's actual freaking space."

"What were you expecting, dearie?" chirruped a high voice.

Maz twisted around.

"Who said that?"

"It's just me, dearie," said the voice.

Was that a Scottish accent? It sounded like a bad Scottish accent. Maz crouched into what she imagined might be a fighting stance, but more closely resembled someone attempting to hover over the seat in a public toilet, and began frantically searching for the source of the noise.

The voice made an alarmed sound. "Please don't damage that," it said.

Maz realised she was still holding the Charles and

Diana plate. She lifted it up and wielded it like a knife at her unseen kidnapper.

"I don't know who you are, but you should know, I've been in a LOT of fights, and you do not want to mess with me."

What she didn't say was that by "fights" she meant the sort of altercation that involves hair pulling and eye gouging and quite a bit of screeching. Not the sort that involves roundhouse kicks and back flips. Her fighting style had been learned on the mean streets of Telford on a Friday night. There wasn't much call for martial arts when you were lunging for Tracey Bellingfield's hoop earrings after she'd called you a slag.

"There's no need for that, dear," chuckled the voice. "We're not going to hurt you."

"That's exactly what a psychopath would say," replied Maz, who was nevertheless beginning to relax her fists.

There was no denying that the woman – if she was a woman – sounded remarkably like Mrs Doubtfire. And who could be afraid of Mrs Doubtfire? She wasn't just Robin Williams, she was Robin Williams with giant breasts and something that Hollywood considered a Scottish accent.

"Och, don't be silly. You're our guest! Do pop the plate down, though, won't you?"

"Guest? Tell me, do you usually suck your guests up into an alien spacecraft and then shut them in your garage?"

Maz regretted her sarcasm immediately. What happened if this old lady was a homicidal maniac? All she had done was antagonise her. She'd be trapped in here forever.

Her thoughts returned to the pile of skin. Perhaps that's what it was – the desiccated corpses of their past abductees, kept as trophies for this hoarding maniac to gloat over.

The voice, however, chuckled once more.

"Oh, yes. I'm sorry about that, hen. There really was no other way of going about it. I did try to invite you along, but you kept ignoring me."

"What do you mean?" said Maz, stepping closer to the source of the voice in an attempt to locate it.

"In the supermarket earlier. I asked you twice if you'd like to visit outer space with me, but you just smiled and nodded and then walked away."

"That…" began Maz, before realising she didn't know how to continue. "… That was you?" she managed finally.

"Yes, dear."

The voice was emanating from an ancient-looking speaker grille in the corner of the room, half hidden behind what Maz suspected might be the alien version of wicker baskets. She approached it as though expecting to find the owner of the voice hiding inside the box – a tiny Scottish alien – but it was just a normal speaker.

"How was I to know you were being serious?" Maz said. "I thought you were a mad old lady."

She thought back to the woman in the supermarket. She hadn't seen her face, just a dark shadow under the hood of an enormous coat.

"Well, that's true."

The second voice made Maz jump, but only from the surprise of hearing someone else speaking. There was nothing to fear in the voice itself. It was a textbook harmless old man voice: querulous, high and wavering.

In fact, it was so on the nose, Maz began to suspect that the voices were actually simulations. Perhaps they had typed in "safe-sounding old people voices" into their version of Google and were simply trying to reassure her that they weren't about to peel her skin from her body and pop her on a barbecue.

"Why don't you come up to the front and meet us properly," said the male voice.

Maz shook her head and shifted on her feet, as though bracing for the speaker to fly across the room and attack her. "No, thank you."

"We don't bite," said the male voice. "I promise."

There followed a gasping sound, which Maz dearly hoped was the right kind of laughter and not the sound of a serial killer amusing himself.

"Ignore him," said the female. "Come up and we'll have a natter, dearie. I've been so eager to meet you."

Maz pictured Robin Williams smiling that lovely lipless smile of his, eyes crinkling with a soft kindness, and she found herself nodding.

"OK," she said casually.

"Wonderful," cooed the voice. "Just follow the ramp up and it's the first door on the right."

"Right-o," said Maz. "I'm coming."

She was not coming. She had no plans to walk up that ramp and go and meet two skin-hoarding aliens who called her dearie. If ever there were red flags, this was them. And the last time she had ignored red flags she had ended up in a relationship with a man who thought foreplay was the highest ply toilet paper posh people bought.

She grabbed a stack of alien magazines – ignoring the unsettlingly moist feeling of the top copy – and placed them carefully in front of the speaker. She had no idea where the camera was, but she was sincerely hoping it was an all-in-one unit. She approached it carefully, creeping as quietly as she could so the aliens wouldn't suspect what she was up to.

"Up the ramp, you say?" she called.

"That's right, luvvie, you can't miss it."

"I'll be right with you. Just, you know, getting my legs working again after that entrance. It's not every day you get sucked up into the rear end of a giant metal box."

She was at the walls now, searching for a latch or doorknob, or anything that might get her out of this place.

"Right behind you, dear," said the voice. "And do pop that plate down before you come, won't you?"

"Why?" said Maz.

"Because it's Roydrick's favourite," said the voice. "He loves Diana, don't you Roy?"

"That I do," agreed the male voice.

"Why me?" said Maz. "Why did you abduct me?"

But the speaker was silent. Perhaps the elderly abductors were preparing their skin peeling death pit and didn't have time for any more chat.

"Pop the plate down and I'll tell you," came the female voice at last.

Maz hesitated. It felt like her only leverage and she was reluctant to give it up. Diana stared out at her, a mute cry for help from one trapped woman to another.

She put the plate down.

"Why did you abduct me," she asked again.

"Oh, that's easy," chirped the female.

"Because you are the Queen of Dross and we need you."

Maz was silent for a moment, waiting for the punchline. No punchline came.

"Ha!" she said, hoping to shame them into admitting the ridiculousness of their claim.

The aliens did not reply.

What a load of old nonsense.

Queen of Dross?

It sounded like the world's worst drag act.

Maz folded her arms. "If you're going to come up with a lie, I'd at least put more effort in."

She peered out at the vastness of space and took stock. The way she saw it, she had two choices: go and meet the skin-peeling aliens, or keep trying to find a way to open the main door so she could fling herself out and freeze like a giant frozen turkey.

Maybe she had special royal powers like Princess Leia. Maybe if she believed hard enough, she could use the Force to keep herself alive as she floated out into the endless vacuum.

Or maybe she would be miraculously scooped up by a band of friendly pirates, happy to listen to her mixtape for the next thirty years and willing to treat her like a cheeky young member of the family.

Except she didn't have a mixtape on her and she was currently neither cheeky, nor all that young. Or at least, she didn't feel it. She had to face it, the odds of her being adopted by adorable comedy space pirates was slim to zero. No, there was nothing else for it.

She attempted to use the Force.

That went as well as she expected.

"Nope," she said.

She was not going to ride the milky way out of here. No rainbow bridge would take her to a planet of hunky gods. No police box would scoop her up and deposit her in a Welsh quarry. She was stuck.

"Looks like it's time to meet the homicidal anal probers," she said.

CHAPTER 3
PROBING QUESTIONS

MAZ WAS STANDING in an old Ford Cortina.

Not that she had ever been inside an old Ford Cortina, but this was what she imagined it would be like. Granted, the cockpit was slightly bigger than a real car, but not by much.

If she had to guess, she'd say the room was only a few metres wide. If she put her arms out, she could almost touch the sides in both directions. She could just about stand, but her head was touching the carpet, which ran from floor to ceiling.

Classy, she thought, staring at the man-made shagpile.

She had expected a sleek, streamlined modern aesthetic (who knew why after she had seen the garage), but this just shouted seventies suburbia.

Not that Maz had the chance to pay too much attention to her surroundings; she had bigger fish to fry. Because, crammed into two driving seats were a pair of what looked to Maz very much like lizards – if lizards walked on two legs, came up to your breasts, and drove carpeted space vehicles.

They were craning their necks around, trying to get a better view of her.

"Welcome, Queen!" said the smaller lizard in a colourful gilet, her querulous, almost-Scottish voice rising high. "I am Vedna Pollup from Sargantana and you are aboard the leisure tourer Lovely Cheryl."

"Lovely Cheryl," echoed Maz.

She wondered if maybe she'd suffered a brain haemorrhage. That might explain things. Was she currently lying unconscious on the pavement, waiting for someone to summon an ambulance?

"And this is my husband, Roydrick," said Vedna.

Next to her, the second lizard person was also wearing a gilet, but this one was beige. Something about the creature said "male" to Maz, and yet it took her a moment to realise what it was.

"Neck feathers," she blurted out, then bit her lip, wishing she hadn't spoken.

"Your majesty," he said, grave as a butler, his bright neck plumage pressed demurely towards his body.

"What do you want? Why have you taken me?"

Maz decided she might as well get down to brass tacks. She wasn't in the mood to indulge their strange fantasies about abducting a queen. Surely even these aliens weren't mad enough to believe they had picked up a member of the royal family by the bins out the back of a Telford housing estate.

Even Prince Andrew hadn't spent time in Telford.

"We don't want anything, dearie," said Vedna in her weird Mrs Doubtfire accent. "We're just your drivers."

"You're my what? Well, in that case, why don't you turn Lovely Cheryl around and take me back home?"

"That's what we're doing, your majesty," came the reedy voice of the male lizard. He was calling to her over one shoulder, since he had one eye on the front windscreen, staring at the nothingness of space as though he might need to turn a corner at any moment.

"Oh, Roydrick, stop pretending you're driving, dear; she's not impressed. Besides, anyone can see that I'm driving."

Maz stared at the female lizard, who had her own steering wheel, but was neither holding it nor looking out of the front window.

"Don't be ridiculous, Vedna, you haven't driven this thing for twenty years. I always drive."

Vedna chuckled and glanced back at Maz, "Don't mind him. He thinks he's driving because I let him think that, but really it's been me all along. He doesn't even have his licence."

"What are you talking about, woman?" Roydrick squawked, his neck feathers flaring out slightly.

"They took it off you, remember?" she elbowed him in the ribs as though trying to shake his memory.

"No, I bloody do not. It was you who got banned from driving after you hit that lad."

There followed a brief squabble, which Maz, her head spinning at the sight of two arguing elderly lizards, tried her best to follow.

How are they speaking English? she wondered.

"Your steering doesn't even work," said Vedna, as though that would put an end to it.

Maybe they've inserted something into my ear, thought Maz.

"Is there some clever tech translating everything?" she said. "But wouldn't that be like watching a dubbed movie where everyone's mouths move independently of their voices?"

The lizards were too focused on their squabble to reply.

"No, your steering doesn't work," retorted Roydrick, continuing the argument. "It broke years ago, remember? We never got round to fixing it."

"Hang on," Maz said. "If no one knows who is driving the spaceship, does that mean that actually no one is? Because this strikes me as a very bad thing. Ideally, if you're being abducted, you'd hope your abductors had a basic grasp of road traffic safety."

"Very true," agreed Vedna.

"Why don't you take it in turns to see who's making a difference?" said Maz.

"That's an idea!" said Roydrick.

The pair of them both lifted their hands from their wheels at the same time.

Nothing happened.

"Right... so maybe now you try doing something, Roydrick," said Maz.

Roydrick took his wheel and turned it. The spaceship began listing gently to the right like an elderly tanker. Roydrick gave a shout of triumph.

"I told you, woman! I'm the one in charge here!"

"Now you try, Vedna," said Maz, feeling complicit in setting the women's equality movement back a couple of light years.

Vedna turned her wheel, and the craft lurched back in the opposite direction.

"Ha! See? I told you I was in control," crowed Vedna. "It's always me keeping us safe."

And with that, Vedna undid her seatbelt.

"Seems like you're both driving it to me," said Maz, eager not to get on the wrong side of the male in case he was the one with the taste for skinning his victims.

"Right, now that's settled," said Vedna, fully satisfied that she had won the argument, "let's get a cup of tea."

She clambered out of her seat and walked past Maz into the hallway behind. Maz's gaze followed Roydrick as he too unbuckled and climbed over his seat.

"We all know that I'm doing the bulk of the driving," he whispered conspiratorially as he passed her.

"And now… Now no one's driving," said Maz.

But she was talking to herself.

For a second time today she was being expected to step into the unknown. She wondered briefly if she could just leap into the seat and drive herself back home. Would her insurance cover her for that? Probably not, she decided.

With a resigned sigh she followed them out of the cockpit and ventured once more into the unknown.

Inside of a spaceship, huh? thought Maz.

She'd seen plenty of sci-fi; she knew what to expect from intergalactic space travel. This looked more like the inside of a poorly maintained static caravan.

"Is that rust?" she said, trying to take a step back to avoid standing on what was possibly an incredibly corroded patch of metal on the floor. She glimpsed a star.

"Can I... can I see into outer space?"

The lizards weren't listening. They were clattering about in a little kitchenette.

"Sorry to keep banging on about this, but shouldn't someone be driving?" said Maz, pointing back towards the door to the cockpit.

"Oh, I'm sure it will be fine," said Roydrick. "There's really no traffic round here. All your planets are far too primitive for intergalactic travel."

"We know you humans like tea, so we thought we'd try to make you some," said Venda.

"No thank you," said Maz, eager not to consume anything that could contain a) sedatives, b) mind-control worms, or c) both.

"Oh go on," said Vedna. "You must be exhausted from being sucked in. It's far more tiring coming that way than just coming in through the door."

"There's a door?" said Maz.

"Yes, dearie," said Vedna. "Of course there's a door. The way you came in was so undignified. Now, won't you have a cuppa?"

"Being abducted does take it out of you somewhat," agreed Maz. "Funny that. It's almost like a massive rush of adrenaline and cortisol isn't a great experience for homo sapiens."

"Bless you. Such a primitive species," said Roydrick.

"Now dear, don't be bigoted. They can't help being a bit backwards. It's due to their limited intellect, through no fault of their own," said Vedna as she brought over a mug of tea.

"What is this?" said Maz, staring at a cup full of brown gunk.

"Tea," said Vedna. "Or, at least, our best guess as to what tea is."

"We found the leaves near where we picked you up," said Roydrick.

"In the park?" said Maz as Vedna nodded enthusiastically.

"An animal was using it as its toilet, so it must have been a special patch."

Maz wondered if this was one of those situations where her captors would take great offence if she didn't drink their offering. She decided to risk it.

"I've actually just given up caffeine," she said, putting the cup down and thinking mournfully of the teabags that were no doubt sprawled out on the pavement next to her frozen peas and Christmas gifts for the twins. A part of her brain – almost certainly the part that liked to think about teabags and peas during an ongoing trauma – alerted her to a realisation.

The Christmas gifts!

"I'm going to have to start my shopping all over again," she muttered.

Granted, Christmas was a month and a half away, but Maz liked to try and get on top of things since Jim had encouraged her to take over doing all the present buying ("You're so much better at it," he told her and she had felt flattered.) Those presents had been a bargain, too.

It was suddenly all a step too far.

"Look, I'm not trying to be rude or anything like that, and I'd be really grateful if you could not get angry and use me for scientific research, or impregnate me, or peel me for your skin pile collection, but can you please just tell me *what the hell you want with me?*

"Why me? I'm a nobody. Why don't you go and abduct someone important? What do you want? Is this an act of war? Are we at war now? Because if we are, I'd appreciate you letting me out so I can join the other faceless refugees, and perhaps you could find an ambassador, or maybe even a real member of the royal family to take as a captive. Preferably Prince Andrew..."

Maz tailed off, aware that she might have just said something treasonous. What if she was being recorded? The British government might strip her of her citizenship, which was the last thing she needed. Especially if she was pregnant with an alien baby and reliant on child support.

Would the British government pay child support for a non-human child?

The question passed briefly through her mind before it was swept away by a more pressing query:

What is the lizard doing?

Vedna was rooting around under a pile of cushions, which were themselves on top of a pile of colourful blankets.

"Aha!" she cried, pulling out what looked like an electronic tablet.

She plonked the gadget down on a cluttered table, clearing aside some coasters and leaflets to make space.

"This is who you are," she said, pressing a button on the edge of the unit.

A small hologram popped up out of the screen, its golden glow making Maz gasp. "Wow!" she said.

Vedna squinted down at the hologram. "Let me see if I can make it a bit bigger."

Vedna picked the unit up and peered at it. Roydrick came over and began interfering.

"Give it to me," he said, taking it from his wife. But after a few seconds, it became clear he was no wiser when it came to finding the zoom.

"Try that thing there," Maz suggested, reaching her hand out to touch a wheel on the side of the unit.

No, dearie, that doesn't do anything," said Vedna. "Bless you for acting like you know what you're doing, though."

They argued for another minute before Maz could no longer cope. She was a gadget person; she liked fiddling with things. Watching these two was sending her insane.

"Honestly, I think you should just try the wheel thing on the side." She tried to reach for it, but Roydrick moved it out of reach.

"I think it might be this button," said Roydrick, turning the wheel Maz had been pointing at.

Roydrick turned the wheel and the hologram exploded in size, taking up nearly all of the tiny camper van space.

"Oh! Well done!" cried Vedna, holding her hands together in satisfaction. She issued a gentle back-handed tap to Roydrick's stomach. "I told you it was that button."

"Excuse me, what?" said Maz.

"You see?" said Roydrick, pointing at the giant hologram. "This is you."

Maz stared at the hologram.

"How so?" she said. "I don't get it."

She was looking at a jumble of what looked like code. It reminded her of moments in films when people stare at reams of tumbling zeros and ones and act like they understand it.

"Her mind's too tiny, remember," said Vedna. "Humanoids can't read the code."

"Er, excuse me," said Maz. "Let's remember who just worked out where the zoom button was."

"Unfortunately, dear, you aren't evolved enough to understand this. Hmm, let's see. Perhaps we can put it into toddler mode."

Another minute passed as the lizards tried to fathom the settings.

"There!" said Roydrick with joy. "Done it!"

The image before Maz changed.

"It's me," she said.

"No," said Roydrick. "That is your mother."

"My mother?" said Maz, suddenly mesmerised. She wanted to argue. She wanted to explain that she had no mother, but she couldn't tear her eyes away from the vision before her.

"Isn't she beautiful?" said Roydrick. "For a humanoid, anyway. Obviously, I prefer them a little more cold-blooded." He winked at Vedna who elbowed him joyfully.

"Och, you old charmer!" Vedna turned back to Maz. "You look just like her, dearie."

"I don't have a mother," said Maz faintly.

"Of course you do," said Vedna. "There are many types of lifeforms in this galaxy, and the vast majority are created by parents of some kind or another."

"With some notable exceptions, of course," said Roydrick suddenly. "I once had the privilege of witnessing a Bennojabi splitting and it was really quite something."

"But…," said Maz, before realising her brain hadn't yet managed to frame a question.

"Take a look at this, hen. It will tell you all about it," said Vedna.

Fifteen minutes later, Vedna and Roydrick had worked out how to get the clip to play, and Maz watched in utter amazement as a short film explained how her parents, the Grand High Rulers of Dross, had been forced into exile by an invading army.

"In desperation," intoned a deep voice, "they placed the Princess Marion into an escape pod and sent her to a distant planet, where a humanoid species was just about to invent a TV with live pause."

"Like a superhero," murmured Maz.

"What's that?" said Roydrick.

"I'm like a superhero… Wait, do I have any powers?"

"Not as far as we know, hen," said Vedna "but we're not actually from Dross, you know? To tell the truth, not many people are."

"What do you mean? Is it still there? Will I get to meet my parents?"

Vedna hung her head, her second eyelids closing sadly.

"I'm afraid not, dearie. Your parents were killed in the one hundred and sixty-fifth war."

"One hundred and sixty-fifth?" said Maz. "One hundred and *sixty-fifth*? That is a LOT of wars. Some might say too many. Is this a warlike planet? Am I about to become the puppet head of a totalitarian state? Is that what this is?"

"That was a while ago, of course," said Roydrick. "There's been quite a few more since then."

Maz glanced from Roydrick to Vedna. "Wait, are you taking me to a war zone?"

Vedna gave Roydrick a swivelling glance with one of her eyeballs. "Not exactly…" she said.

"There isn't a war on at the moment," said Roydrick.

"At least, we don't think there is. It's so hard to keep up."

"We should probably explain," said Roydrick.

"Yes, good idea," said Maz. "I'll just be a minute. I think I might have left something…"

She pointed vaguely and scurried off towards the cockpit door without finishing her sentence. She had to get away. That's all she knew. She couldn't fling herself into the cold reaches of space, but she could try to overpower the lizard people and drive herself back home. Screw the insurance.

Sure, she knew nothing at all about driving a spacecraft, but neither, apparently, did Vedna and Roydrick.

How hard could it be?

The cockpit looked and felt like a classic car. Surely it was just a case of pointing the Lovely Cheryl towards Earth? Then she could guide the ship back towards the UK. Or maybe, she reflected, one of the bigger countries, since her aim might not be that accurate.

She just needed to navigate past all the satellites and whatnot, and she had a vague notion about how she might want to avoid burning up on re-entry. That felt important. Then it was a simple case of not drowning when she inevitably landed in the middle of the Atlantic Ocean.

It would be a doddle.

She jumped into Vedna's seat and began frantically looking for an escape hatch, or an ejector seat button, or really anything at all that could get her off this ship and back to Telford.

    She reached out to touch some buttons, her hands hovering over the console like a Reiki healer. She was hit by an agony of indecision. One wrong move and she'd be in the sea without even a whistle to blow.

    "Oh bums," she said and put her head in her hands.

    She was trapped here! Doomed to be stuck with two genial hostage-takers until… Until who knew what? She took a breath.

    'Get a grip,' she told herself.

    She needed to be brave. She was going to fly herself home.

    "Right, Marion. You can do this. You are a strong and powerful woman." She grasped Vedna's wheel.

    Just then, Lovely Cheryl crashed.

CHAPTER 4
AFTER THE CRASH

MAZ'S EYELIDS FLUTTERED. Had it all been just a strange dream? She reached out, feeling for the bags of shopping, hoping for cold tarmac and scattered peas. Instead, her fingers sank into the soft pile of a shag carpet.

Her heart sank.

She was still in the spaceship.

Above her, a loose cable sent out sprays of gold sparks, while a pipe near the doorway puffed with what Maz sincerely hoped was clouds of harmless smoke.

She clambered slowly to her feet and did a quick assessment. Nothing was damaged – not on her body, anyway. Lovely Cheryl had seen better days, however. A small fire began burning merrily on Roydrick's control console before Maz smothered it with a nearby doily.

"Vedna?" she called out. "Roydrick?"

No reply. She tried to open the door that would take her back into the living area, but something was wedging it shut. She shoved it harder, hoping she wasn't pulverising one of the Pollups in the process, and eventually the door gave way enough for her to reach her hand around and discover the source of the blockage.

A draught excluder was caught under the door panel.

Maz had a brief moment to consider whether there were draughts on a spaceship before she shoved it to one side and pushed her way into the room.

Vedna and Roydrick were on the floor. Vedna groaned gently and tried to sit up. Maz rushed over to help.

"Are you OK?" she said.

The elderly alien rubbed her head. "I think I had a bit of a bonk on the head."

Maz patted her hand and turned to Roydrick, who was lying still with his eyes staring at the ceiling. She felt dread rising in her, but then the lizard's second eyelids blinked, followed by his first eyelids, and he turned and gave her a watery smile.

"I think it might be time to paint that ceiling," he said. "There's a few cracks."

If by "a few cracks," Roydrick meant the gaping hole that had opened up on impact, Maz would have to agree with him.

"I think it might take a bit more than a lick of paint," she said, patting Roydrick's scaly hand.

He smiled at her weakly, and Maz felt a pang of sympathy for the couple.

"Well," she said. "I suppose I should go and find help or something? Do you know where we are? What did we hit?"

Vedna pressed her head back against a stack of crocheted blankets.

"You're home, hen," she said. "This is Dross."

"We're there already?"

"Och yes," said Vedna. "We should be at the Presley Service Station."

"Presley?" said Maz, amazed that somewhere in outer space would be named something so Earth-like.

"Yes," said Vedna. "One of the most popular stops in the whole quadrant."

"Is it safe to go out?" Maz said.

Vedna nodded. "Yes, all service stations use Smart Air these days. No need for a helmet like there was in my day."

"I was thinking more about the thousands of alien life forms, but that's good to hear," said Maz, hoping Smart Air meant what she imagined it meant. She slapped her thighs before standing.

"Right, well, I guess I'll go and find some help. Or maybe a proper cup of tea," she said, heading for the gaping hole and out into daylight.

They'd crashed in the middle of a vast and busy parking area, packed with craft of many shapes and sizes. A million eyes were now on her. Admittedly, those eyes came from just one alien, who loomed over her, keen to tell her how bad her parking was.

"You are barely in a bay," he said in a very nasal, official tone, pointing to the ground as at least half its eyes blinked at once. "And if you were any closer to my ship, you'd have dented my Ergolister Transponder Cone."

Maz's brain segmented into the part that couldn't believe what she was seeing, and the part that knew never to accept responsibility in a car accident. The latter took control of her vocal chords.

"I think you'll find your ship is too big for its bay!" she replied, pointing to a fin-tip which had definitely crossed a white line painted on the ground. "Which, if you used even a tenth of your eyeballs, you could plainly see for yourself!"

"How rude!" said the alien.

Maz got the impression he wasn't used to being spoken to like this. His eyes shot upwards. He crossed something which may have been arms and strutted off in a huff.

That particular crisis handled, Maz turned her attention to the next one. That is, the nervous breakdown she was currently trying to suppress.

She took a moment to breathe, and for the first time, she noted the peculiar metallic taste to the air. Space exhaust fumes, she thought vaguely. Vaguely was about the best she could do when it came to thinking – given her current circumstances. Her brain was trying to disassociate, but some primal instinct was forcing her to stay in reality.

Wherever she looked were aliens. There were creatures with eyeballs on their elbows or elbows on their knees. Some with noses where their bums should be, and skin of every colour in the rainbow and in every possible texture. There were short ones, tall ones, skinny ones, slimy ones; something that looked like a deck chair, and something that seemed to have been created from a collection of joke shop dentures.

To Maz's left, a large beetle-like alien was deep in conversation with what appeared to be a child's attempt to fashion a life-size human being out of play dough. To her right, an ancient goat-man was arguing with a mass of swarming bees.

And nearly all of them were scurrying, hopping, squelching, sliding, floating, moseying and lumbering in one very distinct direction: to the grey building up ahead.

"Looks like the Telford shopping centre," Maz muttered.

But before the familiarity could give her any comfort, Maz was reminded that she was definitely not in Telford by the sight of a three-headed plant-like alien waving its leaves and she felt a wave of shock that made her want to curl up in a ball and start whimpering.

She wanted to shrink down into nothing and hide under a rock.

She wanted to dig a burrow and live the rest of her life as an antisocial marmot.

Her legs quivered as she tried and failed to force herself into action. She needed to get help. Vedna and Roydrick might right now be dying of internal bleeding, or convulsing in shock, or suffering a fatal heart attack. It was too awful to contemplate.

She frowned.

"Hang on," she said. "What am I thinking?"

She had been kidnapped! Why was she worrying about the wellbeing of her kidnappers? This was classic Stockholm Syndrome. These lizards weren't her friends, even if they did seem like they'd make a mean sandwich.

No. She had to get away. She needed to find a ride home.

She looked around. Perhaps there was some kind of taxi rank here, or the space equivalent of a Megabus? Maybe some generous couple would agree to drive her home after a couple of years of indentured servitude.

She was prepared to pay anything – or nearly anything – to return home. To the place where her friends were people like Brenda and her partner was Jim, an older man who had chatted her up while she was still in school and convinced her to drop out and get a job in a call centre. He loved her, she told herself. Suddenly, the Aztec and Inca didn't seem so bad either. She thought of them now with a kind of fondness…

With historic effort, Maz took a lingering, heavy step towards the service station entrance. Somewhere in that building there had to be one kind soul who could help.

"Good work," she told herself, like a helicopter parent micromanaging a child's first steps. "You can do this!"

She took another step.

"Go Maz!" She applauded herself inwardly.

And then, before she even knew what she was doing, she had broken out into a trot. It was as though her legs had decided that whatever she was scared of in front of her was less terrifying than what she was scared of behind her. She sped up.

"Oh, we're doing this, are we?" she said, "Running straight at a building full of aliens."

And her legs motored on, taking her reluctant brain with them.

CHAPTER 5
THE PRESLEY SERVICES

HER LEGS STOPPED when she entered the building. Maz gaped, staring around the room in disbelief.

"Is that it?" she said.

In spite of her terror, she had to admit that she had never been more underwhelmed in her life, which was saying a lot for someone who'd once visited a petting zoo that consisted of some trapped feral pigeons, five rabid gerbils and a depressed goat. So far, her experience of alien culture had been less than impressive, and the inside of the Presley Services was no different. It looked like a large storage facility, somewhere the police might raid to free a group of modern slaves making illicit cigarettes.

Concrete and brittle yellowed plastic reigned supreme with a faded blue-ish sign above her on the domed plastic roof. At least Maz assumed it was a sign: the imagery was hard to decipher, and the lettering looked like the space equivalent of Comic Sans. Even to Maz's untrained eye, it felt amateurish.

Like someone won a competition, she thought.

Where were all the clean surfaces and the cool white LEDs? Maz had been expecting to be blinded by an ecstasy of immaculate minimalism. It seemed to her that no intelligent life forms would ever agree to spend time in something so soulless. And yet, here it was, a space so bleak that it made the Heston Services look like a holiday resort.

The air was filled with a kind of collective sigh, as though everyone in the building knew that by stopping here, they had signed an unseen contract: feed and water us and we'll try not to cry when we hand over our money.

Sure, the food carts were a bit more exciting-looking than the ones at your standard roadside eateries, but Maz could tell by the way many of the aliens were forking food into whatever it was they were using as a mouth (one of them appeared to be sitting on its plate and Maz didn't want to think about what was going on there), that the meals were just as expensive yet dispiriting as the ones back home.

Despite the slightly bleak surroundings, the strange blend of familiarity and alien sent a thrill up Maz's spine. She was on a different planet! There were alien beings everywhere! If she had come here of her own free will, this would be the best day of her life. Instead, she was now in the position of trying to figure out which of these funky-looking creatures might be willing to drop her home without demanding a blood sacrifice.

Surely, she thought, somewhere here was a lonely trucker ready and willing to kill and eat her?

No, that's not right.

She shook herself. There's bound to be some *friendly* truckers. Not all of them would want to kill and eat her.

Some might simply want to adopt her as an adorable pet.

Maybe one being might drive her home in return for a souvenir of some sort. A limb, perhaps.

Or her self-worth.

Whatever the price, it would be worth it to get back to Telford.

Wouldn't it?

Of course it would.

She scanned the room, assessing her options. In one corner a small mound of earth was having a go on the alien equivalent of a kiddie ride while a larger mound of earth stood watch like a sentient mole hill. And although the mole hill looked like nothing but a pile of soil, Maz was convinced she could sense sleep-deprivation and boredom emanating from it.

Just a normal parent. These were people just like her, weren't they? It gave her a glimmer of hope.

Her attention turned to a friendly looking alien with giant bubble-eyes and a perma-smile.

"Hello!" she began.

The perma-smile opened and a shrill noise hollered something unintelligible, two tongues flicking from the alien's mouth like little streamers.

"OK," Maz said, swerving abruptly to her left. "Avoid the nutters, Marion."

She spotted a group of innocuous looking beings – all squat and round and various shades of grey, like a selection of office carpet tiles, complete with a definite pile. No one that bland could ever be a true threat, she decided. One of them had swept the pile of their grey face into natty zig-zags. Maz guessed it was the leader.

"I don't suppose anyone of you chaps are going near earth are you?" she said, then grimaced. "I'm so sorry, I don't know why I said 'chaps' there. Who says chaps anymore? What am I? An Agatha Christie novel? I'm a bit 'werr' today, you know?"

She pulled a face and spun a finger near the side of her head in what she hoped was an international symbol for "crazy."

"It's not been the best day. I expect all my shopping has defrosted by now…" She tapped two fingers on the table, wishing she had never started this. "You know what? I'm just going to go."

The aliens stared as she backed away, smiling as politely as she could without looking like she might be easy prey. This involved a fine balance of smiling and nodding whilst also frowning occasionally.

"For God's sake, Maz, stop acting like a nut bar," she scolded herself. "And stop talking out loud to yourself."

She stood up straighter, tugging her top down neatly, and smoothing her hair. This time she would act normal.

She approached a table of what had to be a space biker gang. You can spot them anywhere, and experience had taught Maz that the tough-looking bikers who gathered in Telford's mean streets tended to be the most friendly big softies imaginable.

The types of bearded heroes who would always aid a woman in distress.

"Excuse me, gentleman… At least, I think you're gentlemen." She sensed she was already getting off to a shaky start. "No judgement here. I wonder if anyone could help me. I'm looking for a ride back to Earth."

She pointed at a little green man with large black eyes and a bulbous head.

"You look like you might have been there before." The little green man blinked and Maz carried on before her nerve went. "I just thought, if any of you happen to be passing near that particular galaxy or solar system, or whatever it is – I really should know that shouldn't I? It's weird to realise you don't know your own planet's address. I'm sure I do, but it's just I'm under a lot of stress…

"Anyway, if you are passing Earth, maybe you could just drop me off on your way?"

The aliens stared from their plastic seats, one peering down at Maz with eyeballs on huge long stalks high above. Another didn't seem to have eyes, its body covered with a mass of writhing hairs that reached out then pulled backwards like Kate Bush in a music video. It leaned back against a wall of pale breeze blocks and the wall shifted to reveal a giant spade-faced creature the size of a minibus.

A little giggle started to bubble up in her throat when a piggy-looking creature with tusks bulging from its cheeks and eye bags like an elephant's thigh grunted at her. Maz closed her mouth to suppress the giggle and a strange noise forced its way out, like a sleeping dog barking at a nightmare.

"I'm not laughing at you, honest," she said. "I think I'm just having a breakdown." The piggy thing grunted again and Maz hiccupped. "Anyone here speak English by any chance?" Her voice gained half an octave. "No one?"

She started backing away from the huge wall, and the pig thing, and all the rest of them. "I think maybe

I've interrupted your lunch, and it's probably a good time for me to go. In fact, you know what? I could do with a wee. Do people go for wees on alien planets? It's all new to me, but I'm sure most of you have some sort of bladder. Right, anyway. Listen to me jabbering on about bladders. Ha!"

She continued retreating backwards, smiling with a rictus grin; hoping, wishing desperately, that something would swallow her whole. Actually, scratch that: she'd settle for vanishing painlessly. That was better, given the sudden likelihood that something almost certainly *was* about to swallow her whole.

"Everything alright?" said a voice, just as she bumped into its owner. Maz turned to see an alien with twinkling eyes. He was so humanlike had it not been for the ears, which sat high on each side of his head like the wings on a Roman helmet. Or, Maz thought, like her dog Bruce, a sad-eyed whippet who had been in her life for just a few years before succumbing to a short illness and a quick death.

She resisted the urge to pat the dog-eared man on the head.

"You speak English?" she said, really feeling like she might now be safe to cry. "God, I know that probably makes me sound like one of those expat Brits, but I can't tell you how glad I am to hear my own language. Now I understand why they all congregate together in Magaluf."

"I have no idea what you're talking about," said the alien cheerfully.

His accent was American-ish mixed with middle-Eastern. Like a corn-fed hero who might call her ma'am at any moment while also baking a pide. Whatever it was, his voice made him seem warm and wholesome and Maz had to remind herself not to trust him simply because he had sad chocolatey eyes and an earnest expression.

And yet, the reminder of her dog Bruce made her feel even more vulnerable, since Bruce had not only been a very good boy, but also her first great love – and the only male who had loved her even when she stank of morning farts and unbrushed teeth (which was only fair, given Bruce himself smelled like that all the time).

She decided to trust this dog-man.

"I don't suppose you can help me, can you?" she said.

"I sure can," he said, flashing her a broad, toothy smile.

Maz wondered if he liked having his tummy tickled. Was it wrong to slightly fancy a human who looked a bit like a dog? In many ways, anyone sane would consider that the best sort of human, but in other ways, it was decidedly creepy and probably a question best not pursued for fear of giving analysts enough content for a new book.

Anyway, it was only a hint of dog: the ears were, after all, flesh covered and hairless (she ignored the tufts of blond at the tips), and there had been, as yet, no panting or scratching. The rest of him was mostly human, and yet somehow also very definitely doggy. He gave off an odour that was both pleasant and yet earthy. Like he had begun the day clean but had, at some point, rolled in something.

"I need to get back to my home," Maz said. "I'm from a planet called Earth. Have you heard of it?"

"I sure have," he said.

His teeth are all sparkly, she thought, like George Clooney. He had George's eyes, too. Perhaps that was what was drawing her to the man, not the dog ears. What a relief! Sad eyes, she thought.

Like a labrador's.

She cursed inwardly. Apparently, she wasn't out of the woods yet with the weird dog stuff.

"I'm so sorry. How rude am I?" she said, trying to be normal. "My name is Maz Star."

"Eff you," replied the alien.

"OK," said Maz, confused. "No need to be rude."

"Ephew," repeated the alien. "Rhymes with nephew."

"Oh, right! I'm sorry, I got confused because it sounded like you were saying…." She looked at his guileless brown eyes and wondered if he'd realised his name sounded like an insult. "Bless you," she said.

"Oh, ha ha! No," Ephew said, clearly delighted. "That's hilarious."

He became suddenly serious. "Anyway, let's get you home, shall we?"

"YES!" said Maz, finally feeling like she was getting somewhere. She lifted a finger. "But, before we do that, is there any chance I *could* actually find somewhere to have a tinkle?"

"A tinkle?" said Ephew, his face a picture of confusion.

"A wee. A pee. A piddle. A slash? A whizz. A wazz? A–"

"I don't know what you're saying," said Ephew, smiling like a superhero. "Oh, no wait! I think I have it." He clicked his fingers. "You want to expunge the noxious liquids from your skin sack?"

"Er… maybe?" said Maz, unwilling to commit.

"No problem!" said Ephew. "Come with me."

And so Maz found herself following a human-dog-alien into the heart of a space service station. Because following aliens into the unknown was apparently her life now.

CHAPTER 6
BATHROOM BREAK

MANY YEARS WOULD PASS before Maz Star could talk about her first experience in the public toilets of an alien service station.

It would be longer still before she could recount it like it was a fun anecdote.

A decade would go by before she could cut to the section containing, "And at that point I looked up and realised it wasn't a shower," and ending, "but anyway, I didn't drown, that's the main thing, and most of the smell had gone away after a few months," and still have a smile on her face.

The finale, where she got to laugh and say, "Anyway, turns out, I'd gone into the maintenance hatch not the main entrance," continued to cause a series of muscular twitches well into her fifties.

The haunted nine-yard stare that came on once the laughter had ceased stayed with her for the rest of her life.

Maz returned to Ephew soaking wet, having sluiced

herself off under what she hoped were the hand-washing fountains.

"Oh dear," said Ephew.

"It stings," said Maz.

Ephew inhaled deeply. "Boy, you really do have quite an odour there." He inhaled again and it dawned on Maz that he was quite enjoying the stench. "It's a really funky aroma," he said. "Almost makes me want to roll in you."

"Please don't do that," said Maz

"Let's get you some new clothes," Ephew said.

Without really understanding how she knew, Maz could tell that the clothes Ephew bought her were the kinds of garments you get in service stations. Even though they looked so unlike the fleeces and tracksuit bottoms you find next to the beach balls, neck pillows and camping chairs in the UK, something about their neutral tones and their shiny fabric told her that the floor-length steel-coloured sweatshirt and the peach sliders were what truckers bought after they'd got ketchup on their top. Or the blood of a hitchhiker on their shoes.

She stood before him, still jerking slightly from the aftershock of the loo experience. She felt utterly ludicrous. And from the look on Ephew's face, she was right to. Her peach shoes squeaked as she shifted uncomfortably.

"Well, at least you're drier now," he said. Then he smiled and put an arm around her like he was guiding a confused elderly person back into the geriatric ward. "Let's get you home."

"Thanks so much," said Maz, feeling her voice wobble. "I really can't thank you enough."

The two of them walked back out into the car park, hitching a lift for some of the longer stretches on those moving walkways you get in airports. Maz's sliders squeaking with every step.

Now that she was finally going home, she tried to take in all the ships around her. She'd always been a bit of a sci-fi fan. Not a total fanatic – she didn't have time for that in between putting on a load of whites and running the tombola at the PTA fundraiser – but enough that she could stare up at the spacecraft before her with genuine delight.

"That one looks like one of the *Battlestar Galactica* ships!" she said, pointing at a long grey rocket-like craft with the face of a conger eel. "And that one's like the silver thing Princess Amidala flies around in." She nodded towards a seemingly molten bubble of metal.

She searched hopefully for a Millennium Falcon and was disappointed. Eventually, they came to an elderly-looking flying saucer that could have come straight from the front cover of the *Fortean Times*.

"Oh, wow, this must be a popular ship. It's just like the one my captors drove…"

Maz frowned as the penny dropped. She turned, twisting her whole body to pierce Ephew with an accusing stare "It is the one my captors drove, isn't it?"

Ephew's head cocked like a dog trying to solve an equation, his smile becoming desperate as he realised she was not happy.

"Is this not what you wanted, Your Majesty?"

"Coo-ee, hen!" cried Vedna, poking her head out of the door. "Come aboard. We've made you something to eat. Our attempt at your fish and chips. Although we didn't have any fish. Or chips for that matter. Still, I think we might have nailed the mushy peas."

Maz whimpered, and Vedna peered at her more closely.

"Oh my dear. Your hair's all wet... And that smell will attract qipocs."

Maz nodded sadly, resigned to her fate.

"Come in, come in," said Vedna. "Let's get you dried off. And then I've got some beings I'd like you to meet."

"Oh goodie," said Maz.

"OK, so there's been some horrible mix-up and really you need to take me home now," said Maz, emerging from what she hoped this time really was the bathroom, but could quite easily have been a sheep dip for all she knew.

She had sluiced off the worst of the smell and now her hair no longer harboured dubious chunks of things she didn't like to think about. She was wrapping it with a towel, so it was only when she looked up that she realised they were not alone.

Vedna and Roydrick's tiny space caravan played host to three new aliens, all peering at her like cats waiting for their dinner.

"Er... hi," said Maz. "Is it too late to run back into the bathroom and lock myself in?"

"Here she is!" cried Vedna.

Ephew waved at her cheerfully. "This is the welcoming committee. Let me introduce you to everyone."

Maz waved him away. "Oh. No. No thank *you*. I'm good. No introductions needed. I'm not staying."

Ephew gestured to a creature that came up to Maz's shoulder. It looked like a fluted glass salt shaker made of jelly baby, flared at the bottom and robed in layers of sumptuous cloth. Eyes bulging out from a pale yellow head, it approached her with a juddering motion, its body expanding and contracting as it moved across the floor.

"Slug." Maz muttered with a shudder.

"No, this is Smivil," said Ephew. "He's in charge of… stuff. I don't know what, exactly. Not sure anyone does. I expect it's all pretty boring, knowing Smivil. Right, friend?" Ephew laughed and slapped Smivil on the back, the blow landing with a dull thud and sending small ripples through Smivil's face. "He's the one who organised bringing you here."

"You're introducing me to my abductor?" said Maz. "Nice."

"It wasn't an abduction," said Smivil peevishly. "It was a repatriation."

An arm appeared out of the creature's body and extended towards Maz, who looked at the long, wintery fingers and grimaced.

"Like one of those sticky men you throw at a window," she said, trying to smile as she took the hand, cold and clammy in hers. The fingers gave slightly under her grasp, and she half expected the creature to absorb her, arm first. She reclaimed her hand and noticed marks left by her grip.

"Seems like I'm making an impression," she said. "Sorry. I don't know why I said that. I think I might have gone insane."

"It is an honour to meet you, Your Majesty," Smivil said in the nasal voice of a pedant. "Although I must say we were expecting you rather sooner. But no matter."

"Oh, wow," said Maz without really thinking – too busy watching Smivil's fingers resolve themselves back into digits. "Passive aggression exists here too, does it? Good to know. In that case, I'm sorry I wasn't abducted as quickly as you'd have liked. I hope I didn't inconvenience you."

"Well, you did rather," began Smivil.

"I couldn't convince her to come with me," interrupted Vedna. "We had to suck her up through the waste pipe in the end. You know how long that can take."

Maz felt her eye twitch. "Waste pipe?"

She suppressed a flashback to being pressed through a giant sky anus.

"And this," said Ephew, as though he was presenting her with a cake, "Is Marshal Tsin. She's in charge of the military and organises all the surrenders."

If Maz was forced to describe Marshal Tsin, she probably would have managed "jacked blue lobster," and then "…thing," followed by, "in army fatigues," before drifting off in a sea of helplessness.

"Your Majesty," Marshal Tsin growled in what sounded to Maz like a Lancastrian accent and saluted with a giant, deadly looking claw. "It's a pleasure to meet you."

Maz had been too absorbed by the sight of a larger-than-life Northern crustacean to register what Ephew had said, but gradually his words filtered through.

She's in charge of the military and organises all the surrenders.

"What do you mean, surrenders?"

Smivil shifted uncomfortably, but the marshal had something to say.

"It will be an honour to serve you for the brief period we both remain alive on this doomed planet," she said, in a tone that sounded like she'd memorised the lines and practised them in front of a mirror. But then the mask seemed to slip and the marshal's register became a whole lot less formal. "If you don't mind me saying, you're weedier than I like my leaders normally, but if you let me get you on the protein powders and perhaps a 531 programme or some interval training, we can soon bulk you up a bit. Make you less of an prawnish embarrassment to your people."

"Doomed?" said Maz, still catching up. "Hang on, what do you mean weedy? I think I'm pretty str–"

"And this," continued Ephew, pointing to the third and smallest of the aliens, "is the curator, Kamello Koturnuk, who gives these, like, really long lectures about… stuff? And… well, who knows, really?"

Kamello rolled her eyes, which took a while, since not only were they huge – like eggs cracked onto saucers – there were also three of them: two at the front in what Maz would consider the traditional place, and then one on the top front of her head, which gazed upwards as though checking for rain. Yellow irises surrounding deep black pupils rose and fell as they completed their circuit and Maz couldn't help feeling Kamello's disdain would have been more effective if she hadn't looked quite so adorable.

"Welcome, Your Majesty. I am the curator of Dross

and its chief historian. I have spent a lifetime trying to restore and preserve the library and museum of our great planet. Not that anyone cares, mind you."

Maz had been expecting a little child's voice, but the curator sounded rather acidic. Like a sarcastic teacher.

"Wow," said Maz, pressing her hands to her thighs and bending down towards the little alien. "I would like to see that. It sounds like you've worked really har…" She straightened up, noticing the alien's three eyes had all narrowed. "I'm patronising you, aren't I? I'm sorry, it's just that you look like an adorable baby." Then added, "No offence."

Kamello's pale eyebrows extended out on each side of her head, thin strands wafting about like seaweed underwater. She raised one now in evident disapproval. "You're welcome to visit," she said tightly. "The museum is inside the visitor centre just a few hundred metres from the royal quarters and next to the bin store."

"Sounds lovely," said Maz, "but unfortunately there's been a mistake: I shouldn't be here. You've got the wrong person. I have to get back to my own planet to cook tea for the twins. It's Tuesday, things'll be kicking off by now; they'll be wanting their dinosaur shapes. I expect Jim is doing his nut wondering where I am, so if you could just pop me back home, we can say no more about it."

Smivil moved forward. "It is true the people of earth will no doubt miss your glorious presence, but you are of age now, and when we asked the Pollups to transport you here in all majesty, there had been peace for over five years, which really felt like we had broken the back on this whole invasions thing…"

"In all majesty?" said Maz, "If being sucked into the arse-end of a spaceship by a couple of elderly lizards is majestic, I'd pay to see your idea of an undignified entrance."

"We did try to get you in through the door, dearie," said Vedna, suddenly piping up from over by the kitchenette. "Remember when I invited you sightseeing in the soft play?"

"Was that you as well?" said Maz. "I was slightly preoccupied at the time, what with Inca handing me a turd."

"…but, it seems we were wrong about that," said Smivil, still on the previous conversation.

"Shh," said Kamello jabbing Smivil sharply in the ribs. Smivil flinched away from her, an indentation in his robe from where he elbow and landed.

"I can see and hear, you know," said Maz. "What is it you aren't telling me?"

"Oh, Oh! I almost forgot," said Ephew suddenly, slapping his perfect brow, "We got you this gift. You're gonna love it. Wait till you see this."

Seemingly from nowhere, he produced a fluffy mammal-looking creature that squeaked indignantly as he handed it to Maz, its little paws stiffening out as though bracing for landing.

"Is that a wombat?" said Maz. "Or some kind of prairie dog or something?"

"I don't know what any of those words are," said Ephew, "but this is a qipoc. They make great pets once you get used to the biting… and the peeing and pooing. And the occasional vomiting. And if she makes a weird noise, that's a fur ball coming out so it's probably best to put something down to catch it. Her name's Bug."

Maz, who was holding the animal at arm's length, had just enough time to wish her arms were longer before the creature squeaked again, freed itself from her grip and leapt at her face.

"Gah! Get it off!" came Maz's muffled cry as the fat rodent-y thing squirmed up her chest and snuggled into her neck, clinging to her with its strangely human little hands.

"Aww, she likes you!" said Ephew. "At least we assume it's a she. Hard to tell with these little dudes. Just watch out for the poop – it can be a bit explosive."

"Yes, thank you, Ephew," said Smivil, his nasally voice tight with impatience. He smoothed his robes. "Your Majesty, let us begin the welcome procession. Your people await."

CHAPTER 7
WELCOME TO DROSS

THE WELCOME PROCESSION was possibly the single most dispiriting thing Maz had ever seen, which was saying a lot coming from someone who'd lived in both Telford *and* Milton Keynes. She had seen some pretty bleak things in her time, but nothing could top the pure dismalness of a handful of Dross citizens attempting to appear excited to meet her.

It started badly and got progressively worse from there. She had emerged onto the grey sea of tarmac to be met by around a dozen aliens holding a few badly made placards, which said noncommittal things like "Hello" and "You're here".

A small being – Maz presumed a child – proffered a fistful of wilting alien flowers in one hand while picking one of her noses with the other. A cheer rose up with such a pitiful lack of conviction that Maz began to wonder if the crowd had been forced to attend at gunpoint.

"They look like hostage victims," she said.

"You ain't seen nothing yet," said Ephew, grinning.

Then came the parade.

If Maz had thought the initial welcome was lacklustre, it was only because she hadn't yet experienced the parade. Some camping chairs had been placed on the tarmac outside Lovely Cheryl and Maz sat in silent horror at the sight of twenty alien beings plodding past, each one attempting, and horribly failing, to perform some kind of impressive feat.

A troupe of drummers kept the beat, traipsing along with all the zest of death row inmates walking the green mile. Unfortunately, all the beats they kept were different, leading to a bewildering rhythm as though they were doing an interpretative jazz number called "Tachycardia". This was not helped by the band of feathered horn players who parped out a tune that evoked the death throes of a flock of dying vuvuzelas. The only cheerful being in the parade was a baton-twirling, sparkly biped wearing a grin of such inanity that Maz wondered if she was actually suffering from lockjaw and needed medical attention.

"My bum hurts," Maz said. "It actually hurts from the clenching. I have embarrassment cramp"

No one replied.

The welcoming committee seemed to be experiencing their own kinds of personal crises. Smivil looked like he had just glimpsed Medusa and was in the process of turning to stone, his motionless face fixed in a cry for help. Marshal Tsin's feet and feelers were waving around as though she was trying to rip a hole in the fabric of space and time in order to escape. The curator Kamello was frantically orchestrating a multi-camera recording of proceedings, instructing a group of drones to capture history being made from every angle. It was like Scorsese directing *The Last Waltz*.

And Ephew? Ephew was having the time of his life.

"Woo! Yes. Go you!" he cried, applauding as a ginger hamster the size of a pig attempted to breakdance. The furry alien contorted his furry body into a series of shapes, like a cartoon character who's just drunk poison, before twisting up into a headstand and spinning around.

"Is that a good idea?" said Maz just before the pig-sized hamster spun up onto one paw with an audible crunch and landed with a squeak of pain on the tarmac.

"Fantastic. I captured all of that," said Kamello. "This day will go down in infamy as our worst parade."

"Ouch," said Ephew. "Buddy did himself a mischief there, eh?"

They watched as a lumbering troll alien lifted the hamster-the-size-of-a-pig into two of his arms and carried him off. It looked entirely sinister.

Maz felt a jolt of alarm. "Is he going to eat him, or…?"

"He'll be taking him to sick bay," said Kamello.

"Little critter will be back in business in no time," said Marshal Tsin.

"I would like it to all be over now," said Smivil.

A hairy troll-like alien stepped into view and proceeded to throw a collection of colourful balls, each landing with a loud crack, in quick succession, directly on his head.

Maz winced. "Was that part of the act or…?"

"Gerald, you dropped one," heckled Marshal Tsin. "What a prat."

Poor Gerald began grovelling about in the dirt

trying to retrieve his balls. Behind him, a dainty little ballerina creature flew high in the air to pirouette. Round and round she went, her turns increasingly fast and and erratic.

"This seems ill-advised," observed Smivil.

In a dizzy chaos of limbs, the ballerina whirled then fell heavily to the ground, her fall broken by Gerald the troll alien, who collapsed in winded surprise and watched helplessly as his balls scattered once again in every direction.

"That'll be a double concussion," said Tsin sagely.

A kerfuffle at the far end of the procession caught Maz's attention. A hairy alien with one giant eye careened out from behind the legs of the horn section, waving a couple of flaming torches.

"Here comes the big finale," said Kamello, reprogramming the camera drones to switch focus. "It's going to be amazing."

"So far no lives lost," observed Smivil, as though reaching that low bar were an achievement.

"Almost a disappointment if you ask me," muttered the Marshal.

"There's still time yet, Tsin, don't lose hope," said Kamello.

"Has anyone got any sunglasses?" said Maz, eyeballing the flames warily. "Or a welding mask?" The eyeball alien began spitting out gobs of lighter fluid, sending out jets of flame. "Actually, a full set of PPE would be good."

Afterwards, Maz would try to work out if the eyeball had already flambéed the entire row of feather-covered aliens when he began to choke on the lighter fluid, or if it was the other way round. Whichever it was, the outcome was the same: the once feather-covered aliens were left scorched, blinking and naked, while Mr Eyeball hacked and wheezed and slapped his lower eyelid, trying to expel the last of the liquid.

"Woo! Yeah!" shouted Ephew clapping and whistling. "Awesome."

"Nailed it," said Kamello beginning to pack up her recording gear.

"Well, that was one way to end things, I guess," said Maz.

"And no lives lost," repeated Smivil.

"Can't wait to put this in my journal," said Kamello. "The bad reviews write themselves."

The crowd began to disperse and Maz and the welcoming committee were left alone.

"Well," said Smivil. "Now that ordeal is over, it's time to show you to your new royal lodgings."

"I was thinking that instead of doing that," said Maz, clicking a finger and pointing, "you could just pop me back on my planet – which I believe I might have mentioned earlier – and then we can say 'don't worry about it'. Because as you keep telling me, I am a person of great importance, and it's only a matter of time before an army from Earth comes to save me and kill everyone here."

Smivil made a noise somewhere between a gurgle and a titter and Maz felt a dawning realisation.

"Are you laughing?"

"Oh, ho ho," said Smivil like some bad Santa impersonator. "We are well aware that Earth has no interplanetary travel technology. You've barely mastered the printer. If you think anyone's coming for you, you're very much mistaken."

"Just as well," grunted Tsin.

"Quite," agreed Smivil. "The last thing that we need right now is trying to find space on our schedules for any more surrenders. We really are booked out for quite a few years to come on that front. Now, we must dash because check-in at the Royal Lodge closes at lunchtime and you wouldn't want to miss it, especially since you're paying for the whole day."

"I'm paying?" said Maz.

"That's right, soft shell," said the marshal. "Now let's try to get that stink washed off you, because I don't mind saying: you smell like the wrong end of a mouldy honkweasel."

"And those clothes aren't really appropriate for a monarch," said Kamello. "It will have spoiled the footage. You look like the kind of person who goes to the shops in their dressing gown."

"Oh you have those here too, do you?" said Maz, remembering a time she popped out for milk in pyjamas and a long coat and hoping no one here could read minds. "Hang on, you're saying I spoiled the footage? What about the fella who set half the audience on fire? Or the… well, everyone involved, frankly? Everyone involved ruined the footage. I just sat here, minding my own business, with a giant rat round my neck, wondering why you chose to abduct me when I still had a load of whites in the machine that needed hanging out."

Kamello squinted all three eyes. "You'd rather be doing laundry than visiting your new royal apartments?"

"Well," said Maz, hesitating. "When you put it like that… Maybe I'll just go and have a little peek."

"Terrific!" said Smivil, his hands emerging from his body so he could clap them together in satisfaction. "Let us get you booked in, and then we can discuss our next surrender."

"Why do you keep talking about surrender?" asked Maz, but Smivil glided off tight-lipped.

"You are going to love your new pad," said Ephew with infectious enthusiasm. "I cannot wait for you to see it."

CHAPTER 8
THE COMING STORM

RIGHT ABOUT THE moment Maz was experiencing a life-changing trauma in what she had mistakenly believed was the Presley Service Station lavatories, Quinton the robot was wheeling briskly through the corridors of a colossal space frigate.

If Maz had been disappointed with the tech she had seen since her abduction, she would have smiled to see Quinton as he whizzed by – a bona fide robot, complete with sleek white casing, large round head and two giant visor eyes.

Here, now, was Maz's true space aesthetic. The frigate was all blinding blue light strips and acres of white walls. Stand around even for a moment and, before you could say "minimalism", you'd feel a migraine coming on. But no one did stand around on this ship: everyone was heading places, especially Quinton, weaving around the octopus-like lifeforms, careful never to hit anyone, heading straight for the main event.

"Sire," Quinton chirped, his wheels whirring into the vast hangar. "I bring news."

Lord Ctan Thunderbeak, high warlord of the Yendoi – a race of highly evolved amphibious Cephalopod-type beings – lifted a tentacle and Quinton hit the brakes. In the distance, Quinton's receptors picked up the sound of something shrieking getting closer.

"Please," cried the faint voice. "I said I'm sorry. I'll do anything. I'll pay it all back. I'll be your slave. Whatever you ask."

Lord Thunderbeak sighed like a supply teacher about to write, "My name is Mr Butts" on the class whiteboard for the hundredth time in his life. On the mantle above his head, smaller tentacles sat like a little crop of hair, currently flat and lifeless, which expressed his disappointment as elegantly as his strobing skin, which flashed scarlet to puce. He shook his head and the row of golden rings in his fin-like flaps clanked and jangled.

"It would be so much pleasanter if these people could just… not," he said, one limb flicking like a cat's tail. "I could live a happy life never having to hear another grovelling apology ever again."

He waved a rippling tentacle at a retinue of military leaders, civil servants, ministers and other hangers-on who shrank back.

"Take note, everyone: should you ever find yourselves on the wrong end of my ire, and if you ever loved me, please spare me the histrionics and simply surrender quietly to your fate." He gave a broad smile, revealing one large beaky tooth. "It would make Lady Tula and I so happy."

"Me," said Quinton.

"What's that?" said Ctan Thunderbeak.

"It's 'me'," buzzed the robot, his voice seeming to print the sound out like an old dot matrix printer. "Not 'I'."

"What are you talking about?" said Ctan Thunderbeak, confused.

"In this context, where you are the object of the sentence, you would say, 'It would make me happy,' not 'It would make I happy.' So the correct statement is, 'It would make Lady Tula and me so happy.'"

Ctan Thunderbeak turned to the guard closest to him. "Rip his arms off."

Quinton whirred, alarm making his servos spin. "You requested I let you know when you made an error, Your Lordship."

"I can't imagine I did," said Ctan, his huge eyes narrowing.

"You said you wanted to know," Quinton insisted. He attempted to wheel backwards, but hit a wall of security guards who had appeared behind him. "It was after Queen Tula requested the divorce…" Quinton stopped. Even without actual senses, he could tell this conversation wasn't going well. "You said you wanted to 'own your mistakes'," he finished limply.

Outside, in the corridor, the screaming grew louder. Quinton circled round as a prisoner was dragged in.

"I swear, I never did it," cried the poor wretch, throwing himself at Lord Thunderbeak's lower tentacles as his own tentacles spilled onto the floor like dropped spaghetti.

Ctan Thunderbeak tsk-ed. "Let's not have begging. It's so unbecoming. Haven't you heard of suffering in silence? I find that to be a very attractive quality in someone sentenced to death. I was just saying the same to everyone. Which reminds me…" He turned to the nearest guard. "What did I tell you?" he said and gestured towards Quinton.

After his arms had been ripped off, Quinton took a moment. Although robots of the Sinovian Prelode in theory didn't feel pain, there was a strange nagging feeling in his sensors that seemed to him similar to what many lifeforms experienced when hurt. Electrical currents with nowhere to go, cables cut short, ripped from their casing. He would have liked to rub it better, but for that he would need arms. He whirred unhappily.

"Sire, I have news," started Quinton, but Lord Thunderbeak had already moved on.

"Fire up the Preparator," he instructed. "Where's the engineer?"

"Here, Your Lordship," came a voice. Small and deep orange with a mop of brown top tentacles, the engineer scuttled forwards.

"Please, no!" screamed the prisoner, his skin flashing yellow and white.

"Do keep it down, won't you?" sighed Lord Thunderbeak. "I would enjoy this so much more without a lot of racket. Let's have a bit of hush, shall we, for her maiden voyage? I've been so looking forward to this."

Four strong Yendoi warriors ushered along the Preparator. It was a large machine that looked a little like a floating professional food processor. Its monolith-styled metal base and vertical crystal-clear glass entry chute shone brightly under the hangar lights. The machine was buttonless, bar one gigantic knob with a few marked settings at intervals. The Preparator's motor thrummed quietly.

"There she is!" cried Lord Thunderbeak, spotting his pride and joy. "What a beauty. Do you know, Quinton, the Preparator can also slice and dice?" He chuckled. "It truly is the workhorse of the kitchen."

Quinton said nothing as sparks of electricity fizzed from his severed shoulders. The prisoner's guards grappled with the condemned creature, who writhed and flailed with doubled effort as the machine approached.

Upon seeing the deadly machine in the flesh for the first time, Lord Ctan Thunderbeak frowned, recognising a technical hitch: the entry chute was a good five metres up from the ground.

"How's he going to get up there?" he said.

The engineer flushed, skin rippling into textured grey in a bid to fade into the floor.

"Er..." he stuttered.

A short debate followed between the engineer and leaders of the armed forces as well as the ministers and civil servants before it was agreed that a ladder or similar would need to be fitted.

"Well, it's a bit late for that now," said Lord Thunderbeak rather peevishly. "Why did no one think about this beforehand? Honestly, now we're gathered here like a bunch of jelly-limbed idiots. Are you seriously telling me we'll have to postpone the execution?" He looked around accusingly at his ministers who shuffled on their legs in embarrassment, none willing to catch his eye.

"The mezzanine," said Quinton.

"What was that?" said Ctan.

"The level above," said Quinton. "It's the same height as the machine."

Ctan shot his assembled advisers an accusing glare and pointed a tentacle towards Quinton. "How is it that a mere service robot, bought off the peg, can have more imagination than the lot of you put together, hmm? Find him some arms."

Two minutes later, the prisoner had been manhandled back out to the corridor, forced into the lift up to the level above and wrestled towards the railing around the edge of the mezzanine. In that time, Quinton had been handed a set of arms to use and was now trying to recalibrate. Unfortunately, the arms the civil servant had sourced for him were designed for a battle bot and Quinton's previously elegant limbs were now muscular biceps – great beefy guns, at least a third too long for his body. They hung heavily at his side while his internal wiring tried to find workarounds for the compatibility issues.

Lord Thunderbeak didn't notice any of this. He was clapping together a few tentacles, gleeful at the sight of the prisoner being slid like a pizza towards the maw of the giant machine.

"May I?" he asked the engineer.

"Of course, sire, of course!"

Ctan reached out and turned the knob to three o'clock. As a set of blades started to whirr inside, creating a horrific squealing noise, the engineer unravelled a large plastic bag and attached it to an outlet on the Preparator's side.

"We're ready for the condemned," he said. "Push him in."

The guards flipped the wailing creature over the

mezzanine's railing. As he disappeared into the chute, his limbs wrapped around a guard's lower tentacle. A terrific muddle ensued, followed by some shouting and slapping, which resulted in not one execution, but two. The guard and the condemned creature toppled into the machine like lovers in a death pact.

The screaming was cut short by a grinding noise as the pair hit the rotating blades. Quinton flinched as the machine chomped and masticated and, in a slightly anticlimactic finale, spat out a pulpy mush of white meat into the engineer's waiting food bag.

Ctan Thunderbeak turned the knob to six o'clock, and the engineer motioned to the remaining guard on the mezzanine. Taking a lot more care than he would have previously, having seen what happened to his comrade, the guard threw in a sack of mixed vegetables, and the machine hacked them into neat juliennes before depositing the chopped goods into the same bag.

The nearest civil servant approached the bag and tossed in some mixed herbs before sealing it and presenting it to his lord like a crown on a pillow.

Thunderbeak clapped gleefully. "That's it! We've cracked it! The most efficient food processor in the galaxies. Well," he corrected himself, "almost cracked it."

He turned to the engineer.

"Make another one, and this time make it shorter so that we can tip bodies in more efficiently. Add a ramp if needs be."

The engineer looked like he might be able to voice some dissent when Quinton whirred loudly. Instead, the engineer said, "My lord," and backed away respectfully.

"Oh, and find some non-stick coating for it. I don't want them clinging on like that in future. It's very disconcerting."

"Yes, Your Lordship," said the engineer in a tone that suggested his evening plans had been well and truly scuppered.

"Think of the meal prep! The time we will save! Our efficiency will make the universe tremble. It's almost too much to really comprehend."

Actually, Quinton could comprehend it: he was the one who had done the figures. Thanks to the planned fleet of meal prep units, the cooks of the Sinovian Prelode would save 219 billion hours per year in time that would otherwise be spent in the kitchen.

"With everyone's freezers loaded up with neatly stacked bags," said the Yendoi Warlord, arms lifted like a conductor, "not a night will go by when there won't be a fast yet nutritious meal ready to cook without the usual faff."

Lord Thunderbeak's retinue applauded, slapping their tentacles eagerly. If they were nervous, they didn't show it, keeping their skin tones neutral, the texture smooth, their limbs under control, and yet Quinton sensed a certain tenseness – and not only because the prisoner had been, up until very recently, Ctan's chief adviser.

Yes, they were worried Thunderbeak might decide to have them sliced and diced at any moment, but there was more to it than that, and Quinton realised he knew what it was. Because someone recently had given him a strange gift, and that strange gift was giving him what he now knew was called "empathy."

Ctan's people were worried about how to react.

They didn't know what to make of their lord's new obsession. Ever since he had started following a cooking influencer, he had been preoccupied with batch meal prep. The influencer had made her name selling the dream of a freezer full of bags of chopped vegetables, meat, herbs and spices, all ready to be chucked into your preferred cooking device after a busy day at work.

"With these machines we can transform an entire population into ready meals," said Lord Thunderbeak, not for the first time. "Never before has a planet been so on top of its meal planning! Our afternoons will be our own!"

Quinton knew that sorry truth of it was that Thunderbeak's subjects would spend that extra free time exactly how every species in the known galaxies would spend it: farting about on their mobile devices. But if his dear leader wanted to believe he was somehow optimising the efficiency of his people, Quinton wasn't going to tell him otherwise. His programming was capable of evolving based on new data, and he had already learned the hard way what happens when you correct Lord Ctan Thunderbeak – even when you have been specifically instructed to do so. He had upgraded his operating system accordingly, and he wasn't prepared to lose another limb over it. The ones he'd been fitted with were ungainly enough, and now he would be the laughingstock of the other robots of the Sinovian Prelode.

His vocal processor produced a sound not unlike a sigh. He may no longer wish to correct his master, but he had a message to deliver. A message that was meant to have been delivered already.

"My lord," said Quinton. "I have news from Dross."

Lord Thunderbeak's smile dropped. "Oh, alright, what is it? But really, I'm not sure you needed to come wheeling in and spoil the Preparator's maiden voyage. I've been looking forward to this."

"Word from our spy scouts is that Dross had a queen in exile," said Quinton. "And she has returned."

A cloud of anger rained on Lord Ctan Thunderbeak's good humour, and he turned as dark as a thundercloud. Dross had been the easiest conquest of his career, the citizens agreeing to a full surrender before the warships were even in their airspace. He had planned his venture around their demise. Where else would he acquire so much free meat? But now a new leader might put his whole enterprise in jeopardy

"Is that so?" he said. "Well, then, let us teach this Queen of Dross a little lesson on meal prep."

CHAPTER 9
THE ROYAL LODGE

"I'M AN IDIOT, REALLY," said Maz. "I'm not sure what I was expecting. I've only myself to blame."

They were standing in front of what, to Maz's eyes, looked very much like those motels you find next to service stations along any of Britain's busiest roads. She could picture the architect who designed it drawing a two-storey rectangle of brown bricks and colouring in a few brown-framed windows, before popping down their pencil and declaring, "That'll do," before heading off to the pub satisfied with a job badly done. It was the sort of building a terminally unimaginative child might draw – squat and sorry-looking; a giant block of litter on the landscape.

"The Royal Lodge!" announced Smivil proudly, waving his rubbery arm towards the building.

The misleadingly named Royal Lodge was a stone's throw from the service station, connected by a strip of tarmac followed by paving slabs, which cut through a square of grass at the front of the building and took you up to the entrance. A memory bubbled up. Maz was entering a local emergency clinic with the same glass-panelled doorway and vestibule. She was there to have her chin stitched after she climbed a farmer's fence and fell six feet into a metal sheep trough. It had been yet another failed foster home in a long line of duds.

"I'm alright, I think," said Maz. "I'll pass on the royal lodgings. Suddenly, that drum full of white underpants back home doesn't seem so unappealing."

"But don't you want to see your room?" said Ephew. "It's pretty awesome."

"I think I'm probably alright – because if it's anything like the standard room in a Travelodge, I can honestly say I've seen it before."

"Oh no, no, no," said Smivil triumphantly. "The Queen of Dross gets the premier suite."

"Is the premier suite just the same room but slightly bigger and with a bathroom where the toilet doesn't get covered in water from the shower? Because if so, I've seen those before too."

Smivil shifted uncomfortably. "It's too late for a cancellation now," he said peevishly. "You'll still get charged."

"Royal apartments, you said," said Maz accusingly at Kamello.

Kamello shrugged and inspected a fingernail. "I wanted to see your face. It did not disappoint."

"Tell you what, queenie," said Marshal Tsin, "let's get that smell off you and find you an outfit that makes you look less like you bury bodies under your patio on weekends. Then we can discuss your future. How's that sound?"

Maz sighed and thought back to her previous two encounters with the facilities here on Dross. The first memory was something her subconscious mind was busy trying to smother with a pillow and never think of again, while the second – in Vedna's bathroom – was simply a reminder of every camping holiday or festival she had ever been on.

"You're right. I wouldn't want to take back some new alien superbug or something."

"That's the spirit, Your Maj!" said the marshal, thwacking Maz on the back with her larger claw. Maz staggered forwards. "Because right now you smell like my auntie's fungal foot infection. The one that never fully healed. We kept putting the cream on it, but it just kept weeping and stinking. Sometimes we thought she'd died and started decomposing, but it was just the foot, rotting away like nobody's business. Then we'd have to go in and scrape it all out and start again with the cream. Sometimes I'd–"

Maz raised a hand and interrupted. "I think that story's gone on long enough. I get it. I stink." She sighed and gave in. "I'll have a *quick* shower and then you're taking me home."

"Right you are, Your Maj," said Tsin giving a heavy salute. "I'll lead the way."

Maz assessed her room. Apparently, the same unimaginative layabout who had designed the building had also done the interior design work: blue carpet, blue bedspread covering white linen on a blue bed; a narrow brown desk; something that might have been a hairdryer in the top drawer of a brown unit; and thin curtains that didn't quite meet in the middle.

Everything was so familiar. It was almost as though someone from Dross had read an article about the "Five worst roadside service stations in the UK" and had taken it as a challenge. And yet, things were unfamiliar too: holes that might be sockets arranged around the room at intervals; a tablet that beamed out a hologram of a uniformed alien waving in greeting; the occasional whirring sound of a spaceship whizzing by; and a total lack of light switches. When – or if, Maz supposed – it got dark, she would be stuffed.

She inspected the bathroom. It seemed almost like a normal bathroom but with enough alien technology to remind Maz she wasn't in Telford anymore. It was like the facilities on a train, she thought, everything moulded and formed as though it were all just a single experience. Tentatively, she pressed a button and water rained down from the ceiling in one corner. After a further inspection to check it was water, and not some kind of alien goo, and not too hot, Maz was satisfied she could risk it.

Bug, the qipoc, who had spent the entire parade dozing around Maz's neck, jumped off her shoulders. Maz rubbed at her throat which was both clammy and itchy from the creature's hot body. And while Maz stepped into the shower, Bug took the opportunity to explore the small space and take a dump in the far corner.

"Charming," said Maz. when she emerged, towelled head to foot, and the smell hit her nostrils. "I expect that will also be added to my bill."

In the tiny closet, Maz discovered a selection of worn-looking royal robes – like a dress-up cupboard for adults with delusions of grandeur. And yet, despite their threadbare state, every item had a price tag attached. She eventually threw caution to the wind and selected a pale kaftan-type thing with an ornate turquoise silk overcoat embroidered in gold and a pair of gold trousers: somehow the most understated outfit by some margin.

Outside she could see the parking bays empty and fill as visitors came and went. Real spaceships were taking to the skies and shooting off into the distance. Maz tried to imagine where they might be going but her imagination seemed to fail her. It was too much to take in. She assumed there was an actual town here somewhere, not just a sorry-looking service station and a parasitic motel. Perhaps there was a quaint little old town filled with rustic structures thrown up by ancient alien beings? Or maybe even an ultra-modern civic complex filled with beautiful architecture? There might be a lake and a park and something more picturesque than the stamp of grass by the food court filled with grubby picnic tables.

Shame Maz wouldn't get to see any of that because she was out of here.

"Here's Her Maj!" said Marshal Tsin gruffly when Maz appeared in the hotel vestibule, Bug once again ensconced in the space around her neck like a sweaty fat scarf. The welcoming committee had been loitering like teenagers at a bus shelter, waiting for the return of their abducted monarch. Maz raised an eyebrow at the military lobster.

"Aren't you, maybe, meant to show me more deference than that?" she said. "Seems a bit chummy for an armed forces leader."

"Do you know, you might be right," said Tsin,

chuckling. "It's been a long time since we had any royalty, and to be honest, our air force isn't exactly the most organised. It's mainly volunteers. In fact, come to think of it, it's all volunteers. We meet every other week to do a couple of press-ups and some squats."

"But you're so buff," said Maz, without really thinking what she was saying. The Marshal bellowed deeply, her voice making the vertical blinds rattle.

"Oh, no, not at all. Tsin means 'runt' in my language. I was the smallest hatchling in that year's brood of thousands."

"Well, I'd give anything for thighs like that," said Maz. "Although I'd only need two."

A thought occurred to her. "How come you all speak English? Is there some AI tool or something?"

"Oh no," said Smivil, "We switched our national language to English a while ago now. It made sense to learn our queen's tongue."

"You did it for me?" said Maz, suddenly quite touched. "I don't know what to say."

"And there was this amazing dude from Earth who passed through Dross this one time," said Ephew. "They named the service station after him. A lot of his fans learnt the language then."

"Wait," said Maz. "This is the Presley service station, right? Are you seriously telling me that Elvis was actually here?"

"That's right," said Kamello briskly. "He'd been abducted, but he didn't bitch on about it like you. He just accepted he was now the rightful property of his captors and went off to live a quiet life of servitude in a distant galaxy."

"I expect it didn't feel much different to the Vegas

residency," said Maz. "Wow. The King, eh? Imagine that."

"Plus," said Kamello. "English is a brilliant language for idiots with weak minds who can't cope with anything too complex. And since it's happy to absorb other nations' vocabulary, one can really sproik one's donken."

"Yes, it's far better for commerce," agreed Smivil. "Dross has thirty-nine words for surrender, but really no way to ask how much something costs. In fact, since we switched to English, we've been able to get a lot more information from our invaders in advance. And when the invaders leave, they take the language with them, so you'll hear it spoken quite widely."

Maz thought of Jim. The one and only time they'd been on holiday abroad, he had shouted in English at a waiter, asking him why he hadn't learned the language.

"I'm glad Jim isn't around to hear that," she said. "He'd be smug as a testicle in a hard hat."

And she was surprised to realise she meant it: she really was glad Jim wasn't around.

"Speaking of which," continued Smivil, "later today, you will have a short speed-learning session in the language of our new overlords so you can get a head start on negotiating the terms of our–"

"No thank you," interrupted Maz. "I think I'll pass on the speed-learning class. Next, you'll be trying to get me to invest in some pyramid scheme. I'm not an idiot, you know. I know what a scam looks like. I've been there and done that and got the thousands of pounds of debt and the ugly leggings, thank you very much. No, I'm going home now." She glared at the welcoming committee. "And you're going to take me."

The group shuffled uncomfortably.

"Before we do that," said Kamello, "how's about we just show you a little slide show about your parents… and some other stuff?"

Ephew put a cheerful hand on her shoulder and gave the muscle a little massage. "Ooh, great idea! Let's do that!"

"You'll never believe what your family used to be like," said Kamello.

Maz thought of those web articles that promised to show you some celebrities who had aged badly, or a miracle pill that could dissolve fat but which really took you to a spam site that tried to install dodgy software on your computer without ever making good on the initial enticement. She had been tricked by the internet one too many times, so really she should have known better than to be sucked in by the promise of so much. But Maz couldn't help it. She wanted to know more about her parents. How could she not? She had spent a lifetime believing she was an abandoned orphan, growing up in care.

"I promise this time it won't be a crushing disappointment," said Kamello.

Maz clicked the metaphorical link.

"OK," she said. "Tell me."

CHAPTER 10
A SHORT HISTORY OF DROSS

MANY, many thousands of years before Maz's birth, the people of Dross had been a mostly peaceful bunch, minding their own business as they trudged through the prehistorical mud and tried to keep the damp from their caves. But then the invaders had arrived, appearing through the clouds like space Vikings from the space mist.

The first thing the new arrivals did, after murdering anyone who looked at them sideways, was establish there was nothing much worth staying for before marching sixty per cent of the population onto large space frigates and heading home again with a hold full of slaves. This was not, the invaders quickly realised, a planet worth hanging around on.

And yet, a few stragglers from the invading force remained: some afflicted with jockey rot from the damp air; others suffering malnutrition and bone density loss due to the limitations of early space travel. A good half dozen had been abandoned simply for being irritating little weasels, petty, pedantic and peevish – the ones most likely to point out a missing apostrophe on a funeral wreath. Some simply missed the announcement and came back to discover the entire fleet had left without them.

Of course, over time, the story of the first invaders became apocryphal: after all, no one really remembered who had been the original inhabitants of Dross, and no venerable cleric or proto-historian had been around to document it. But, given the fate of the planet in the millennia to come, chances are it was pretty much spot on. Because, in the years that followed, and after records began, Dross was invaded at least four hundred and fifty-six times – more than any other known planet.

And each time, the invaders lost interest when they discovered the planet's almost total lack of neat stuff. There were no fun parties or exciting night spots; no arty bit where the cool people sprayed graffiti and started tiny overpriced coffee shops inside their vintage record stores; no fancy building where the great and the good gathered to watch ballet or opera or listen to intelligent talks; no dodgy area where you could score drugs and experience an illegal rave; no huge park where you could walk your pet and tut at other pet owners; no grand architecture or clever technology. In fact, there was nothing much to do at all, especially on the Dross equivalent of Sunday afternoon.

What there was in spades, however, was swamps, drizzle, and the general lethargy of the inhabitants. And eventually, as the centuries rolled round, there was a service station for interstellar travellers on their way somewhere else, a downbeat motel and a shopping mall filled with all the most disappointing chain stores.

Thanks to its position as a strategic outpost en route

to other galaxies and quadrants, Dross remained popular with invaders. They arrived full of hope, but soon left disappointed, like kids with a swing-ball set. Some did settle for a time, adding the small planet to their expanding empires, but running the place was considered a duff gig: no one wanted to be the governor of Dross.

Invariably the empires sent their least able, least popular civil servants to run the place. And those new leaders would often find themselves caught in the middle of the next invasion. Despite the constant churn of extremely average underachievers, a few capable souls from each new invasion did occasionally chose to stay. Sometimes because they truly appreciated the raw murky beauty of the bogs or because they liked the steady hum of air traffic overheard, but usually because they were already locked into a fixed rate on their mortgage and couldn't afford the early break fee.

And like those first invaders from legend, some simply got left behind by mistake. Carvan Deendle of the Ritulans was busy doing a number three in the Presley Service Station lavatories when his people left. Many years later, Maz Star would spend a month trying to get the smell of that number three out of her hair and Carvan Deendle would be running a small business mending shoes in a kiosk by the front entrance and wondering if his family ever thought of him.

And so, Dross came to be inhabited almost entirely by mediocre beings with very little get-up-and-go and next to no self-worth… and those in debt. This was a planet populated by creatures who would really rather be anywhere else, or who couldn't be bothered to imagine anything better. The dampness of the swamps and the humidity and the small biting insects that descended en masse every spring, the corruption of the politicians and the dismalness of work opportunities all contributed to creating a planet that, for the most part, didn't think too highly of itself and would have quite liked a holiday somewhere where fungal spores weren't constantly trying to send up mushrooms in any fold of skin.

Perhaps if Maz had been given this history, she might have felt able to understand her people a little better. After all, she came from the Welsh borderlands, a damp and hilly place that had played host to numerous battles over the years between the Ancient Britons and the invading armies of Romans, Angles, Saxons, Jutes, Vikings, Normans and, finally, the melting pot that was the English. She might even have felt some pride in Dross, which, in spite of its centuries of invasion, persisted. And given the unmistakable similarity between her birth planet and the concrete delights of Telford, she might have started to feel a little more at home.

Unfortunately, this was not the history Maz was given. Instead, right when you were reading that, Maz was sitting in the Visitor Centre listening to Smivil explain how many Investors In People awards the local council had been given, and hearing about plans to extend the service station to create a slightly larger indoor dining space with more unisex bathrooms.

And the "The Visitor Centre" Maz had been taken to turned out to be a large shed, about the size of an old cricket pavilion or bowls hut, across from the Royal Lodge. It had a table covered in a few leaflets; a back room Kamello boldly called the "museum," but which was actually just a roomful of boxes and research papers; and a poster on the wall saying "Total Dross: experience everything we have to offer in under five hours."

Before Maz took over running Jim's household, she had been slowly rising through the ranks at a part-baked bread company. From temp to marketing assistant and from there, who knew? She might have moved into sales or distribution, maybe she could have gone on the road as a rep, demonstrating how to bake the rest of the bread in-store to sell fresh and hot. She could have worked her way up to middle management. Perhaps she could even have been on the leadership team one day. But that career path was never trodden: Maz gave it all up to raise someone else's children and get a part-time job as a dental nurse.

Even so, she had done her time in the heady world of corporate bakery. And during that era, she had made and seen a LOT of PowerPoint presentations. And despite the high-tech nature of the 3D model being beamed straight into her eyeballs right now, she knew a poorly made slide deck when she saw one. No care had been lavished on the layout; there were far too many words per slide.

Thankfully, after another half an hour – during which time Smivil discussed the local pothole problem, their workplace incident records (five fatalities on one day being one of the many low points) and talked about health and safety initiatives alongside a training course called "Aligning and Leveraging Synergies" designed to bring together all Dross inhabitants – it was Kamel-lo's turn to speak.

That's when Maz finally got to hear about her planet's scrappy survival against the odds.

"And so, as you can see, Dross really isn't much different to Telford, except you get to be in charge of it," Kamello finished lamely.

"I don't think that's quite the selling point you think it is," said Maz.

"Pretty great though, don't you think?" said Ephew, oblivious to Maz's tone. "Dross certainly has a unique culture, am I right?"

"When you say 'unique culture' what do you mean precisely?" Maz asked. "Because so far all I've seen is a service station and something suspiciously similar to a Travelodge. It's not exactly City of Culture stuff, is it?"

"Well," began Ephew, as though he was going to say something profound. But Ephew had never said anything profound in his life – not unless you counted the time he once belched something vaguely resembling the opening line from "If" by Rudyard Kipling. And so, inevitably, he just went with, "nope."

"But we need you here, Your Maj," said Marshal Tsin. "I mean, we've got a lot of work to do before our next surrender and–"

"How about," interrupted Kamello, giving Tsin a meaningful stare, "How about we give you a proper tour and you can see that Dross is a lot more than just a service station?"

"Yeah," agreed Ephew, "It's also a swamp and there's a large scrap heap, and we have one of the biggest roundabouts in the galaxy that we're sure to get the funds to finish some day."

"Righty-ho," said Tsin. "Shall we begin?"

"No!" shouted Maz with a sudden fury that

surprised even her. "You lot need to return me to my planet now. I've had enough. You promised me a slide show about my parents and they were barely mentioned."

"Fair point," said Kamello.

"I've seen your little space motel and I've experienced your plumbing and your incontinent pets and now I want to get home to my family."

Bug squeaked as though she had understood the insult and the smell of farts wafted in a little miasma around Maz's neck.

"Perfect," said Maz.

"But," began Smivil.

"No buts, Mr Jelly Baby. Put me back where you found me." She prodded him in the head, leaving an impression of her finger, before pulling herself up to full height and speaking in an imperious tone. "I command you to take me back to Earth because it's bin night and our recycling has got out of control. It'll be two weeks before they come again, and I'm not sure we can last that long."

Maz realised that the longer her speech had gone on, the more she had lost the dignity and command that she had begun with. "So, if you could just sort that out, I'd be very grateful," she added, pulling at the sleeves on her jacket and trying to look assertive.

"For Grud's sake, Your Majesty," said Kamello, rolling her eyes. "How many times do we have to tell you that you're not going anywhere? We're about to be invaded. What part of that don't you understand? We can't go flying around the galaxy on some fool's errand, we've got a surrender to organise and an invading force upon us. And even if we could return you, how do you think you'd get there? Vedna's spaceship is still being repaired, and unless you want to try to hitch a ride with one of the random people you find in the service station café – and good luck with not being killed and eaten there – then I'm afraid you're stuck here until you've surrendered on our behalf."

"I'm sorry, what?" said Maz, looking at the little curator who was staring at her balefully with all three eyes (no mean feat for the one that normally gazed exclusively at the sky).

"That's right, soft shell," said Marshal Tsin cheerfully. "You have to surrender on our behalf."

And with that, all their talk of invasions and surrender filtered into Maz's brain and she realised she had been too preoccupied with her ongoing status as an alien abductee to really digest the full meaning of what they were saying.

"Surrender on your behalf to an invading army? Absolutely not, no. I won't be doing that. Why on earth would I?" Maz laughed a little to herself at the preposterousness of the suggestion. Then a thought struck her. "Or is it 'why on Dross would I'? Doesn't have quite the same ring to it. Anyway, the point is, I won't be surrendering on behalf of anyone or anything any time soon. No way."

"Yeah, see," said Tsin, "The thing is, you kind of have to."

"Have to?" said Maz.

"We've had a message," said Kamello.

"We had better show her the footage," sighed Smivil.

He pressed something on the tablet in his hand. Maz's eyeballs were bathed with light and she found herself staring into what looked like a large white warehouse filled with blinding white and blue LED strips. A large octopus was staring directly at her – or at the camera recording his speech, that is. It was like having a newsreader invade your mind's eye.

"We have heard about your queen," said the octopus in a voice that seemed to combine classic Hollywood mid-Atlantic with something Tom Hardy might cook up. "And I'm afraid it really won't do you any good. We'll be with you in just a few space-time days and we have this marvellous machine ready to go."

Maz's eyes were fed an image of what looked like a huge food processor with a self-service checkout bagging area attached. The image changed, and she was being shown a terrified octopus being pushed and shoved by guards towards the top opening of the chute. She watched in horror as the terrified octopus and one of the guards tumbled into the chute.

Maz put a hand over her mouth and wished she could shut her eyes to the horror, but the image stayed with her, whether her eyes were open or closed. Before long, the machine had done its worst, and the remains of the two octopus people and a load of chopped vegetables had filled a plastic bag at the base of the unit.

"So you see, we have big plans for you and your subjects," the large octopus said, turning to the camera and holding up the bag triumphantly. "You will be a central part in our drive for maximum meal prep efficiency. The Yendoi will never go hungry again, which is why we need your immediate surrender. But here's something we can promise you, Majesty."

He leaned in towards the camera, his eyeballs looming closer so that Maz took an involuntary step back. "We will save you for afters. That way, before you die, you can watch as every last one of your subjects is sliced and diced into oblivion and witness a civilisation truly at the peak of its food planning prowess."

The alien turned as if he were going to scuttle away, but then he looked back to the camera. "I expect to receive your surrender in person by the bleat of the neggle." He waved a tentacle. "I am only fair. If you surrender without trouble, I promise to stun you first so you don't feel anything. But if you try to evacuate, I will chase you down like clams. And if you choose to fight? Well, then I'm afraid I will kill you all slowly and painfully. And, once we have filled our freezers, I will move my meal prep operations elsewhere."

He leaned briefly out of shot. In a whisper Maz heard him say: "Where are we going next?"

He returned to the screen, his huge eyes seeming to grow even bigger. "And by elsewhere, I mean a primitive planet called Earth."

The footage ended and Maz found herself once again staring at the welcoming committee, except now they were looking shifty and sheepish. All except Marshal Tsin, that is, who seemed to take the whole thing in her many-footed stride.

"Not the best news, is it, soft shell?" she said, clacking her largest claw together.

"You've basically brought me here to die?" she said.

"Looks like it," said the marshal.

"Not intentionally," said Smivil pedantically. "We thought we'd turned a corner with the worst of the invasions."

"Usually it's just indentured servitude for a few years tops," said Ephew. "Which isn't so bad."

"We haven't had a total annihilation for a few centuries now," said Kamello.

"Great. Perfect," said Maz. "So, if I don't surrender, they kill us and everyone on Earth?" said Maz.

"You heard the guy," said Kamello.

"And if I do surrender, they kill us all anyway?" said Maz.

"'Fraid so, cockle" said the marshal.

"But it will be worse if you don't," said Smivil.

"Wow, you've really stitched me up here," said Maz.

"It's certainly less than ideal," said Smivil.

"You could try to return to Earth," said Kamello, "but it's highly unlikely you'll survive the journey. You heard Thunderbeak say he's going to round up any evacuees."

"And even if you made it out alive, you'd soon be rounded up and minced once you reach Earth," said Tsin. "Probably not worth the effort, to my mind."

"Terrific," said Maz.

"So we just need you to board our royal ship and travel to Lord Thunderbeak's vessel on behalf of our planet," said Tsin soothingly. "And this time next week, once conditions have been met, this whole sorry mess will be over."

"Because we will all be dead," added Smivil, as though that needed clarifying.

"It's going to be a major bummer," said Ephew, his usually cheerful face turning forlorn. "I had, like, plans and everything. Maybe camping, or something. Or, I dunno, driving around."

"Yes, it is VERY inconvenient," said Kamello, tapping a neat foot irritably. "I had only just finished reconfiguring the underlying architecture on our archive. A whole database of every invasion we have on record, fully searchable, detailing every atrocity."

"That's nice," Maz managed. She would have liked to respond more appropriately, maybe say something about the news of their impending demise, but her brain wasn't functioning in any meaningful way. Aside from operating its usual jobs – getting her digestive system in line, keeping her blood pumping round the various major organs – it was almost totally out of action. If she tried to form a thought, her brain simply played a high-pitched squealing sound. Like an eighties TV playing the test signal.

But something in her body somewhere must have still been in charge, because without a word, she found herself turning on her heel and walking out of the shack and into the drab grey light of the afternoon.

CHAPTER 11
THE HOG AND THE FAIRY

MAZ WAS GOING FOR A WALK.

Booze had been her first thought. She had considered trying to track down a bar in the motel, but she had read enough books and watched enough films to know that going to an alien bar always ended in a fight.

Or, if there wasn't a brawl, she knew she would inevitably order a drink that her primitive ape system wouldn't be able to handle. And then, who knows? She would wake, blind and paralysed down one side, probably wearing a clown outfit, or entirely naked, with no memory of who or what she was.

So, walking was the next best option. Her final foster mum – the one she had liked the best – would have seen her face and said, "Maz is in a huff. She's got the hump. She's going for one of her stomps."

And it was true. It was how she coped with life.

When she was growing up in care, she would often go for a walk just to have a break from the madness of the kids' home. Or to escape the children of her foster parents when she was tired of their baleful stares, which served as a constant reminder that she was the reason they didn't have their own bedrooms.

More than once she had packed a tent and sleeping bag and made for the hills, setting up camp in the ruins of an old lead miner's cottage on the hills of the Shropshire Stiperstones, truffling out the magic mushrooms that grew amongst the moss and sheep-clipped grass, and scoffing them alone as she gazed up at the stars and imagined what life would be like on another planet.

More fool her.

The countryside calmed her. It reminded her she was a creature on this earth, or – she corrected herself – this Dross. It reminded her that all things pass. Or at least they used to. Currently, it seemed more likely that all things *end*.

Painfully.

And they end with her watching an entire planet being bagged and labelled into evening meals while she awaited the same fate.

All things considered, what with the turd in the soft play and the abduction and the mix-up over the bathroom situation and the godawful parade and the immediate threat of being turned into dinner, she was prepared to call it: this wasn't the best day she'd ever had.

Her foot landed with a squelch as she stepped off the slab paving and onto the grass sending a spurt of dirty water up her leg. She sighed and prised Bug from the resting spot around her neck before plonking the heavy rodent down on the grass.

"Maybe take this opportunity to do your business," she said.

Bug gave Maz a look that said, "You know where

you can stick that suggestion." Nevertheless the qipoc loped tentatively onto the damp grass and began sniffing around while Maz rubbed her neck, sweaty from hot rodent.

To their right was the picnic area for the food court, while to the left was the entrance for the Royal Lodge. Behind, just beyond the Visitor Centre, was the bin area. Maz caught herself wondering if Jim had remembered to put out the recycling and laughed to herself.

As if.

Thinking about recycling was strangely soothing. The past few hours had mainly been about her current status as an alien abductee: letting her brain move onto more familiar subjects was a comfort. Like finding an old teddy to cuddle as the tornado chews apart your house.

She squelched onwards through soggy grass, Bug tiptoeing gingerly through the damp after her. They passed the giant dumpsters and beyond the back wall of the service station, where Maz half expected to see a fuelling point. Instead, the pathway opened out, and she was staring at a collection of spaceships.

She had stumbled into a spaceship dealer forecourt. A collection of classic and state-of-the-art spacecraft lined up like beautiful show ponies along with an assortment of rather more sorry looking vehicles waiting to be fixed. Many of the more "classic" spaceships looked like drawings of the future from early sci-fi book covers, all shiny and silver and streamlined.

One was like a rocket, long and lean and ready to pierce the sky at a moment's notice. Another made the shape of a giant 'V', bright lights dotted up each side like an illuminated sign. And dotted between the more retro UFOs were some modern-looking vehicles: large liquid teardrops; a rubbery flat purple manta ray-shaped machine; connected glossy orbs that could have been rendered by AI. Maz walked past each machine enjoying the wonder of so much alien technology.

"Cor," she said, reaching out to the closest one.

"Don't touch that," barked a voice.

Maz snapped her hand back and whirled round like a naughty child. Towering above her was a dark wire-haired monster that looked more like an enraged warthog than anything else. Maz's heart began thumping in her eyeballs as the monster glowered down at her. Bug leapt up into her arms and scrambled with soggy paws onto her neck, quivering in fright.

"I come in pieces!" Maz spluttered. "That is, I mean, I come in peace. I come in peace." She took a step sideways and another, crab-walking her way along the edge of the spacecraft, getting ready to run for it. "I'm really just totally harmless and… And you shouldn't worry about me at all."

She pressed back against the vehicle.

"Whoa, there," she heard herself say. "Easy. Easy, now."

Who the hell do you think you are, Marion? said a voice in her head. The Horse Whisperer?

And the creature seemed to hear her thoughts.

"Who are you and what are you doing here?" it bellowed, sending a puff of hot rageful air onto her face.

"I just wanted to go for a walk," Maz said meekly.

"Well, find somewhere else to do it. You're not wanted here."

You're not wanted here.

Perhaps it was the rudeness, or perhaps it was that

she had spent her life hearing something similar, or maybe it was just because she had been abducted but now she was being told to go away, but somewhere in the monkey part of her brain, something snapped.

"I'm not WANTED here?" she said, her voice becoming louder. "Oh REALLY? Try telling that to the clowns in your TIN POT government or whatever the FUDGE they are. Try telling it to the bunch of aliens who ABDUCTED me from my OWN PLANET while I was MINDING MY OWN BUSINESS. Maybe you can convince them to send me BACK WHERE I CAME FROM, because I sure as hell can't and I can tell you that I have had ENOUGH."

Maz flung her arms around in such a fury of impotent frustration that the large alien took a step back. And as he did, Maz realised he wasn't so huge after all, and he wasn't quite so warthoggy as she had first thought, either. Yes, there was still a vibe of something a bit pig-like about him, but really he seemed almost human-looking.

"Fudge?" he said.

"What?" she said.

"Fudge? 'Whatever the fudge they are.' That's what you said."

She sighed. "Look, if you spent most of your day speaking to people under the age of five, you'd self-censor too. It's a habit. OK?"

He narrowed his eyes, which no longer seemed yellow and alien.

"Who are you?"

Maz shifted, suddenly aware that while she was observing his slow transformation – into something if not entirely human than no longer entirely monster either – she too was being evaluated by him. "I'm Maz Star," she said. And then, in the hope that namedropping might help: "The Queen."

He grunted. Well, he wasn't bowing and scraping, but he was at least not eating her, and at this stage in her day, Maz was going to go ahead and chalk that up as a win.

"And… you are?" she said.

There was a pause that was so long that Maz began to wonder if she had actually spoken.

"Denx."

"Nice to meet you," she lied.

There were many things she could say about how it felt to meet him, and "nice" wasn't one of them. He grunted again and then, without warning, started bashing out a dent in the side of the ship nearest to him. A ship, Maz realised, that she recognised.

"The Lovely Cheryl. It's Vedna and Roydrick's caravan."

"Some idiot drove it into the tarmac," said Denx.

She knew it was better just to flee now that she had survived her encounter with whatever Denx was, but curiosity overwhelmed her.

"Do you mind if I take a look?" she said, gesturing to the array of show ponies. "I promise not to touch, so there will be no need to eat me or anything, if that's what you're into."

Denx grunted yet again, apparently his preferred mode of communication.

"I'm going to take that as a yes," she muttered almost to herself, resisting the urge to add, "use your words."

With regular glances back at Denx to reassure

herself he wasn't about to launch a one-man stampede or fling his hammer at her head, Maz began wandering about, admiring each vehicle like a Sunday tyre kicker at a car forecourt. Bug clambered down and began skittering along next to her and, with considerable self-control, Maz went from ship to ship, resisting the urge to stroke the shiny silver of these beautiful machines.

She stopped at one that rose high up into the sky. It was like a matte black yacht, complete with a long keel that was twice her height. But where what Maz thought of as the "boaty section" would normally be was an open cockpit that looked like a motorbike saddle.

"Black Beauty," she said, remembering the children's book about a horse who was constantly being sent to new homes. She had read it in foster care and the irony had not been lost on her.

"Yes, she is, isn't she?" said a small, cheerful voice.

Maz turned to see a a sprightly little creature advancing towards her. If the being didn't quite float, she certainly gave that impression. Standing approximately three feet tall, the alien seemed to create her own halo of light, a silver glow like a bad social media filter. Although her face was diffuse with a soft focus, Maz could see it was delicate and elfin, with a pale metallic purple tinge. To finish the effect, the alien wore a floaty outfit of pale purple and peach, with a skirt like gossamer petals.

"A fairy," said Maz, gaping. "A real-life fairy."

The fairy laughed and then dropped into a strange mix of a bow and a curtsey.

"It is an honour to meet you, Your Majesty. I am Sammiel, of the Alfarr people."

"Hello Sammiel, I'm Maz," said Maz. "No need to

call me Your Majesty. Feels a bit weird, to be honest. I'm usually just called "Maz" or "bitch-face" in my house."

"Well, it is a pleasure, Maz," said Sammiel with a sweet smile.

Bug trotted over and stood on her hind legs to sniff the fairy's skirt edge, one little paw pressing into the alien's knee. Sammiel reached down to tickle Bug under the chin and the qipoc made a buzzing sound that Maz assumed was a qipoc purr.

"Please ignore Denx," Sammiel said. She sounded faintly Icelandic mixed with cockney. Like Björk, thought Maz. "He cannot help himself. He has no manners. It was how he was raised, you see."

Maz glanced over to where Denx had been, but he was no longer there.

"You have lots of very beautiful spaceships here," she said.

"Most are not ours, sadly. We simply restore them for clients. Some have been here many years."

"Abandoned?"

"I think perhaps, yes."

"Interesting… Does that mean some of them are for sale?"

"Why? Are you thinking of buying one?"

"Would any of them get me back to a planet called Earth?"

"Nearly all are short range. Pleasure vehicles not suited to long distances. This one has a broken extreme distance engine, but it could just about make it if." She pointed to Lovely Cheryl. "But the owners are waiting for her."

"What about this one?" said Maz, walking over to Black Beauty, the beautiful yacht-like ship.

There was no reply. When she turned, Sammiel had gone. Instead, Denx was approaching. Bug leaped back onto Maz's neck and made a grumbling sound.

"You can't afford it," Denx said.

"What happened to Sammiel? Did you eat her?" said Maz. "Or, wait. Was she a figment of my imagination? Am I seeing things now? Or did someone say they don't believe in fairies? Do we need to clap or something."

She clapped anyway, just in case.

"She's a free spirit," said Denx. "She comes and goes as she pleases."

"She really is a fairy, isn't she? A really big fairy. Does she vanish into thin air because I'd really like to see that."

He grunted and Maz suddenly registered what he'd said earlier.

"How do you know I can't afford it?" she said. "Actually, I think you'll find my credit rating is much better now I've nearly paid off that store card and–"

"The Dross royal family is in a lot of debt," Denx cut in. "Cash only for the likes of you."

Maz frowned. It seemed her credit rating had followed her.

"Which one can I afford, then?" she said "And do you take contactless?"

His wordless stare was all the answer she needed.

"I don't really have anything of value," she said. But then she remembered the engagement ring Jim had given her, blue sapphire surrounded by small diamonds. An heirloom, he claimed. "Would this get me anything?"

Denx looked as she held the ring out for him to

inspect. A small half-smile stole briefly over his face and he led her to the far corner of the yard and gestured towards a spaceship.

It looked like someone had taken a can of fizzy drink, crushed it in one of those can crushing devices, and then attempted to restore it back to its former can-shaped glory with almost no success. The whole creation was a mass of dents and chips. The two blade-like wings that sliced backwards from the battered body would have looked impressive had they not both been at slightly different angles and pocked with holes.

"This is in your price range," he said.

"I asked for a spaceship," said Maz. "This looks like an art installation on the subject of desolation"

"Which is all that ring will get you," said Denx.

"Will it even fly?"

Denx shrugged and gave the hint of an amused grin. "Only one way to find out."

"Is there? Really? Only one way to find out? No simulation software you can run first to check for aerodynamic… whatever?" She realised she was out of her depth, but flailed metaphorically onwards. "No safety droid or something who can take the test flight?" Indignance rose like a bubble. "Is this seriously all my ring will get me?"

"Your ring, plus another four thousand."

Maz didn't spend time considering four thousand of what because the fact was, it made no difference if it was socks or silver pieces: she didn't have four thousand anythings.

"I don't think you understand. I really need to get home. I've been abducted. I shouldn't be here. I have a family to get back to."

"Sucks to be you," he said, and Maz suppressed the urge to smack him round the head. All those years without a family, fending for herself, had taught her that violence sometimes was the answer.

She eyed him suspiciously. "What kind of mechanic are you, anyway?"

"I'm the only mechanic."

There was a hint of danger in his voice, as though he had killed and eaten the others, and Maz decided not to enquire further. Instead, she found herself nodding at the inevitability that on this entire planet – and on the site of an intergalactic service station – there was somehow only one mechanic. And that one mechanic was a grumpy arse with absolutely no gallant urge to save a damsel in distress.

"Can I get Sammiel back?" she said, casting about in the air for the alien fairy as though she were hovering above them, invisible. "I'd rather talk to her. She works with you, right? What is she? Your partner? I expect she should have a say here."

"She's not here," he said, staring at her bullishly.

"Oh," said Maz, feeling hope ebb away. She sighed and stared off glumly into the middle distance.

She heard Denx cough and she looked back to see him shifting awkwardly. "I tell you what, since you're new here. I'll be kind to a first-time customer. It's yours for the ring. Forget about the four thousand."

Maz felt the prick of tears, but she caught herself before they fell. "Thank you," she said in a voice thick with emotion. "That really means a lot. I can't tell you what kind of day I've ha–"

Denx turned on his heel. "And if I get you the documents do you promise to keep it that way?"

"Yep," said Maz regaining her desire to clout him round the head.

She waited for him to disappear into the shabby building beside the garage, counted to two, and then raced over to the big black yacht ship. If she was going to take another space flight, there was no way she was going in the old rust bucket Denx was trying to palm her off with: she was going to steal Black Beauty.

There was just one problem: how to get into the thing. Assessing the machine, Maz decided she would have to find a way to get from the ground to the motorbike-style controls at the top. It was going to be a bit of a climb. She put a foot into what looked like a stirrup and searched for a hand hold to pull herself up. There was a whirr and, in one fluid motion, the step began lifting up, taking her foot with it.

"Woah," she said as she was dragged upside down.

With one foot caught fast in the stirrup her other limbs were free to flail about like a flipped beetle. It was only when she reached the top that she discovered the handrail right next to her. Presumably the one she was meant to have held onto this whole time. She grasped it now and tried to hoist her body upright. With a grunt of extreme exertion she gracelessly scrabbled her free arm and leg up and onto the saddle before slowly mounting the saddle seat. She felt a rush of exhilaration. She was a cowboy about to break out of jail and flee on his trusty steed. She smiled in triumph.

A bubble of rippling material appeared from somewhere, covering and surrounding her in something like a thick agar, heavy and warm, and yet Maz found she could breathe without any problem. She reached out to grab the handlebars, expecting to be thwarted by the need for keys or fingerprint recognition, or any number of other unknown technologies, but as soon as she touched the grips, the spacecraft purred into life.

"This is going to be amazing, Bug," Maz said.

Somehow, through all of Maz's escapades, Bug hadn't moved an inch and now, around her neck, surrounded in the protective jelly, the creature gave a little unconvinced grunt. Maz twisted the throttle in her right hand, waiting for the ship to take her home.

Except, of course, this wasn't a motorbike and the thing in her right hand wasn't a throttle, and she had no idea how to either drive or navigate an interstellar flight.

The not-throttle did absolutely nothing.

She waggled it. Still nothing.

"What are you doing?" shouted Denx, appearing from the garage and looking up in horror. Maz gripped the handlebars tighter.

"For god's sake, just GO," she said, followed immediately by, "Yneeeeccccchhhhhh" as the ship bucked into life under her instruction and began moving at what felt like warp seed.

Unfortunately, the direction it was moving in was backwards.

Maz glanced behind and saw the Visitor Centre – or, more pressingly, the brick wall holding up one side of the Visitor Centre – getting rapidly closer. She twisted the not-throttle forwards and felt the craft switch from accelerating backwards at breakneck speed to accelerating forwards at breakneck speed.

"Oh, fuuuuuuuudge," she said.

Now it was Denx's workshop that was looming large in Maz's vision. She would have crashed into it had she not twisted her hand and felt the machine shift into reverse once more.

"Who the hell twists something forwards to go backwards?" she shouted angrily, as though this were all Denx's fault. It seemed like the kind of thing he would do just to really annoy people. Below, she could see him shaking his fist at her as the ship hurtled towards both him and his workshop. At the last second, he leapt out of the way just as Maz twisted her hand again and the ship returned to its backwards trajectory.

This scene continued on for longer than Maz would later care to admit, every panicked twist of her hand sending the ship backwards and then forwards between the workshop and the Visitor Centre like a a never-ending tennis rally, until finally, Maz managed to force her hand to a middle position and the craft slammed to a standstill. Now Beauty was floating just above Denx, who was back on his feet and once again shaking his fist like some kind of cartoon baddy.

"Great," Maz said to Beauty. "Now, go higher."

And now the craft lifted into the air at such a velocity that Maz felt her whole body compress. She began to believe she might literally be about to kiss her backside goodbye. Yet somehow the pressure continued to increase, as her ribs concertinaed into her abdomen. Bug seemed to weigh fifty kilos, his bulk pressing down on Maz's shoulders

"Too high," she managed to gasp.

Black Beauty stopped instantly and for a split-second Maz felt relief. But then the ship began plummeting to earth and Maz's stomach lurched so hard she puked right into her gel bubble, the chunks held in place like insects set in amber. Time seemed to stand still as Maz eyeballed the vomit in suspended animation right in front of her, but the next moment she was back to hurtling, at speed, towards the ground, hearing a crunch as the ship's long rudder pierced a spaceship below.

"Stop!" she screeched and her body lifted from the saddle as the ship halted.

"OK," she said, taking a breath and feeling she was at last taking control of the situation. "I've got it now."

She glanced over and noticed Denx waving his arms and yelling. She grinned at him.

She raised a one-fingered salute with her left hand, revved the throttle with the other and shouted, "Go."

The precise moment she remembered it wasn't a throttle, was the precise moment Black Beauty shot backwards at full speed and crashed into the Visitor Centre.

CHAPTER 12
SICK BAY

"HAEMORRHOIDS CREAM," muttered Maz.

It was all coming back to her now. She had forgotten Jim's cream. She would pop back and get it when she collected the twins from pre-school. Jim had been unbearably grumpy of late thanks to his piles, so really she would be doing herself a favour as much as him.

"Who is this Haemorrhoid and why are they screaming?" came a voice.

Maz frowned, her mind reaching for recognition.

"I do hope they're not planning on invading us." continued the voice. "That would be most inconvenient."

Maz could almost place it. The owner's name was on the tip of her tongue. It sounded like her old geography teacher. Nasally and bland.

"Hold on a bit, she's waking up," said another voice. This one was gravelly, like a bag of rocks being eaten by an angry Northern bear and yet somehow female. "You alright, cockle?"

"If she doesn't wake up soon I'm leaving," said a

third voice impatiently. "I need to get the museum packed away before the invasion. And, now the Visitor Centre has been destroyed, I'll have to reorganise that, too. You know the first thing invaders always come for is the culture of the previous inhabitants."

Maz was struggling to see how any of this related to the haemorrhoids cream. She wondered if perhaps she had fallen asleep with the TV on.

And then, slowly, like treacle off a spoon, the realisation came: this isn't a dream; there would be no visiting that Tesco Metro anytime soon; Jim's haemorrhoids would live to throb another day.

Maz opened her eyes.

"Umpf," she said, which roughly translated as, "Oh, yes, I'd forgotten about the alien abduction bit of the day, but it looks like that definitely did happen after all."

She managed to take in her surroundings.

"There you are!" said Ephew, smiling up at her.

He was remarkably cheerful, Maz thought, for someone covered in building debris. She looked down at him from her saddle. He was also dangerously close to the edge of Black Beauty's sharp keel, which must have been centimetres away from ploughing into him.

"Ephew," Maz managed.

"Same to you," said Kamello sourly. All around them pamphlets fell like rain. "I'd just sorted those," she said.

"I think that's the least of your worries," said Marshal Tsin as a chunk of wall tumbled to the ground.

"Someone's going to have to pay for all this," said Smivil.

The bubble around Maz opened. Bug, apparently

unharmed, hopped smartly off her neck and into Ephew's arms. The vomit, previously suspended in the jelly, splattered down into Maz's lap.

"How are we, soft shell?" said Tsin. "Everything still where it should be?"

"I think I might be a little–" Maz began. "What's the word for when your entire body hurts and your ego is dented, and you just smashed a building thanks to gross incompetence, and got concussion for possibly the third time in one day, and you've been abducted by a group of aliens who also appear to be inept members of local government, and they expect you to go and meet a homicidal maniac in the hope that he might not mince you into a frozen dinner, and despite washing twice you still smell like a haunted toilet?"

"I think the expression you're looking for is, 'totally fudged'," said Denx, appearing at the hole in the wall.

"Oh great," said Maz. "Just when you think your day can't get any worse."

And then, since she hadn't thought to touch wood, the universe rewarded her for tempting fate. She swung her leg over the saddle and reached for the rail. She nearly had it, too, but the stirrup-pedal immediately began its descent and Maz found herself falling backwards. She supposed she should be grateful when her foot caught, but, hanging by one leg as she hurtled to the ground, gratitude was hard to find. Unlike the floor is going to be, she thought morosely, just before she thudded in a tangled heap onto the Visitor Centre concrete.

"Ouch," she said.

"Let's get you a once-over at the hospital shall we,

soft shell?" said Tsin, peering down at her. "Check that bonce isn't broken."

Hospital was overselling it. Tent in a field was more accurate. The sort of place you see in films about the world wars. Rows of temporary beds on top of hessian on top of grass. The whole set up protected only by a thin layer of green canvas that wrestled with every breeze.

"Welcome to our military field hospital," said Marshal Tsin proudly.

"Thanks," said Maz. She was lying on a rickety camp bed surrounded by the welcoming committee.

"It's actually the only hospital," said Kamello. "Unless you count the first aid room in the Presley Services, and I wouldn't. They were the reason we had five deaths on our health and safety record last year."

"That wasn't in Smivil's PowerPoint," said Maz.

"Yes it was," said Marshall Tsin. "It's the only section I remember."

Smivil tapped the tablet in his hand and gave a satisfied look. "This has worked out surprisingly well with our itinerary," he said "We were scheduled to show you this bit next."

"Oh, great," said Maz.

"But maybe you could try not to destroy this building," said Kamello. "Just a thought."

"It WAS pretty awesome though," said Ephew. "Like something a superhero would do."

He frowned. "Except I guess they would miss the building and not stink of vomit."

"Quite," agreed Kamello.

"Ouch," said Maz, rubbing her arm. A large preying mantis-looking alien with a green carapace had just injected her with something and she looked up at it suspiciously. Maz really hoped the insect was a medical professional of some sort.

"I meant to say, 'this is going to sting'," said the beetle, slapping one of its legs to its head and clacking its mandibles. "I always forget that bit. I guess it's not in my nature to warn my vict– I mean patients."

"What have you done to me?" Maz shouted. "What have you injected me with?" She eyeballed the insect suspiciously. "Is this some kind of bug serum or something? Am I going to turn into a bug now."

The insect's shell split and it buzzed a set of wings slightly in a gesture that seemed to suggest its feelings had been hurt. "It's just some vaccinations. All pretty routine stuff."

Around her, the welcoming committee shuffled and Maz felt suddenly embarrassed.

"Oh, vaccinations, eh?" she said, attempting a jocular tone. We all know what that means. Am I right?" She winked. "I suppose you've inserted a microchip into me now, eh?"

"Yes, that's right," agreed the insect.

"It will be much easier to keep track of you now," said Tsin.

Maz's smile dropped. "What?"

"No more wandering off, creating havoc, destroying community spaces," said Kamello. "You've really been quite tedious so far."

Smivil presented her with his tablet. "Now, if you could just sign this," he said.

Maz peered at a chaos of diagrams and symbols. "What is this? I can't read it."

"No need to worry. It's just you accepting liability for theft of a yacht-bike and smashing into that long range ship and destroying the Visitor Centre and ruining the yacht-bike, and then a bill for your treatment."

"How much is the treatment? I only had one injection!"

"Actually, you had a few more than that," said the insect, raising a hand like a student needing the toilet. "And I fixed your sprained ankle after you passed out."

"Why don't I remember this?" said Maz. "Did you drug me?"

"Yes, that's right," agreed the insect.

"The bill comes to four million kronogs," said Smivil. "I believe that is about 240,000 of your Great British pounds."

"For an injection?"

"And the ankle," said the beetle, keen that shouldn't be overlooked.

"Well, only in part," said Smivil. "The medical bill is just 230,000 kronogs, which is approximately £13,800."

"What?" said Maz. "What is this? America? Haven't you people heard of "free at the point of use"?" She inspected the tablet. "And what's this here?" she said, prodding at a long string of symbols.

"That's the cost of your journey to Dross," said Smivil.

"I'm sorry, what?" said Maz. "I think maybe my hearing might have been affected by the two spaceship crashes I've been in today and the bit where I fell on my head and got drugged by an insect. Did I just hear you right?"

"Yes, the payment to Vedna and Roydrick, the Pollups who transported you here."

"You're charging me for my own abduction?"

"There's a slight fee for their crash too, although they do accept some of the liability for that themselves."

"Excuse me? Are you saying I have to PAY for Vedna and Roydrick's bad driving?" Maz attempted to climb out of bed, but the beetle used a couple of hairy limbs to press her back down gently but firmly.

"Well, someone has to pay for it," said Smivil, as though she had personally insulted him. "And the Crown usually covers its own expenses. It's been like that for centuries now. Ever since invasion three-hundred and forty-three."

"The Collodorians, if I remember correctly," said Kamello. "And I always do."

"Yes, it was their decree that the puppet royal family accept liability for their costs, and that is what has put the family in debt ever since," explained Smivil. "This is the clothes on your back, and this is the lodgings deposit, and–"

"OK, that is IT!" said Maz, shoving the insect out of the way and clambering out of bed. "I DEMAND as your QUEEN that you take me back to Earth. To my fiancé and my sort-of-step-children and my friends."

"What friends?" snorted Kamello. "You don't have any friends."

Maz glared at the small alien, whose cute little face was turned up to hers with an expression that was both adorable and mocking.

"Yes I do have friends. Belinda is my friend."

"She is not your friend," said Kamello. "She's just the woman who lives across the street."

It was true, Maz had lost touch with a lot of her mates when she started seeing Jim, and even before that she didn't have many thanks to years spent moving from place to place and school to school, not to mention her unappealing personality, but she still felt Kamello was being unfair.

"She is too my friend," she said. "We share a lottery subscription."

"Which won a hundred quid last week, and she kept all the money," said Kamello. "Oh, and she's sleeping with Jim."

"Steady on," said Tsin. "Did you need to mention that?"

"She what?" said Maz. "She kept the hundred quid?"

Her brain, which hadn't been quite what it was since the abduction (and the concussions), took another second to register the bit about Jim.

"She's boffing Jim?"

And then the next thought shattered her entire life. "Why would she want to do that?"

Kamello raised an eyebrow. "And there we are. Her Majesty has reached enlightenment."

"Now about this signature," said Smivil.

The welcoming committee had been politely instructed to leave by their queen – if being ordered to go forth and multiply in Maz's least child-friendly language counted as polite instruction. Smivil had tried to raise some points of order and had mentioned various different statutes and by-laws that he seemed to think would prevent Maz from booting them out, but Maz had been adamant and eventually the large insect had popped a couple of feet down about the disruption, and the welcoming committee had been obliged to leave.

Now Maz was alone in her camp bed, with only the clatter of the insect doctor's mandibles for company as it organised its instruments of torture for the next unsuspecting patient.

Alone, except, that is, for the alien in the bed next to her. She hadn't noticed him before now, assuming the fluffball she could see was just a blanket. But as he wriggled himself upright against the pillows, she realised it was the hamster-the-size-of-a-pig who had injured himself during the welcome parade.

"That sounded stressful," he said.

"Oh! Hello!" she said. "I thought you were a rug."

Not her best opening line, she thought, on reflection.

"Sorry, that was a bit rude. I've had one of those days. Let me start again." She took a breath and smiled. "Hello! I'm Maz Star." She paused, feeling the need to add: "From Earth."

"Hello Mazstar! I am Rolypoly Lemonsqueezy of the Epidorean race," said the hamster-the-size-of-a-pig.

"No, you are not," said Maz, guffawing.

A few moments passed during which Maz insisted the hamster-the-size-of-a-pig was pulling her leg, and the hamster-the-size-of-a-pig assured her he wasn't. And eventually, after an awful lot of back and forth, Maz had to concede perhaps he really was called Rolypoly Lemonsqueezy – or something very like it.

During this exchange Rolypoly Lemonsqueezy had

become increasingly prickly and so Maz, feeling guilty, cheered him up by talking him through the horrors of the past twenty-four hours of her life, including the bit about the poo in the soft play and finishing with the crash and the discovery that her fiancé was cheating on her with her only friend.

"And she won a hundred quid on the lottery last week and didn't share it with me like she was meant to," she finished. That final injustice apparently providing the real sting.

"This sounds all-too familiar to me," said Rolypoly Lemonsqueezy mournfully. "Last breeding season, I tried to enter the burrow of my mate only to discover she had already allowed another Epidorean to mate with her."

Maz made a suitably appalled sound, and Rolypoly Lemonsqueezy continued.

"At that point, I was faced with a stark choice: eat all of her offspring or remain uncoupled."

Maz laughed. "Ha! Just imagine if that really was the choice."

Rolypoly Lemonsqueezy turned mournfully into the middle distance.

"That was a pretty tough meal to swallow, I don't mind saying," he said. "Eating those kids was the worst thing I've ever done."

"Excuse me, doctor?" said Maz, putting a finger up to get the insect's attention. "I'm all better now and I'd like to leave."

CHAPTER 13
DROSS ASSEMBLE

SAMMIEL WAS STANDING outside the tent when Maz emerged.

"I am glad to see you are recovered," said the dainty alien in her soft cockney-Icelandic tones. "Denx and I were worried about you."

Maz hadn't given much thought to her theft of the vehicle, justifying it as a necessary evil in trying to escape a planet that was holding her against her will. But staring at Sammiel's china doll face, she felt quite sheepish.

"Yeah, about that…I'm sorry about the ship. I hope it can be fixed?"

"Oh, I am sure," said Sammiel. "Once we have pulled it from the broken building."

"Sorry," Maz repeated, unable to think of anything better to say. "I expect Denx is really angry."

"Of course," laughed Sammiel, "But I do not blame you for trying to escape."

Maz couldn't help being slightly pleased that she

had annoyed Denx. "What's his deal, anyway? I'm sure he was an angry pig-headed beast when I met him. Which, I have to admit, feels a bit on the nose. But then he looked more like a human – albeit one with an underlying hog vibe. Or was I just hallucinating?"

"He is a Gurnox. They shift their appearance to match their moods. Something they cannot always control." The fairy looked suddenly quite pensive, her little forehead creasing in a delightful frown. "If I had known this before, I might not have partnered with him. But," she continued, smiling at Maz, "I would not change it. He is a good person at heart."

Maz remained unconvinced. "Very deep down, I'm sure he's a pussycat," she said. "A really mean, feral pussy cat. But listen," she continued, seriously, "I AM truly sorry about the ship."

Sammiel grinned. "I think perhaps we must get you some flight lessons," she said.

"Oh, no need," said Maz, waving a hand, but briefly delighted at the idea. "We're all going to die any day now, so it would almost certainly be a waste of everyone's time."

Sammiel cocked her head. "Why are you so sure?"

Maz realised too late that not everyone on the planet might know about their imminent appointment with a meat grinder. "Sorry, was that a surprise?"

"Oh, no, most of us know," said Sammiel. "The ones who don't chose not to come to the meeting. Some people prefer ignorance. I cannot blame them."

"And you're not worried?" said Maz.

"When you have been invaded as many times as we have, you tend to get a little philosophical about it," shrugged the fairy. "Countless tribes and species have tried to destroy the people of Dross over the centuries and yet," she spread out her hands, "here we are."

"Yes, you are," said Maz thoughtfully. "You most definitely are."

"What is it?" said Sammiel, seeing Maz's expression.

And just like that, Maz knew what she needed to do.

"Sorry, Sammiel, I've got to go."

"Oh yes?" said Sammiel.

"I think I've got a fight to win."

A smile lightened Sammiel's face.

"In that case, may I join you?" said the fairy. "Denx and I are surprisingly useful in a scrape."

"Sure," said Maz. "More the merrier. Where is Denx anyway?"

"I am never entirely sure," said Sammiel. "But wherever I am, he can usually also be found. We do everything together."

"Oh, you're partner-partners? Not just business partners?" said Maz, amazed that a creature as kind and beautiful as Sammiel would go within a two-mile radius of a grumpy brute like Denx.

"We are very close, but we are not lovers if that is what you mean," said Sammiel. "It is complicated."

"I hear that, sister," said Maz, readying herself for a full bonding session over Sammiel's relationship woes, but by then they had arrived at the Visitor Centre and when she turned to say, "Tell me all about it," Sammiel had vanished.

All around, aliens of every hue and species worked to move the rubble from the building so that the crashed ship could be retrieved. The welcoming committee had been overseeing things, but when Maz entered, they descended on her like wasps on a picnic.

"We are repairing the royal vessel for you, your majesty," said Smivil. He gestured towards Denx, who emerged from behind the crashed craft and greeted the group with a grunt.

"By the end of the week," continued Smivil, "the Yendoi warships will be within range and you will need to be ready to give our full surrender."

The tablet computer Smivil carried everywhere buzzed. He withdrew it from a vast pocket in his cape and showed it to Maz.

"And right on cue, we have an incoming missive from Lord Ctan Thunderbeak, grand ruler of the Yendoi people," he said. "Perfect timing."

"No!" said Maz, putting out her hand to prevent him from connecting the call. But it was too late and suddenly she was looking at a live feed of a giant octopus.

"Greetings, Earthling," said Lord Thunderbeak.

"Hi," said Maz. "This isn't actually a great time. Can I call you back?"

She mimed a throat cutting sign at Smivil, but he just carried on holding the tablet up like the world's most infuriating iPad stand.

"I've just got a few bits and pieces to do, and then I can call you straight back," she continued.

"I trust you are ready to meet us in the outer atmosphere in order to provide a timely surrender?" boomed the octopus, waving a tentacle. "It's just we have a lot of meat processing to do, and I am eager for things to stick to the schedule."

"I'm afraid I'm not going to do that," said Maz.

"What did you say?" said Lord Thunderbeak. "What did she say?" he said to someone to his left, off camera.

"Knew it," muttered Denx, as though he had won a bet with himself.

"What does that mean?" said Maz, turning to Denx, suddenly annoyed.

"I knew you wouldn't be able to surrender," he said.

"I'll come with you, soft shell," said Marshal Tsin. "No need to be afraid."

"Aside from the fact that you are almost certainly going to die, that is," added Smivil.

"That's not what I meant," said Maz, wrong-footed. "I didn't mean I am literally afraid. It's a turn of phrase. I just meant," she turned back to the screen and raised her voice in an attempt to sound imperious, "I will not be surrendering to the invaders."

Judging from the way Lord Ctan Thunderbeak's skin changed from a pale white to a hundred shades of angry swirling red, this news had not been well received.

"Well," said Smivil, "that puts us in a bit of a pickle."

"Oh great," said Kamello grumpily. "I guess we'll have to do it, then, will we? Bloody typical." She lifted her head. "You know, this is the reason why I've never liked having a Royal Family. Total layabouts who just cost the state money and never contribute anything."

"Er, excuse me," said Maz, stepping towards the tiny alien. "Firstly, I do too contribute something. Have you seen the size of my tab? Apparently, I'm even paying for my own abduction. And anyway, I thought you were meant to be a fan of Dross history."

"I wish you wouldn't call it that," said Smivil. "It was a repatriation."

"And SECONDLY," continued Maz, eyes swivelling towards the civil servant. "What I MEANT was: *none* of us will be surrendering to the Yendoi. The Dross will not give in to tyrants. The Dross will stand and fight."

Maz had intended to look heroic at this moment, but she was still smarting at Kamello's rude comments about her family and Denx's sarcasm and somehow she found herself saying, "So there," and sticking her tongue in her chin at the welcoming committee.

But it seemed as though the committee had more pressing concerns and her insult was lost in the chaos of everyone talking at once.

"What do you mean, we're not surrendering?" said Smivil, his yellow eyeballs goggling.

"I like this one!" cried the marshal. "She's got more fire in her belly than a fire-bellied raddleberk"

"Cool," said Ephew. "You tell 'em, your holiness."

"I do like Dross history," said Kamello, primly. "I'm just not sure a monarchy is the best system of government."

"Oh really?" said Maz, tilting her head in a combative gesture. But suddenly she straightened. "No, fair enough, I'd probably agree with you on that."

"SILENCE!" screeched Lord Thunderbeak. He was now a deep, dark grey and had grown longer and taller, the web around his legs spread wide.

"Oh crikey," said Maz.

The Dross quietened and stood shifting from foot to foot like naughty children.

"By your insolence you have brought down the wrath of the Yendoi," Ctan said. "I will no longer offer you such leniency. Your people will die painfully and, as queen, you will watch them suffer. And when we are done," he somehow lengthened even more, his large eyes just slits of malice, "we will take our legion of Preparators – and the new slicing and dicing add-ons that I'm excited to try – to the planet you call Earth and we will destroy every last one of your pathetic–"

Maz reached forward and smacked the screen out of Smivil's rubbery arms.

"Hey!" he said.

"I think we'd got the gist there," said Maz. "Blah blah, you're all going to die horribly."

Denx raised his head and looked at Maz, a twinkle of humour in his eye. If an outsider had been watching, they would have thought he was taking a liking to this strange spaceship-stealing human called Maz.

"So then, your majesty, what's the plan?" he said. "How do you propose to stop us all getting eaten?"

And now the welcoming committee plus Denx were all staring at her expectantly, Maz had to admit that having a plan might have been a good idea. Possibly, you could argue it was the bare minimum. Some might even go as far as saying that without a plan you had just doomed an entire planet to a truly grim fate that was worse than the original already pretty grim fate.

Perhaps she hadn't thought this through.

"I was thinking we should maybe workshop some ideas," she said, clicking her fingers like a corporate jazz musician. "You know – no bad ideas and all that?

Proper blue sky thinking, get out the dry wipe markers, couple of flip charts or whatever. What do you say?"

Denx's smile evaporated.

The committee began to share glances. The kind of glances that said, 'You pin her down while I ring the institution.'

"Hey, I'm not saying I've got all the answers here," she said, trying to win them round but hearing her voice raise a semitone. "I'm just saying we can't give up that easily. Because I for one quite like living and I'm sure you all do too. Right?"

This time they looked anywhere but at her and she heard someone – she thought maybe it was Smivil – say "not really."

"I do!" said Ephew.

"There we go!" said Maz. She gestured triumphantly at the smiling alien. "Ephew here knows life is worth living."

"And what's so great about your life?" said Kamello. "From what I've seen, your life is an endless array of laundry, school runs and shopping trips. By all accounts, you haven't had a night of passion since the Queen of Britain died."

"Jim was very shaken up by her majesty's passing," said Maz defensively.

"Belinda would say otherwise," said Kamello, raising a shaggy eyebrow.

Maz had the sudden urge to grab her by those hairy eyebrows and swing her off into outer space, but she took a breath.

"Anyway, we're going to just skirt right on past how it is you know so much about my love life and my lottery numbers, because frankly we don't have time for it right now. Let's get some ideas going, shall we?"

They exchanged glances again and Maz sighed.

"Look, I'm going to set the bar really low and say we just need any ideas that might prevent us being mashed up into ready meals. We don't need to triumph or thrive or anything. Let's just not end up as dinner."

"What sort of thing were you imagining?" said Smivil, uncomfortable with the current turn of events. He would much rather stick to the original plan, surrender and live a quiet life right up until his inevitable demise.

"Is there some sort of mutually assured destruction we can call upon, Smivil? Have you, by any chance, been building some kind of Death Star for the last twenty years? Is there a crack team of assassins we can unleash? Or failing that," Maz continued, growing increasingly desperate as she stared into the blank faces of the committee, "is there anywhere really good we can hide? Maybe for the next six to twelve months? Or years."

She began to wonder if there was a limit to how many times you could stare at the same blank expressions before you went mad. Perhaps she had already gone mad. Perhaps this whole thing was just a terrible nightmare, and she was actually wearing an open-backed hospital gown and a pair of paper knickers in a secure facility somewhere in the Welsh countryside. The thought of it calmed her. With any luck the medication should start to kick in soon and she would no longer be trapped in this nightmare. Because at this stage, sitting in an armchair, staring blankly out of a window, high on diazepam, barely able to conjure up her own name, would be a blessing.

"You're wasting your time," said Denx.

"Oh good, you're still here, are you?" said Maz, although she knew full well he was, since his was the only face that wasn't staring at her blankly. He was too busy half-smiling with a kind of smug amusement, as though he had a secret and the secret was that Maz was an idiot.

"Don't you have a spaceship to fix?" she snapped.

"Still waiting for it to be dragged from the rubble," said Denx, "because some idiot crashed it into the side of a building."

Maz flushed red. "I didn't mean that one, *actually*," she said, giving full emphasis to the word actually, as though it were a funny comeback. "I meant the ship I'm meant to be surrendering in."

"Oh, right! That one. Well, that one needs to be fixed after some idiot smashed a fin keel into it," said Denx. "And the only other one available also needs to be fixed because *some idiot* smashed it into a parking bay."

"I'm sorry?" said Maz, moving towards him. "Are you talking about Lovely Cheryl? Because there's no way I'm taking the blame for that. I can tell you that *this idiot* only crashed into two things and neither of them were this planet." She hesitated. "And that all came out worse than I wanted it to, because I am NOT an idiot."

"OK," said Denx, raising his hands in sarcastic surrender. "If the lady says she's not an idiot, who am I to call her a liar? After all, she's going to come up with some great scheme to save us all. And how is that working out for you so far, Your Majesty?"

"It's going brilliantly, actually," said Maz, jutting out

her chin defiantly. "We're just at the spitballing stage of the process. The really good ideas will come later, when we've warmed up. Maybe order in some pizzas." She turned to Smivil. "Can we do that? Order in some pizzas?"

"What are pizzas?" said Smivil. "And do you have any money?"

"And then," continued Maz, pretending he hadn't replied, "we can start really brainstorming this problem." She thought of her time in the part-baked bread company. "Maybe we need to do a SWOT chart."

And she was vibrating with a kind of nervous energy now, giving off the sort of deluded self-confidence that always ends in a breakdown. The committee watched as she tried to remember what the initials of SWOT stood for.

"Strengths, Weaknesses, Or… On… something and Treats. Yes, that's it! Treats. That's the bit where we all have some chocolate." She pointed suddenly at Smivil, "And don't say, 'What's chocolate?' because so help me god, I will break. The news about pizza was enough of a blow. You can't take away my chocolate too."

"Is anyone else feeling like they're watching a car crash happen?" said Kamello. "I almost can't take my eyes off her and yet morally speaking I probably should."

"Should we intervene?" said Smivil, wincing. "Because I'd rather stay out of it if I'm honest."

"Do you maybe need a time out?" said Ephew. "That's what I do when I'm feeling a little buzzed. Just get myself out and have a little run, or maybe use one of the massage chairs in the service station. You know? Kick back."

"Listen, soft shell," said Tsin. "I for one think it's great that you're coming out all guns blazing. And I'm not entirely sure what you think you're doing, but I applaud the instincts and the effort."

"Thank you, Marshal," said Maz, feeling thoroughly vindicated. "It's good to see someone believes in me."

"But before you get any more carried away," continued the giant crustacean. "I think you should probably come and meet our army."

CHAPTER 14
COUNCIL OF PRESLEY

MAZ HAD NEVER SEEN A MORE dispirited bunch of losers in her life, and that was saying something because she once played in a relegation match for an under-elevens remedial Sunday league.

She had been growing accustomed to the many varied types of aliens that inhabited this planet, but even she could tell that the six soldiers in front of her really did represent the dregs of Dross. From the scrawny bird-like one, to the puffing, bloated Rhino-like one, to the anaemic-looking blob one, every sorry individual seemed to be representative of the very worst of their species. They were marching back and forth with all the energy of a Covid test queue at the height of the pandemic, but she would have forgiven them all of their faults if it hadn't been that there were only six of them.

"Where are all the rest?" she said, looking around as though they might be hiding. "Are they off on some kind of mission somewhere?"

"Yes," said Tsin. "Beob's been off for a few days with

a bit of a tickly cough. It's really knocked him sideways. Other than that, the full complement is here."

They were standing in what could best be described as a small paddock just to the south of the service station, right next to the medical centre where Maz had been treated. She had missed the training ground because it looked more like somewhere you might keep a geriatric donkey rather than an entire planet's military capability.

"No, seriously," said Maz. "Where are the rest of them? This cannot represent our only interplanetary defence?"

"Oh, that's a fancy name," said the marshal, cackling. "Sounds like someone's got ideas above her station."

"If you think this is bad," said Kamello, "you should have seen what we had this time last year."

"Yes," said Ephew. "We didn't have the training ground: it was still being used as a pet lavatory."

"And our army was less than half this size," said Smivil. "We have gone to some lengths to shore up our defences."

"I'm sorry," said Maz. "Are you expecting me to be impressed because you now have an ex-dog toilet to stand around in, and you've gone from two soldiers to six?"

"Yes, it's pretty sweet, isn't it?" agreed Ephew happily.

"Three to seven," corrected Marshal Tsin. "Don't forget Beob."

"I apologise if I'm not quite as thrilled as you," said Maz, ignoring the marshal. "It's just that I've seen better security in a Budgens." She put a hand to her hip and lifted her eyes wearily to the sky. "Sweet Lord, what have I done?"

"Do you want to meet them?" said Smivil.

Maz sighed.

"They're very excited," said Tsin. "Just look at Cullton's face."

Tsin gestured to a blob creature. Colton looked like something that was dredged up by a deep-sea submersible and then walloped repeatedly with a spade. Gelatinous, with no discernible features beyond a large bulbous nose, he resembled a mournful sneeze.

"Yeah, give them a few words of encouragement," said Denx, enjoying the look on Maz's face. "I'm sure it would mean a lot to hear the grand plan directly from your mouth."

Maz moved closer to the troops and they stopped abruptly as Marshal Tsin barked an order. There was a slight scuffle as the bird-like creature bumped into the rhino, who staggered slightly and trod on the edge of Cullton. Cullton, despite having no mouth, let out a shrill scream and seemed to shrivel into himself like a trampled jellyfish. Still, the troops attempted to stand to attention and Maz, sensing their embarrassment, decided it was better to pretend nothing had happened.

Marshal Tsin barked another command and the soldiers gave what Maz assumed was a salute, all of them using whatever limbs they had to slap their foreheads, Cullton merely quivering like a smacked blancmanche.

"It figures," said Maz. "It makes total sense that the Dross salute looks like a facepalm."

She responded in kind, slapping her head as though remembering she'd left the hob on.

"How has this become my life now?" she asked nobody.

"I can give you the presentation again if it helps," suggested Smivil.

"No, you're alright," said Maz.

The Marshal gestured for Maz to start walking along so she could admire each soldier in turn, which she duly did.

"Very good," she heard herself saying in a fake posh accent. "Carry on. As you were," she continued as she walked past each soldier. "At ease."

"What is she saying?" said Denx to Kamello.

"I don't know," said Kamello, "but I wish she would stop. I'm the person who has to record all this in the Dross official history."

"Lovely," said Maz to the soldiers. "Marvellous. Jolly good. Thank you for your time."

She turned and her smile dropped as she started ushering everyone out of the paddock.

"We have a situation on our hands," she said.

They were eating fries in the food court of the Presley Service Station. Or at least Maz was. She had been relieved to discover they have chips in space: it seemed fried carbohydrates were essential food sources for every life form.

"Elvis introduced them," explained Ephew. "It's one of the reasons he is so revered."

He gestured and Maz looked up to discover she was sitting beneath a poorly cast giant gold statue of the king himself. Elvis stood with one arm raised, holding a mic in the other. His face looked more like a swollen Ken doll than Elvis, but Maz could tell it was him because his expression was frozen into the famous sneer, one side of his lip curled up in a gesture both strange and alluring.

Did she detect a silent cry for help behind those eyes? She thought so. To her he looked like a man taken hostage by aliens and forced to perform for their entertainment, but perhaps she was projecting. She wondered briefly if there was a statue for her father, the actual King and she was about to ask when Smivil called the meeting to order.

"I call this meeting to order," he said, his nasally voice cutting through their potato-based chit-chat.

And with that, the whole welcoming committee plus Denx turned to Maz expectantly. Maz swallowed her mouthful of fries, the large gulp masking the large gulp she would have been doing otherwise.

"These are really good fries!" she said, clearing her throat and wishing she had a glass of cola to swill them down with. "Now let's get this show on the road."

"What road?" asked Ephew.

"It doesn't matter," said Maz.

"What show?" said Kamello. "Not another procession to record?"

Maz caught herself under the spotlight of their stares.

"I'm sorry. I really think I might have slightly lost my mind," she said, holding her forehead like she was giving a Dross salute. "I've never been abducted by aliens and then had to organise a military campaign with aliens who don't understand me against a giant angry octopus who wants to chop me up into mouthfuls."

"Can we keep our voices down?" urged Smivil. "We don't want to drive away customers."

"Why?" said Maz. "Do we need the money for something? Have we got time to spend it all before ol' Thunderbum arrives?"

"Actually, we don't earn anything from the services," said Smivil.

"What do you mean, we don't earn anything from the services?" said Maz. "I thought it was the planet's main income?"

"It is the main income. It's just not our income," explained Smivil.

"Whose income is it, then?" said Maz.

"We're not entirely sure," said Smivil.

"It's complicated," said Kamello.

"Well then, is there any chance you could uncomplicate it and maybe just give me the really simple version for idiots?" said Maz.

"The fact is, we don't know where the money goes," said Smivil.

"Okay, so it might as well be ours," said Maz. "Can we have it?"

"Why?" asked Kamello. "You just said yourself we don't have time to spend any of the money before we're killed and eaten."

"Yeah, but now it feels like a matter of principle," said Maz. "Maybe my first proclamation as queen is to declare the Presley Service Station the property of the people of planet Dross."

Smivil looked like he was unsure whether to weep or die of excitement.

"This is going to mean an awful lot of legal paperwork," he said.

"Brilliant," she said. "Sounds like a win for you. Make it so," she announced, waving a hand. "Because we're going to need all of that money once we've come through this–"

She was going to say invasion, but she didn't want to upset the clientele – especially as their money would soon be hers.

"Set back," she finished.

"So then, what's the plan?" said Kamello. "I'm really looking forward to hearing how we're not going to get killed."

Maz stared at her a moment, hoping something really clever would occur to her, but unfortunately nothing even slightly intelligent entered her mind. In fact, she was pretty sure she could feel her IQ plummeting the longer the silence stretched out. Eventually, she slumped forward onto the table, her hair spilling across the melamine.

"Everything all right there, soft shell?" said the marshal.

Maz made a quiet whimpering sound, but then abruptly she took a breath, lifted up her head, flicked her hair back, and spoke.

"The fact is, I don't know what the hell I'm doing. But," and here she looked each one in the eye and tried to sound confident, "I honestly believe you lot do."

"I wouldn't be so sure," said Kamello.

"I agree," said Smivil. "Best to assume incompetence unless informed otherwise."

"I don't even know why we're here," said Ephew, smiling.

"No, really. I'm serious." said Maz. "I believe in you?"

"The obvious question mark stole some of the power from that statement," observed Denx.

"But because I believe in you," said Maz, ignoring him, "I actually do think I have a plan."

The committee leaned in, Marshal Tsin's bulk causing her moulded chair to buckle. Maz opened her mouth, hoping against hope that her brain would come up with something while she was talking. "So," she began, "I want you, Marshal Tsin, to…" The Marshall looked at her expectantly, eye stalks pointed steadily at Maz's open mouth. Maz felt a flicker of thought and leaned into it."…Marshal. Yes, that's it. Start marshalling." She thought of all the films she'd seen where the plucky underdogs prepare for an onslaught. They would need some sort of exercise montage. "Get your troops ready for battle. I need them to be as fit as you can get them in the next few days."

"Right–o, cockle. If you say so."

"Denx, I need you to ready every ship you can. We're going to need a fleet."

Denx made a rumbling noise like he was going to protest, but Maz ignored him.

"Smivil," she continued, turning to the civil servant. What the hell could a bureaucrat do in a war? She clicked her fingers. "I'd like you to… do a spreadsheet."

"Go on," said Smivil, his interest well and truly piqued.

"Put together a list of all the nations who have invaded us in recent times and find any soldiers left behind who may still be available to serve."

Smivil's arm emerged from the side of his body and he raised it to ask a question, but Maz ploughed on.

"And Ephew… Well, Ephew, I don't actually know what you do."

"I'm the one who cleared the poo from the training field," he said cheerfully.

"Right. Good…"

"Some of the qipoc turds exploded in my face." He barked out a laugh that was a little too desperate. "It was quite a day."

"In that case, how about you help the marshal get the new recruits into shape?" said Maz. "Maybe some agility training?"

"The current recruits could do with that too," said Kamello out of the side of her mouth.

"Hey!" said Tsin, snapping her largest claw. "I told you, they've been resting in preparation for the surrender. And there's been that tickly cough going round."

"Kamello," said Maz, trying to stop them from derailing her flow. "We need a plan."

"And that's my problem how?" said Kamello.

Maz puffed out her chest and attempted her most rousing voice. "Because, curator, you are the keeper of the records. You have an encyclopaedic knowledge of every single invasion we have ever suffered. You are fully versed in every plot and scheme to destroy this civilisation. You know where the bodies are buried and how they were put there. And somewhere in those records are the strategies we need to defeat these…" Maz deflated suddenly, losing her confidence. "What do we call them? People? I'm not sure I've really got the right term. Is people offensive? Anyway, doesn't matter. My point is, you're the one who needs to go through our history and find some way we can outmanoeuvre these… whatever they are."

She gave Kamello her most serious, most regal look. "We need a plan of attack."

"You look like you need a poo, but whatever," said Kamello, leaning back. "I'll go through some of the archives, but I wouldn't hold your breath. It's not like we've ever successfully defeated an invasion. All the documents are going to tell us is how to take over a planet populated with idiots, not defend one."

"You know, sometimes with you, I can't work out if I'm talking to a sarcastic teenager or a mean old person," said Maz. "How old are you, anyway?" She held up her hand, realising she was getting sidetracked. "You know what? Doesn't matter. Just do your best. Ok?"

Given a choice, Maz would have quite liked the welcoming committee to leap from their seats and hurry off to do her bidding. She had an image in her mind of them snapping to attention, feeling inspired by her leadership, rushing from the service station to ready the planet for the coming storm. Sadly for Maz, the minutes following her instructions were spent fielding a seemingly endless supply of quibbles and queries.

Everything from the myriad problems of drawing up short-notice recruitment laws to the exact form of callisthenics Maz thought would be best for bulking up soldiers in under a week. It was a real insight into what it would be like to be in middle management at that part-baked company, and Maz didn't like it one bit.

"Is there not some sort of prime minister or president who can deal with all this?" she said wearily.

"Some chief of staff or, I dunno, special adviser or something?"

"Not really," said Kamello. "The last invaders executed parliament and ruled as a dictatorship until they left."

"So, what's been happening since then?" asked Maz. Kamello shrugged.

"Not sure, really?" said Marshal Tsin, as though she were just realising for the first time that no one was in charge of the planet.

"Yeah? What has been happening?" said Ephew.

"Well, obviously," said Denx with a sigh, "Smivil has been running everything. Or did you not notice?"

Smivil's jelly baby flesh turned pink. "Oh, I don't know about that. The other members of the civil service helped."

"Did they?" said Maz. "Maybe I should meet them."

"I wouldn't recommend it," said Denx, "If you think Smivil is boring you've got another far more boring think coming."

"It's true," said Smivil, "The Quontrarians are renowned as the least interesting beings in the known galaxies. They thrive on tedium, pedantry and bureaucracy."

"Their invasion really was a dark time in Dross history," said Kamello. "I'll be honest. I've never made it through a full account of their rule. They seemed to conquer simply by boring everyone to death."

"What happened to them? Who pushed them out?" said Maz.

"No one," replied Kamello. "Once they'd assumed power, everyone just acted like they weren't here. It wasn't so much that they got overthrown as overlooked. And they didn't have the charisma or might to resist the next invasion. Their best weapon is bogging everyone down in bureaucracy, which many of the invaders found quite useful for distracting the populace. Everyone was too busy filling in forms to notice another occupation in progress."

"One day, I'm going to need to hear how each of your people invaded," said Maz. "But for now, we've got an industrial-sized food processor to swerve. So, let's get a wiggle on, eh?"

It only took another half hour of questions before the committee finally left. Before they went, she made an important decision.

"I've decided," she said. "In the absence of a government or leadership team or whatever, you are no longer just the welcoming committee: you're now the Queen's official council. I'll think of titles for you all once we've avoided being killed. Saves wasted effort if we end up mashed into dinner."

"Sensible," agreed Tsin.

"Should I have that drawn up as your first proclamation?" said Smivil.

"Maybe do the one about the service station first, just to be on the safe side," said Maz. "Then the one about the army enrolment, and after that, knock yourself out."

He looked confused, so she added, "Not literally, obviously."

Denx got up to leave.

"Where are you going?" said Maz.

"You wanted a fleet, Your Majesty," he said, being sure to say "Your Majesty" with enough sarcasm that Maz couldn't mistake it for respect.

"But you're on my council too, right?" she said. "I need a royal… mechanic."

This came out less confident than Maz had hoped and for a moment she thought he was going to say no. But then he sighed.

"You're the boss."

"And tell Sammiel I want her to be on the council too," she called as he walked away. He lifted an arm to show he'd heard and would do as he was told, but he didn't look back.

"Right," she said to her council. "Let's get going."

CHAPTER 15
A VERY LONG MONTAGE

CUE MUSIC, roll cameras.

This is where Maz's montage begins. Or, at least, where this is where she wished it would begin. There should be a series of scenes: the marshal signing on hundreds of smiling recruits, Ephew helping with fitness drills, Denx, covered in oil smears and wearing a tight vest, sweating as he fixed the spacecraft, and Smivil finishing up a long document, before dotting an "I", crossing a "T" and pulling a satisfied expression. Kamello, meanwhile, would be running her long grey fingers down an index file before selecting exactly the right document from her vast library. Maz would spend this montage appearing in clips with each member of the committee, pointing at things, looking at things, smiling at things. Then they'd be together again, maybe sharing a meal, and she'd laugh and they would laugh too, and then it would all be over, and they would be ready to defend the entire planet from an alien horde in the space of a three minute inspirational power ballad.

Perfect.

Unfortunately, life didn't happen that way. Instead, Maz spent what felt like the entirety of her adult life listening to Smivil explain the minutiae of complex legal proceedings and trying to pay attention as he listed all the problems in drafting an emergency national service bill. It was like having physics, geography, and a health and safety briefing all at the same time, given by the least charismatic being on the planet. At one point she dropped off only to wake and discover he was still making the same laboured point.

"So as you can see, it's quite a knotty problem," he concluded, giving a nasal chuckle of delight.

Maz smiled and nodded, and wondered if it was possible for her spirit to leave her body out of pure despair.

"Smivil, how do I explain to you that literally no one will read this document so it doesn't matter where the comma goes?" she said.

He was still laughing at the brilliance of her joke when, desperate to stretch her legs, she escaped to see how the troops were getting on.

Marshal Tsin had already conscripted a few new recruits by steering some service station workers hanging out near the bins on their break into the army training paddock on the promise of a nicer lunch spot. Once they had finished their food, the crustacean politely barred the gate and explained they now belonged to her.

Normally Maz would have tried to step in to save these innocents from indentured slavery, but given they were all going to be dead soon, it hardly seemed to matter. She wondered if this was how all tyrants started out. Justifying every loss of freedom as a means to an end for the greater good before finding themselves standing over a table, nodding approvingly as the architects rolled out the first blueprints for a gulag. She should, she mused, keep an eye on that. Becoming a tyrant wasn't on her bucket list.

Then again, her bucket list didn't contain anything more adventurous than, "go to Pompeii", so she should probably revisit all her life goals at some point – now that she had a benchmark that was a little higher than, "visit Italy." Planning to defend a planet from an alien invasion put a few plaster-of-Paris humans into the shade. Hell, eating chips in an alien space diner probably topped anything she had ever imagined doing. Up until now, Maz's idea of a grand adventure had been visiting a craft market in Shrewsbury.

"Hey, Your Majesty!" called Ephew cheerfully.

Maz waved back. Marshal Tsin came over on her many legs and stood by the gate. Amazing how quickly you can get used to standing in a field with a giant lobster person, thought Maz. She supposed at some point she would have some kind of meltdown, but in the meantime, her brain seemed to be greeting the sight of a huge crustacean with eyes like black marbles and a claw the size of her torso with incredible aplomb.

"Looks like your ranks are swelling," she said.

"Oh, no, one of them is always that big," said Tsin. "It's why I walk funny."

"I meant your army," said Maz.

"Yes," agreed Tsin, waving her one giant claw around. "It is a very big army."

Maz wondered if it was worth asking for a do-over on the whole conversation, but decided it was unlikely to yield much success. Instead, she opted to make another foolish error: she attempted a joke.

"Where does a marshal keep her army?" she said.

"Right here," replied the marshal waving her claw. "Are you alright? Is the concussion finally kicking in or something?"

"It was a joke," said Maz. "Never mind." She tried so hard to stop speaking, but she couldn't help herself. "It's just, you know, one of those jokes we have on Earth. 'Where does the General keep his armies? Up his sleevies.' It's a play on words. Do you have those here?"

"Soft shell," said Tsin, clacking her large claw. "Can I give you a bit of advice?"

"Maybe?" said Maz, clenching her jaw.

"Leave the comedy to the professionals, because – and I say this with all due respect and deference to Your Majesty, our Queen – you really are terrible at it."

"Right–o," said Maz. "Sorry. Maybe I've just spent too much time with four-year-old twins recently. Their idea of funny is handing me a turd in a ball pit."

"Now that is the kind of humour I like," said Tsin once she had stopped crying with laughter.

"Oh good," said Maz. "Well, I'm glad I could be of assistance. I admit, it seemed less funny when I couldn't get the smell out of my hand."

In the field, Ephew had the new army doing high knees, demonstrating the action with enthusiasm. It was like watching a Labrador puppy lead a fitness class.

"Amazing what happens when you mix a bit of dog DNA into the gene pool," said Tsin.

"I'm sorry, what?" said Maz.

"Ephew," said Tsin, waving a claw in his direction.

"He's the result of a human-dog DNA cloning experiment."

"I'm sorry, what?" repeated Maz.

"We've had a few despotic scientists invade over the years, and this one dude spent the entire time fiddling about with cloning things. Ephew there, was his only successful creation."

"Ephew's a clone?"

"That's right. Gene-spliced or something, I don't pretend to understand it. He was the man's son, combined with his dog. A beast which I believe originated on your adopted planet – like humans?"

Maz had so many questions. The first one being, what kind of man would clone his own son with the added genes of his dog? But for some reason her brain went with, "They have dogs in space?"

"The first explorers went to earth, saw dogs, and said to themselves, 'They're too good to leave behind,'" said the marshal.

"I mean, who could blame them?" said Maz. "Who doesn't love dogs?"

"But once they'd decided they weren't as tasty as they'd first thought, they decided just to keep them as pets."

"Oh good," said Maz.

"They've proven remarkably popular. Almost more popular than the qipoc, given they're less likely to take a dump in your hair."

At this Bug – who had been nestled around Maz's increasingly sweaty neck for the past few hours – roused herself, gave a squeak of indignation and leapt onto the ground, before squatting in the field, back legs quivering.

"I guess I should be grateful she didn't do that on me," said Maz.

"Wouldn't want you exploding on us, soft shell," barked the marshal cheerfully.

Over in the centre of the field, a recruit had just fallen and twisted what Maz assumed was their ankle.

"Best get back to it," said Tsin. She pointed to the turd. "And you need to clean that up. Mind it doesn't blow."

She scuttled off on her many legs to the injured soldier, leaving Maz and Bug alone.

"Ephew," called Maz, pointing to the steaming pile. "I've got a job for you."

In the absence of a montage, Maz trudged up to the garage forecourt to find out how Denx was getting on. Sammiel greeted her.

"How's it going?" said Maz.

"How do you describe something that is not going well?" replied Sammiel.

"Like you just did," said Maz. "What's the problem?"

"I don't know if you have noticed this," said Sammiel. "But my partner is a little… shall we say…"

"Grumpy?" said Maz.

"I was going to say, 'furious', but grumpy also works," said Sammiel.

"I did notice that, yes," said Maz.

"Well, unfortunately, some of the parts we need are unavailable to us."

"What has that got to do with Denx being grumpy?" said Maz.

"The people who have the parts don't like him very much," the fairy alien explained. "They're refusing to sell us what we need."

"Surely that can be easily resolved? You could go and get them. Everyone loves you. Who could be angry with an Icelandic pixie?"

"That is very kind, but unfortunately, that won't work. The beings who have the parts we need know who I am. They will not sell them to me because that would be the same as selling them to Denx."

"Can't Denx just apologise?" said Maz.

"This is the problem," said Sammiel, "Denx never apologises. This is one of his defining qualities."

"That and the thing where his face looks like a warthog when he's angry," observed Maz.

"Yes, that too," said Sammiel.

"But this is ridiculous," said Maz. "You can't destroy a business relationship just because you're too proud to say sorry. This is like toddlers squabbling over toys in a sandpit. What is Denx supposed to have done, anyway?"

Sammiel squirmed. "I think that is for him to tell," she said.

"Well, now I really want to know."

But Sammiel's lips were sealed and Maz eventually gave up trying to prise the story from her.

"How about I go down there and see if I can charm them into giving us the parts we need?" Maz suggested. "Maybe they'll be excited to meet a queen. They might even give it to us for free!"

"I would not hold your breath," said Sammiel. "I do

not believe they would be in the least interested in you."

"OK, good to know." Maz paused. "Did Denx mention I wanted you to join my council? It would be good to have someone to remind me not to get a big head."

"Is that a problem with your species? Expanding heads?"

"Metaphorically, yes, it does seem to be a problem. We do tend to get a bit big for our boots."

"Enlarging feet too? Truly, you are a novel species. I have never heard of this. Big heads and large feet."

"But luckily, someone like you, with your straight speaking and inability to understand idioms, can really help keep a person's feet on the ground."

"Oh dear, we are also floating off, are we? This is a problem. I can see this. Yes, in that case, I will be on your council, even though the thought of it bores me greatly and I will certainly be looking for ways to escape whenever I can."

"Sure," said Maz. "I mean, that's a given. Me too, frankly."

"You can find the Steelers in the junkyard," said Sammiel. "Perhaps you can make a difference where I have not."

Maz tried to pay attention while Sammiel gave her directions. However, Maz was not immune from the human condition. Like any normal person, as soon as someone started trying to give her directions, her brain simply started playing hold music while she nodded dumbly, slack-jawed like a chimp in a commercial.

"Got it," she said when Sammiel had finished.

"Oh, and that qipoc around your neck," said Sammiel, "do not take it with you."

"Why's that?"

"The qipoc occasionally eat the Steelers. This would not be conducive to establishing a working relationship."

Bug attempted to bite Maz's hand as she extricated herself from the qipoc's hot embrace.

"Will you take her?" she asked, holding Bug out.

"No," said Sammiel. "I am allergic – as are you."

"I am?" said Maz.

"Your skin is malformed and incorrectly coloured."

Maz touched her neck and was suddenly aware of how itchy it was.

"Great," she said. "Where's Ephew? I've got another job for him."

Having dumped Bug on Ephew, who cheerfully agreed to look after the creature, Maz set out to find the junkyard. Of course, finding the place turned out to be as disastrous as everything else she had attempted so far. But, she reflected, at least being a bit lost was less likely to cause long-term trauma than what had happened to her in the service station bathroom. Nor had she knocked down any buildings or witnessed a bipedal hamster called Rolypoly Lemonsqueezy – or something very like it – break a paw. So, as far as she was concerned, things were looking up.

Twenty minutes later she was feeling less buoyant. In fact, she was beginning to wonder if she was better off attempting to retrace her steps and ask Sammiel to draw a map. So far, she could only see acres of what appeared to be bog land to one side and concrete to the other, the latter presumably overspill from the expansive parking area. Its emptiness created an eerie atmosphere and was yet another reminder that this planet was hardly the thriving metropolis she expected from an alien civilisation.

And then, right when she was ready to give up, the path opened up into a winding view down into a valley. Her destination turned out to be exactly how it sounded: the junkyard was just a massive pile of scrap dumped on the landscape. All around lay the carcasses of alien spacecraft, giant bolts, sheets of metal, rusted bed frames, decaying household appliances: it was all so familiar, and yet the alien nature of the junk gave it an uncanny valley quality, as though the whole vista had been rendered by a misfiring AI.

Towering above her were machines that would take the breath of any right-thinking nerd. She walked through the avenue of scrap like a tourist in Manhattan, gazing up at each stack of junk in amazement.

"Hello, is anyone there?" Her voice echoed around the silence of the junkyard. "I come in peace," she added pointlessly.

But there was no-one.

She started to daydream, staring up at the three pale suns slightly hidden behind a blue-green fug of pollution. It was quite pretty in a sort of wintry sunset kind of way. Pollution had its positives, she thought. Her daydream didn't last long; the unmistakable sound of a gun cocking put a stop to that.

"Put your limbs in the air," said a voice. Or, more

accurately, a chorus of voices, all perfectly in sync. "Put them up, or we'll shoot."

CHAPTER 16
BUTTERFLIES AND BATTERIES

QUINTON THE ROBOT tried to keep his eyes facing forward as Lord Ctan Thunderbeak, noble warlord of the Yendoi, ancient race of the Sinovian Prelode, sat at a vast silver dining table with glass bowls full of squirming creatures, paused his viewing screen, which was playing a short video about the fastest way to dice vegetables, and flung out his tentacles in anger.

"HOW IS IT POSSIBLE," he cried, "that a planet as PATHETIC as Dross could resist ME?"

The Yendoi Lord had been going on like this for quite some time and Quinton feared his battery might run out before Ctan had finished his complaint. If that were to happen, there was a risk Quinton might never wake up, since there was no one here who would take the trouble to wheel him down to a charging bay and juice him up.

Without moving, Quinton slid his eyes to the right and caught sight of Lord Thunderbeak waving limbs around like a cowboy throwing multiple lassos.

"Was it truly so hard for you to give me the correct information about the new queen?" Thunderbeak shrieked.

Standing before him, his advisers quaked, their skin pale as snow with food poisoning.

One of them, Quinton noticed, was crying, fat salty tears falling from his huge cephalopod eyes, a tentacle occasionally reaching up to dash away another drop. And because a very special Yendoi had recently inserted a very special little chip into a slot in his maintenance panel, Quinton found that the tears provoked some unexpected feelings. Which is to say, he felt sorry for the crying adviser. If he was being perfectly honest – and because of his programming, he always was – he wasn't sure he liked it.

If anything, it was a bit of a drag.

"You are all worthless," clacked Lord Thunderbeak. "Luckily for you, I always have a back-up plan. And in this case, Quinton here has informed me that the queen has just made herself a powerful enemy."

All eyes turned to Quinton, and he whirred into life, using precious battery to appear alert and ready. But Ctan had already moved on, pushing back his seat and rising to his tentacles.

"Tell me," he said, turning to a small orange Yendoi. Quinton recognised the quivering creature as the engineer of the food prep machines. "Tell me, did you finish the new model?"

"Yes, my Lord," said the engineer.

"Excellent. Bring it."

The engineer signalled feebly and four larger Yendoi wheeled in the newly improved Preparator. It was smaller, more compact, with a ramp leading to the entry chute at the top.

"And tell me," said Lord Thunderbeak, "did you fix the interior?"

"Yes, my Lord," said the engineer timorously. "The interior now has a special nonstick coating."

Something in Quinton's circuit boards started to fizzle and buzz; something he couldn't quite understand. It gave him a strange sensation in his stomach. He didn't have a stomach, not really, but that's where the sensation seemed to be. And that sensation was telling him something, and that something was this: bad things are about to happen.

Quinton was unsure what to make of this funny feeling and this sudden conviction. He had never had a premonition before, never had a feeling of dread in his stomach; he didn't even recognise them as being those particular things.

All he knew was that this moment would not end well.

"Good, good," Thunderbeak was saying. "That is very good news."

Quinton felt a bit more of his battery ebb away. Shame he couldn't turn off the butterflies in his stomach, since they must surely be consuming power. And he didn't need the bad feeling to prophesy a bad outcome: simple mathematics did that It had been long enough since the warlord's last act of cold-blooded violence and Quinton had been at enough of Thunderbeak's staff meetings to know how they generally played out. The engineer was currently on very shaky ground.

But whichever sense he used, from gut instinct to

mathematical probability, he still couldn't identify the exact moment that Lord Ctan Thunderbeak switched from screaming rage to cold-blooded psychopath; he couldn't pinpoint that split second when the octopus warlord decided to commit another atrocity. But it was around now.

"Show me," said Lord Ctan Thunderbeak.

The engineer's eyes widened. Quinton wondered if this was the moment the engineer began to have his own premonition.

"Certainly, your Lordship," he said, apparently determined to brave it out – a tactic Quinton had never seen work. The engineer clapped two of his tentacles, and the burly subordinates moved the machine closer.

"You may feel for yourself, my Lord," said the engineer, "how the non-stick coating is impossible for our tentacles to cling to."

"Wonderful. That is very good news." There was a brief pause that seemed to span the ages. And then Ctan Thunderbeak spoke again.

"Show me."

The atmosphere in the room, already cooled by fear, dropped by another ten degrees. Smiles froze, sweat beaded into icy droplets, their breath seemed to hang in the air.

The engineer swallowed and seemed to resign himself to his fate. He nodded.

"Yes, my Lord," he said.

He began climbing sadly into the funnel of the machine.

The blades began to whirr, and Quinton looked away.

"Quinton," said Lord Ctan when it was over. "Get me the Zorothian."

"Your Lordship," Quinton managed.

On his communications panel he located the being in question, his battery level flickering lower by the second, and then he connected the call.

After, Quinton wheeled his slowly failing body out and down the corridor, past the many Yendoi making their way through the arteries of the frigate. They were doing their jobs, heading about their business, unable to change the fact their master was a monster.

Quinton made it to the charging bay just in time. His belly cavity popped open and he unfurled a charging cable. Slowly, sluggishly, he plugged himself in and powered down while he waited for the charge to replenish his battery.

But the fluttering in his stomach never stopped.

CHAPTER 17
SCRAPHEAP CHALLENGE

"PUT your limb parts where we can see them," said a small voice.

Maz raised her hands slowly and felt her heart in her mouth. She took the opportunity to once again ponder life's rich tapestry in the context of recent events and concluded that life's rich tapestry could bugger off. She glanced around carefully, trying to locate the source of the noise, but couldn't see anything.

"I come in peace," she said to the air, adding, "promise," as though that might seal the deal.

"You will remain where you are," commanded the small voice – or, more accurately, small voices, plural. It sounded to Maz like a tiny chorus, all chanting in perfect unison.

"I'm the Queen of Dross," she said, feeling idiotic; hands raised, claiming to be a senior member of the monarchy, shouting at air. "I have come to apologise on behalf of Denx."

If she had hoped that would placate them, she was sorely disappointed. The voices set up a strange kind of caterwauling, and it took her a moment to realise it was simply all of them shouting different angry curses at the same time. Apparently, the speaking-in-unison trick didn't work for cussing. The noise continued until they ran out of ways to swear and, having spent enough steam, they spoke in unison again, a little chanting tone that would have been pleasant had they not still been so furious.

"We will not have his name uttered in our presence. You besmirch the air with your utterances. Be gone, foul creature. We do not like your kind around here."

"My kind?" said Maz. "What do you mean by 'my kind'?"

Normally, Maz would have invited them all out for a fight at this perceived insult, but it was hard to get angry at thin air, and besides, it didn't fit with her current diplomatic mission as a peacemaker.

"Can I also just say," she added as a parenthesis, "that was a very complex sentence to say in unison. You don't hear 'besmirch' and 'utterances' much these days and I, for one, think that is a shame."

"We speak of your kind – the big folk," they said. "You are not welcome. Depart! Depart immediately and never return. This is our hallowed ground."

"What... the rubbish heap?" said Maz, wondering if there was a temple nearby she had overlooked somewhere in all the rusting metal.

The wailing sound began again and Maz realised that she had caused offence.

"Sorry, sorry," she said, putting one hand down slightly in a placating gesture. "I meant nothing by it. I was just asking. It's a lovely junkyard. One of the best I've seen. In fact, come to think of it, the only one I've seen. It's just that where I'm from, the scrapheap... well, it's not what we'd describe as 'hallowed'. It's more just a place where we get rid of things we don't want to think about anymore."

The caterwauling struck up even louder this time. Maz's efforts to charm the creatures were not going as well as she'd hoped. Part of the problem was she still couldn't see them, so there was nothing to focus on. She slowly cast her eyes around, hands still raised, body bent slightly at the knees as though that would somehow help should anyone decide to shoot.

"I'm sorry," she said. "Let me start again. My name is..."

"Yes, yes, we know who you are," the little voices interrupted. "You are the ruler of the large folk. We have no interest in your kind, no."

Maz moved as slowly as she could, and although some creatures made angry noises, she had not yet been shot.

"I just wanted to come and say, 'Hi'. Introduce myself, get to know you a bit better; find out a bit more about my subjects, you know? I thought this would be a good place to start because..." A thought struck her and she hoped her idea would pay off, "as I mentioned, I've never been to a scrapyard before."

"What?" cried the voices, their horror evident. "You have never visited the Scrap?"

"No," she replied. "That was always something Jim did. He liked going to the tip."

"What is the tip?" they said, curiosity in their voices.

"Where I'm from," she explained. "The tip is where we drive to on the weekends when we want to sit in a long queue of traffic and wait our turn to be allowed to discard all of our old appliances, furniture, and other rubbish."

"But this is not rubbish!" the creatures cried. "This is treasure. Yes, yes. The junk is the treasure of the planet."

"Is that why you came here?" asked Maz.

"Yes, yes. We came for the Scrap. The Scrap called to us and we came."

"I see. And how's that going for you?"

"It is not good."

"Oh? Why is that?"

"People keep asking us for the Scrap," they cried, "but it is our Scrap,"

"I see." Maz paused. "But, I believe you have some kind of shop here, right?"

"Shop? Yes," they grumbled. "Yes, we have the Shop. But never before have people wanted to buy things from the Shop."

"I don't want to speak out of turn here, but isn't the defining quality of a shop that people buy things from it? That it sells things to people?"

"NO!" they shouted, and Maz raised her hands higher again as they continued. "Where we are from, everyone owns a Scrap Shop. There is no need to buy, no. We simply swap our Scrap for other Scrap. That way, our treasures never leave."

"Right... okay. But, what if we were to tell you that we really, really need the Scrap," she said. "Like, your junk is currently the most important thing on the whole planet."

"We already know this, yes," came the little voices in a sea of outrage. "We are well aware that the Scrap is the most important thing on the planet. It has always been – it was ever thus. Do not mock us by speaking such foolish words with your giant flapping tongue."

"Right. OK. Listen," said Maz, glancing carefully around. "Would it be alright if I lowered my hands?"

"NO!" they screeched. "The enormous stupid arms will remain lifted."

At that moment, Maz caught sight of movement just to her left. She turned her head quickly and glimpsed out of the corner of her eye a tiny figure. It was not human. In fact, Maz had the faint sense that she had caught sight of a beetle on its hind legs, and given how her life was currently, that seemed entirely plausible.

"I just want to have a little chat about your scrap. I'm not going to hurt you," she said. "Plus, I'll be honest, I don't think I have the upper body strength to keep my hands up much longer."

There was a grumbling that suggested the creatures were open to reconsidering, and Maz jumped at it. "I promise I won't take anything and I promise I'll never besmirch any air by mentioning the person-who-shall-not-be-named's name again. Agreed?"

There was further muttering and grumbling and eventually Maz heard a reluctant, "Yes, OK then," from the group.

"Great," she said. "First things first: let's see you."

Slowly, with much grumbling, the creatures stepped out from their hiding places among the rubbish. Two very different thoughts went through Maz's brain at the same time. The first was, Oh cute. Little alien bug people. The second was, *No! Get it away! Yuck! Stamp on them. Kill them. Squish.*

"Hi," she managed, her voice quavering between the registers like a broken accordion. "I think I might sit down, if you don't mind. Wouldn't want to accidentally smash you all to smithereens with my feet and cause another diplomatic headache."

She tried to laugh like she was joking, but there was no masking the fact that it was taking all of her willpower not to start stomping indiscriminately.

The Steelers stood, shiny and upright on their back limbs, every colour of the rainbow and more besides, from black pearl to acid green. Their body shapes were equally varied, running the full range in body type, build and height, from a few centimetres to a few inches; from skinny little flower beetle to plump scarab and burly stag. Four more limbs, further up their thorax, appeared very much like human arms would if they were covered in black fuzz and had fine spurs instead of hands and fingers. They stared with their wide, dark eyes as Maz lowered herself carefully to the ground and rested her hands on her knees.

"Good!" she said, masking a shudder. "Now we're all more comfortable…" She gave a pointed look at their weapons and the bugs took the hint and began holstering them in tiny pouches that were slung around their bodies like tourist handbags. Not that Maz was worried about the guns at this stage. She assumed it would be like being shot with a pebble. And really, how much could that hurt?

"How…" she searched for the right words. "How can we *resolve* this?"

The question came to her from an old part-baked bread company meeting she had attended. The manager had been trying to settle a dispute over parking spaces and she remembered being impressed by how he could dispense corporate waffle like a human vending machine. For some reason, she decided that corporate waffle would be a good path to take here, a choice she would never be able to explain – to herself or anyone else.

"What can we do to ring-fence your psychological safety and facilitate a comfortable resolution?" she said, already regretting everything that had led her to this moment, wondering how long she could keep going before she ran out of nonsense. "How can I think outside the box to mediate this conflict to help you thrive and bring your whole self to work?"

She realised she had reached the end of her jargon and decided just to give up.

"What do you want?" she said.

"We demand an apology!" The creatures said.

It was a very clever trick – how they all spoke in unison. It was a mystery how they did it, but Maz was sure it would be a useful skill to have. She was about to ask for tips when one of the creatures began shouting independently.

"I, Taridan, will never forgive what the beast-man did! That creature may never have our precious Scrap."

Maz looked at the diminutive round bug. It – Maz assumed she – stood defiant, holding what looked like a spear, her antennae waving, palps gesticulating, back legs straight and proud, the glossy shell like petrol on water.

"Can I ask, what did he do exactly?" Maz said.

"He is a brute!" announced the little beetle.

"Yes, I think we can all agree on that, Taridan," said Maz. "No two ways about it, the man is a beast. Or sometimes," she said, reflecting, "he's actually more man than beast. It really depends on his mood. But anyway, you get what I mean. He's not a very personable bloke is what I'm saying."

"I hate him!" said the beetle, bashing her spear on the ground.

"Settle down, Taridan," said the other beetles in unison. "We will listen to the large lady speak before we make a decision."

Taridan looked ready to begin an argument, lifting her chin in defiance and putting her hands to her glossy carapace.

"We must hear her out," the unison continued, "and then we will decide."

Maz cleared her throat and tried again: "What did he actually do wrong?"

"He is a racist," shouted the bugs.

"A racist?" she said, hastily rearranging her face into seriousness. "Really? Wow, that is a surprise, I'll admit. Of all the things I guessed you might say, that was not one of them. I can imagine sexist, I can see my way towards sizeist, maybe a bit ageist. But racist? I have to say, I'm disappointed." And she really was.

The bugs agreed that, yes indeed, it definitely was disappointing. "Especially as he has so much lovely Scrap."

"And, may I ask? What did he say exactly that was racist?" said Maz. "Do I need a trigger warning first?"

They took a breath.

"He said that we were silly little bugs."

Maz cleared her throat. Anyone who knew her well might suspect she was smothering a laugh.

"Yes, that does sound problematic, doesn't it?" She began hastily reorganising her own thoughts to ensure she never referred to them as silly, little, or bugs at any point. "And which particular word of those three was it that most offended you?"

"We are not silly," they said in offended unison.

"Ah, right."

"We are a proud and serious race."

"Of course you are."

"Actually," said Taridan, once again going solo. "Matthew is quite silly."

"Yes, yes," they agreed. "Yes, Matthew is quite silly. Sometimes Matthew is silly. That is agreed. But other than that, we are a serious race and we do not like to be–"

"And also," interrupted Taridan, "it could be argued that Caroline is sometimes quite silly too."

"Yes, yes, that is true. I am quite silly," agreed a taller red bug standing on a piece of metal. "Remember the other day when I forgot that I had been running a bath, and the water spilled everywhere."

They murmured at this, their antennae waving. "Yes, yes, that was quite silly, wasn't it?" they agreed. "But other than that," they said, "we are a proud and serious race."

"And then there was that time when I was leaving, but I forgot about my drink and I left it on top of my spacecraft. And I flew all the way to where I was going and discovered it still on the top of my spacecraft when I arrived. Remember that?" said Caroline.

"Yes, that was very silly," agreed the aliens.

A beefy looking horned beetle began chuckling at the memory. "Yes, that was silly," he said.

"Right," said Maz, "so we can agree that sometimes Caroline and Matthew can be a little silly. Is that right?"

"We are not little," the beetles shrieked.

"Oh, no. Sorry. I meant a tiny amount silly. Not as in stature. No, no, no." Maz put out a hand and shook it, hoping to wave away any insults. "No one would ever dream of calling you that. And I think when Den… I mean, when he-who-shall-not-be-named had been talking, that's what I believe he meant. He didn't mean that you were small in stature. He meant little as in… It's just a turn of phrase. Let's face it, I could call him a silly little idiot for causing this dispute in the first place over something so… er… silly." She was struggling to find any words at all that might not accidentally cause offence. "It's just, I think what we have here," she said, "is just one of those misunderstandings when a lot of different peoples come together and try to learn how to live as one, you know. And yet, isn't it beautiful?"

"Beautiful?" they said, confounded.

"There are so many different species living here, all in harmony."

They laughed bitterly at this. "We do not live in harmony. These creatures are all our mortal enemies."

"I'm not trying to gaslight or anything," Maz said hastily. "It's not for me to question your lived experience and all that stuff… but are you sure about that? It's just… Well, it seems like you've been given your very own tip to live in. Is that not what you came here for?"

"Yes, yes, it is. We agree that yes, we did get what we came here for." They chatted about this for a while, in fact, and agreed that yes, indeed they had got what they wanted in that regard, and, really, they had no complaints there. "The creatures here gave us the scrapheap when we demanded it. No questions asked."

"Right, so perhaps the other beings aren't your mortal enemies?"

"Maybe," they said, reluctantly. Maz noticed Taridan kicking the ground and looking down, like a child being forced to hear reason.

"And I believe–" Maz began and then realised she had nothing left to say. It had all been going so well, but here she was, empty of anything useful to add. Her mind was tired, her thoughts empty, but her mouth continued to speak.

"Yes, he's a jerk, but we can make it work."

The bugs leaned in, disarmed by Maz's words. "The lady speaks poetry," they cried.

"Do I?" she said, looking down at them. "I mean, I guess the words rhymed."

"Say more!" said the creatures.

Was the culture shock kicking in at last? Was this delayed jet lag? Was her repressed trauma finally forcing its way into her conscious mind? Whatever was happening was very odd. Maz tried to think of poems, but her brain failed her.

"I'm a poet and I did not know it?" she finally managed, feeling miserable about the whole matter.

"Once again, poems!" the creatures cried.

"Oh, well, you know," she said.

"Please, more!" pleaded the creatures.

It was like no other song or poem ever existed. Maz couldn't think of a single one. Eventually, after casting about her brain desperately, something came to her, something the twins requested every night before bed.

"Twinkle, twinkle, little star… No! I mean, Twinkle, twinkle, *normal*-sized star. How I wonder what you are."

Maz was going to finish there, maybe with an abject apology, but the creatures were looking at her with such evident delight that she felt it was only fair to continue. Haltingly, she started to sing. "Up above the sky so high, like a diamond in the sky. Twinkle, twinkle, average sized star. How I wonder what you are."

"Ooh!" said the bugs in unison. "We love this one!"

"You do?"

"It's a favourite of all bugs throughout the galaxy."

Maz didn't know what was stranger, the proliferation of *Twinkle, Twinkle Little Star* throughout the universe, or the fact she was singing it to insect aliens. Whatever, they were all delighted. Maz felt herself redden under the sound of their tiny insect limbs clapping.

"Let's find a way to get you what you want," she said. "Did I hear you right when you said that on your planet – which you really must tell me about someday – no junk is ever sold?"

"This is correct," they agreed.

"And that's what's upsetting you – aside from the fact that, as we've agreed, your mortal enemy is a rude *silly little* idiot."

They laughed at this, now very much on her side, and agreed that, yes indeed, aside from the rude silly little idiot, they were mostly upset at parting with their beloved scrap.

"So, then," said Maz. "How about we do a trade?"

―

"No, absolutely not," said Denx.

"Oh, please," said Maz. They were standing in Denx's mechanics yard, doing what they seemed to be best at, which was arguing.

Denx shook his head. "Nope. There is absolutely no way in hell I'm letting those creatures into my garage."

"Look," said Maz, "be reasonable."

"I am being reasonable," he said. "I know what they're like. They're going to come in and they're going to strip the entire place for every spare part that we have lying around."

"Yes, and then they're going to give you exactly the spare parts that you need."

"But then I won't have any of my other spare parts."

"Right," she said, "OK, yes, I see. I haven't fully thought this through. I'm doing my best here. I'm winging it, you know, blue sky thinking or whatever it is."

"Well," he said, "your blue sky thinking needs more thought."

"Thank you for your appraisal," she said, giving him her most withering stare. He ignored her. At this stage, he was already part warthog, and she wondered if his intelligence took a dive at the same time. Certainly, he didn't seem to be appreciating her sarcasm.

"But what harm can they really do?" she said, attempting to wheedle him into submission. "They're only tiny."

"Tiny little sh–"

"Shh!" Maz interrupted, glancing around to check no one heard. "No more calling them little, alright? And I shouldn't have said tiny either. That was a mistake. They might be listening in. Who knows where those itty bitty critters get to." She put a hand on her hip. "And now I've just heard myself. Amazing how hard it is not to accidentally refer to their size, isn't it?

From now on, let's just refer to them by their names, which is the…" she trailed off. "I forget. Or did I ever know? Honestly, there have been too many new words for me to learn recently. Did Sammiel call them Steelers?"

"They're from Carabid," said Denx. "The dung and scrap planet."

"Sounds delightful."

"Half of it blew up due to a methane build up," said Denx. "Which is why they came here. People call them Steelers because they pinch metal – or anything not nailed down. Until they've stolen all the nails, of course, and then–"

"But we're not going to call them that, though, are we?" interrupted Maz. "Because that might cause another diplomatic incident."

Denx grunted an assent.

"So," said Maz, "are you going to work with them, or what?"

"No," he said.

"Fudging hell." Maz was suddenly quite grumpy. "I think my blood sugar levels have dropped. Someone's going to have to find me some chocolate. I realise that might make me sound like a diva, but so would anyone at this stage in the afternoon without a sniff of a biscuit or a cup of tea."

Ephew appeared with Bug – who was now attached to a lead.

"She kept trying to go in the training ground," Ephew explained.

"Ephew, do you think you could find me a cup of tea or coffee?" said Maz.

"A cup of teaorcoffee," Ephew said, pronouncing it

as one word. He gave her two finger guns, walking backwards. "Got it."

Maz had a sudden dark thought.

"Don't ask Vedna," she said, remembering the leaves and the mud Vedna had brewed up for her.

"Gotcha," he said, this time giving her a double thumbs up. "I'll be back in a jiffy."

"Good boy," said Maz, then cringed. "I mean, thank you."

But there was something about Ephew that gave Maz the sense that spiritually, if not literally, his tail was wagging. He trotted off.

Maz turned to Denx. "Look, we need to find some sort of solution. Where is Sammiel? I need to speak to someone who's willing to listen to reason."

"This has nothing to do with her," Denx replied, the warthog part of him erupting once again. "Leave her out of this. You can't go running to her every time you're frustrated by something I've said."

"Can't I?" said Maz. "Well, that's annoying. In which case, you're going to have to come up with a solution yourself. I've told them they can use your yard to scout for new toys and in return they'll give you the parts you need. Seems like a perfect plan to me."

"Well it isn't."

"How about if we agree that they're not to take anything without your say so and you agree that you're not to call them any further racial slurs?"

"I did not call them any racial slurs," Denx said, now entirely warthog and growing taller by the second.

"All right, calm down, Mr Literal Metaphor For Chauvinism." She took a breath. "Let's agree that they can come here – with your say so – and in return, you can have the spare parts you need, and you will no longer call them any names, or speak to them, or stare at them funny, or do anything at all that might contribute to them getting in any way cheesed off. Because, frankly, we don't have the time for that, and because – I don't know if you're aware – this time in a few days, we're all going to be someone's chicken dinner, alright?"

He began shrinking, and Maz, feeling quite light-headed after her speech, took that as a sign of assent.

"But they're not taking anything from this side," he said, waving his hand.

Maz looked over at 'this side'. "It's exactly the same as the other side," she said.

"No," he said, gritting his teeth. "It's not. There are some very important things on this side."

"Well, you keep clinging to that version of your reality and we'll just crack on if that's alright? The Carabid are only allowed on this side. Got it. And I think we can all agree that this is a lovely solution to a very silly problem."

"OK," he said, mollified, but still huffing through his warthoggy nostrils.

"Good."

She walked off and Sammiel caught up with her a few seconds later.

"It sounds like you have resolved everything to everyone's satisfaction," she said.

"Oh, is that what I did?" said Maz. "Because it sure as hell felt like I've just annoyed everyone and created more chaos."

"No, no," Sammiel said. "You must be satisfied in

the knowledge that you are almost doing a good job, which I believe is probably best you can do."

"Thank you," said Maz. "I'm going to take that as a compliment."

"Oh, no," said Sammiel. "It wasn't quite a compliment. I will let you know when I am ready to give you one of those."

"Good, good," said Maz.

Ephew appeared holding a paper cup.

"One teaorcoffee," he announced.

"Which is it?" she said, staring dubiously at the brown liquid. "Tea or coffee?"

"Yes," said Ephew, looking pleased with himself.

Tentatively, suspiciously, Maz took a sip.

"Holy cow, what is that?" she said, after she had spat it out.

"I did like you said," said Ephew. "I asked Vedna."

"Brilliant," said Maz. "Well, let's hope I don't get worms or something, because that really would be the icing on the cake right now."

She handed him the cup.

"Do you people not drink any stimulants?" she said.

"Oh, sure," said Ephew cheerfully. "We have loads of drinks with drugs in."

"Perfect," said Maz. "Get me one of those."

"No problem," said Ephew

Although he had his mouth shut, he still somehow had the air of a Labrador panting excitedly. He darted off and Maz watched him, enjoying his innocent enthusiasm for all things. Then she turned to Sammiel.

"I think I'm gonna go and get insulted by Kamello," she said. "That somehow feels simpler than all this."

"If you prefer to stay, I also can insult you," said Sammiel.

"Thanks," said Maz. "But I fancy a change."

And with that, she headed off to see the curator.

Kamello's third, lofty eye caught sight of Maz as she approached.

"Go away," the curator said, without lifting her head. "I'm busy."

Kamello was surrounded by shelves filled with old leather tomes, stacks of loose, yellowing paper and what looked like rolls of scrolls. There was also an old computer shoved on a shelf, no longer in use, but probably storing all kinds of vital information that someone intended to get around to copying off there some day. On Kamello's littered desk sat another computer, with a monitor like a tiny projector which, as Maz had already discovered, beamed the information directly into your pupils.

The room itself was like every draughty community centre office, dusty, cluttered and quietly dismal. It was larger than a minicab control room and slightly less grotty than the room where mechanics write their invoices. Hardly the place you'd expect to find a planet's entire written history.

"Lucky I didn't drive into this bit of the building, isn't it?" said Maz.

Kamello's third eyeball seemed to bore into Maz, but she still didn't look up.

"I hope I didn't destroy any of your work?" Maz added.

"No, it's fine," said Kamello, finally levelling Maz with a glare from her two main eyes. "I absolutely love having to tidy up after idiots."

"Sorry. In my defence, I was under a considerable amount of stress. Imagine how you'd feel if you'd been abducted by aliens."

"How do you think I got here? Not everyone came willingly, you know."

"Were you abducted?" said Maz, horrified.

"My parents made me come."

Fifteen, thought Maz. She's definitely fifteen.

"You think being abducted from your home planet is the same as being made to move by your parents?" said Maz.

Kamello shrugged.

"They worked for the government. It was a pain."

Maz was finding it hard to sympathise with someone who probably grew up with every luxury. "Oppressing the locals was a drag, was it?"

"I wasn't allowed to talk to anyone."

"Why not?" said Maz, winding her neck in slightly. That did, after all, sound quite bad.

Kamello shifted in her seat, clearly uncomfortable with the personal turn the conversation had taken. "I was a princess."

A few beats passed while Maz let that sink in. A small part of her felt deflated. It made sense, she supposed, that there would be other royal families here on Dross, given its history of conquests, but for a moment she had enjoyed being special.

"Your parents were the rulers?"

"Sort of," said Kamello. "They were puppets for the government."

"Oh," said Maz. "That's awful."

"Thankfully," said Kamello, "I have no need to talk about it. So, if you don't mind," she gestured to her papers, making it clear she was eager to return to them.

"But if your parents were the rulers, what happened to them?" asked Maz.

"They were killed when the next invaders came," said Kamello, levelling all three eyeballs at her.

"Sorry," said Maz. "I shouldn't have asked."

"No, it's fine," said Kamello. "We weren't close."

"How old were you?" said Maz. "…Fifteen maybe?"

"Old enough," replied Kamello.

"And what happened to your people?"

"They left."

"Why didn't you go with them?"

"Oh, I had stories I wanted to collect," said Kamello. "All those people I haven't been allowed to talk to were suddenly available to me. I wanted to know more about them."

"So how come you're not the queen?" said Maz.

Kamello turned her chair slightly towards Maz and put her fingers together.

"It's an interesting question, isn't it?" she said. "Who is in charge of a planet that has been invaded so many times?"

"So why me?"

"Because your family were the kindest," said Kamello. "They were the ones who brought us together. Your family took charge whenever the planet was at its most fractured and despairing, and they didn't kill everyone."

"Good to hear."

"Just one or two here and there. A few painful punishments, the odd lifetime incarcerations, a handful of quiet assassinations. But their strictness brought stability, and that's really all the people need."

"So my family were the least bad?"

"That's one way to put it," said Kamello, "and probably true. But how else do we choose who rules us? What form of government is best? What kind of leadership? Because ultimately, when it comes down to it, people are dreadful and anyone who wants to be in charge probably shouldn't be. Just like your family, you seemed like the least bad option."

"Wow," said Maz, "you certainly know how to make a girl feel good about herself."

"Just don't mess it up," said Kamello. "I don't mean this next bit: if we die, we die. That was always going to happen. I just mean until that moment, just try not to be a total vulka."

"No need to translate 'vulka'. I think I can work it out from context," said Maz.

Kamello returned to her books.

"So, how is your research going?" asked Maz.

"For some reason I can't concentrate… because someone keeps talking to me."

"Do we have a plan of defence, yet?"

"No," said Kamello.

"Thanks for the amazing pep talk."

"You're welcome," said Kamello.

Maz stood for a few seconds while Kamello continued to look down at her books. Eventually, Kamello's top eye swivelled down to glare at her.

"Can I get back to my work?" said the curator.

"Actually," said Maz. "I think it might be time for a meeting with the council to assess how things are going in Operation 'Let's Not Be Dinner'."

"Oh goodie," said Kamello.

CHAPTER 18
THE LAST ZOROTHIAN

THE COUNCIL HAD ASSEMBLED at their table at the service station diner. The building was emptier than usual and strangely silent. No hum of people heading for the facilities or choosing between two disappointing sandwiches. No clinking of china or plastic trays. It was mostly just Presley food court employees waiting for something to fry. Word had got round that Dross was about to experience yet another invasion, and tourists were unsurprisingly finding alternative stop-offs along their route.

"Fussy, if you ask me," said Kamello.

"Yes," agreed Maz. "That's how I'd describe it. Fussy. Fussy old tourists, not wanting to be turned into a casserole."

"Afraid of a little confrontation," scoffed Marshal Tsin.

"After all," said Maz, "Who doesn't like a threat to life when they're on holiday?"

"Precisely!" agreed the marshal. "Bunch of lily-livered wimps."

"Smivil," said Maz, "do you want to call this meeting to order?"

Smivil looked like it was his birthday.

"I call this meeting to order," he said. "First on the agenda. Denx, how is the fleet coming along?"

"We will soon have fifty operational vehicles," Denx replied. He looked less pleased about this than you might have expected. The détente with the Carabid (or "Beetle People", as Maz still kept accidentally calling them) had turned out to be a good deal more successful than anyone could have hoped. Anyone except Denx, that is. The bugs had taken a keen interest in his machines, suggesting parts that Denx had never considered. Even better, they had helped him install the smaller fiddlier parts and had begun assisting him in everything. They were soon a highly effective mechanics team, ready and willing to support in any way. And Denx was less than thrilled about it.

"They get everywhere," he said. "Always scuttling about being helpful and efficient."

"Sounds awful," agreed Kamello.

"Look at what you've achieved, though!" said Maz.

"If I accidentally tread on one, it's on your head," said Denx.

"Won't it be on your foot?" said Ephew, confused.

"Marshal Tsin, how is the army recruiting getting on?" Maz asked, turning to the great blue lobster creature.

The marshal crossed a few of her legs and rested her largest claw on her knees. "I'll admit things could be better," she said. "I was hoping we'd have press-ganged a few more victims by now."

"Volunteers," Maz said. "I think we should call them volunteers, who are definitely… volunteering."

"If you like," shrugged the marshal. "We've tracked down a few old soldiers from previous invading forces, but we simply haven't got enough of them. I also scooped up a few… volunteers… who'd just lost everything on the slot machines over there, but other than that, things have slowed considerably. Word started to get around and everyone's avoiding this area like there's about to be an invasion by a hostile planet. Like I said, wimps."

"Well," continued Maz, determined not to be put off, "Keep going."

She turned to Smivil.

"How is the new source of income coming along?" she asked. "Does the state now own the Presley Services or…?"

Smivil lit up and Maz sensed there was about to be a long speech about contracts. "I'm pleased to say that we have surmounted many obstacles, not least establishing what legal entity actually owned the building and the land…"

Here Maz zoned out for a moment. Her eye was caught by the sight of an alien in what looked like full-body armour, carrying a large weapon, heading through the service station and towards the food court. Towards them, in fact.

"And so," Smivil was saying, "We had to re-look at the covenants. That's when we discovered some potential restrictions that could very well cause future problems. With that in mind, we began…"

Maz squinted at the armoured alien. He was walking with a very purposeful gait, as though he'd just spotted the shortest queue in the supermarket and was making a beeline for it.

"…Then we discovered a confusion – and confusion really is an understatement here – with the freehold. But, we held firm, and we found some workarounds that I believe are satisfactory. I will just briefly go over some of the key points."

"Smivil," said Maz, still looking at the approaching alien, "is there any chance you could skip to the end?"

"First," said Smivil, "we had to agree the boundary line, which as I'm sure you can imagine, was less straightforward than one would hope – I mean these things always are–"

"Please Grud, while we're young," said Kamello, jabbing Smivil in his soft rib and leaving an impression that slowly resolved itself as he continued talking about boundaries.

"Denx, who is that over there?" said Maz, pointing towards the approaching alien.

"Then, of course," continued Smivil, "we had to consider public rights of way, and if there were any access rights for freeholders of neighbouring plots. And let me tell you, that's where things got really interesting."

"I don't know," said Denx, narrowing his eyes and, Maz noted with alarm, turning slightly more warthoggish.

"He doesn't look very happy, whoever he is," said Tsin, looking over.

Ephew turned to see and stiffened like a pointer, a low rumble emerging from deep in his throat. Even Bug, who was firmly wrapped about Ephew's neck, had raised her head.

"I smell trouble," said Ephew.

"Smivil!" ordered Maz, still looking at the armoured alien. "Skip to the end."

"…And I'm pleased to say we are now the official owners of the Presley Service Station," said Smivil, a little ruffled at being rushed. He unfurled a scroll that had appeared from somewhere inside his robes. "I took the opportunity to have this proclamation drawn up and shared on the Dross central noticeboard, which is located–"

"Fantastic!" Maz took the scroll and rose from her seat, still looking at the alien as he pounded ever closer. "Let's get out of here, shall we?"

And that's when she heard the furious scorch of laser blast.

Maz's breath left her body as something heavy knocked her onto the floor. She felt herself pinned down, her face pressed to the grotty tiles so that she could just see the feet of the armoured alien, standing about ten metres beyond. Others were running away or crawling along the ground, trying to get away. Maz attempted to move but couldn't, and it took her a moment to realise what was going on.

"Denx," she said. "Get off!"

The weight lifted slightly and the huge warthog-like creature stared down at her.

"You OK?" he said.

"No, I'm not," she croaked. "There's a massive pig-man lying on top of me."

He moved aside and Maz managed to crawl out. All around, people were hiding behind bins and chip wrappers and whatever they could find. Maz would have liked to have done the same, but she suddenly felt a gun pressed to her temple.

"Rise to your puny lower limbs," said the alien.

"Oh good," Maz said bitterly. "I was just starting to think things were settling down. God forbid my life should become boring."

She clambered wearily to her feet. Denx growled, and the alien turned the gun towards him.

"Step back, farm-faced creature," said the gunman.

"Hey!" said Maz. "Only I get to call him that."

The alien pressed the gun into Denx's leathery cheek and Maz froze. "Denx, do as he says."

Denx looked like he was about to grab the gun and beat the alien to death with it, but Maz put a hand on his arm. "Please," she said.

Denx moved back and, when the alien gestured with his gun, moved back even further where he stood, taking grunting breaths like an angry bull.

"What do you want, then?" Maz said, turning to the alien. "Who's been offended? What do I owe you? What's your grievance? Let's get this over and done with."

This seemed to baffle the alien, who took a couple of steps back, waving his gun around and glancing at the people all around as they fled and hid. Up close, Maz could see his armour more clearly. Slate grey, with a sheen like pencil lead, every part of him was covered in sections of metal, including his face, which was latticed with a metal grille, showing hints of a dark purple-skinned alien beneath, like an aubergine in a colander. But while the armour looked impressive from a distance, up close its age was evident, wear and tear on every join and edge, dents and rust marks, chips and cracks, and an overall shabbiness that suggested this armour's best days were behind it. The armour, thought Maz, looks as knackered as I feel.

"How can I help you?" she said. She knew she should probably be afraid, but somehow she couldn't summon up the energy.

"He is a Zorothian!" shouted Kamello from her hiding place behind the tray stacking area.

"OK," said Maz. "And what does that mean?"

The Zorothian looked at her and she could just make out an indignant expression from beneath the mesh. "My people own this planet!" he shouted. "You are not welcome here."

"Given I was literally kidnapped and brought here specifically, I think there are some other beings here who might disagree with you on that. But–" she put her hands out, hoping to calm him, "you're entitled to your opinion. This is a free country."

"No, it isn't," said Smivil's voice from somewhere.

The Zorothian swept his gun around, and those who were still on their feet ducked for cover again.

"Any chance you could stop waving that about the place?" Maz said, crouching. "It's just that I've had a very long week and I'm starting to get a bit fed up with having weapons aimed my way."

"No, I cannot," he shouted, his voice turning a little shrill. "I am here to avenge my people."

"Right," said Maz. "Let's talk about this. I'll tell you what, I'm going to just sit down because I'm feeling pretty tired, and it's been days since I had any form of caffeine. I haven't been offered a single cup of tea or coffee since I arrived, unless you count the two mugs of leafy mud water, which I have to say, I do not. Someone promised me a drink with drugs in, but that never materialised."

She shot an accusing look at Ephew's hiding spot, then sat down with a weary grunt on her usual plastic seat. The Zorothian made an incredulous squeaking sound, but did nothing.

"Come on then," said Maz, once she was settled, "tell me what the problem is."

"You have stolen our service station," he said.

"Your service station? I thought it was the planet's service station?" She twisted around. "Smivil, can you come out here, please?"

Smivil poked his head out reluctantly from behind his chair.

"Smivil, this man says that he owns the Presley Service Station. Is that true?"

"Well," said Smivil, "I suppose technically, his species did build it, yes."

"Great," said Maz, throwing her hands up in despair. "So he owns it, does he? I thought you said it didn't belong to anyone anymore, and that's why we could claim it?"

"Now, well," began Smivil, and Maz felt her heart sink.

"Is this going to be one of those long technical explanations?" she asked. "Because if so, I might tell the Zorothian just to shoot me. Any chance you could just fast forward to the end bit where you tell me yes or no."

"Ah, well," said Smivil, raising a yellow jellybean finger.

"Enough!" cried the warrior. "This is not a debate. We are not here for fun. You need to hand over the service station and return it to my people."

"And where are your people?"

The warrior hesitated. "They left."

"Oh, they left, did they? Right. OK. So is it just you, or—?"

"They will return," he said, sounding defensive.

"Good. Good to know. That's nice. So they're going to return. And how long is that likely to be, do you think? Only, it would be nice to be have some warning, given we're already in the middle of an ongoing invasion."

"They left forty years ago," supplied Kamello from her hiding place, "with a note that read, 'We're off and we're not coming back. This place is a turd hole.'"

"Ouch! Sounds pretty final," Maz said, turning to the warrior. "What do you make of that, then?"

"Lies," he said. "They would not have left me on my own."

"You'd hope not, wouldn't you?" said Maz. "Doesn't seem like a very nice thing to do to one of your own. Although, as far as I can tell, none of these invading types are particularly nice people, are they? They get these warriors to up-end their lives, they make them move to a foreign planet, and then they just abandon them when they've had enough."

"This is my planet and my people will return for me," insisted the alien.

"Hope's the real killer, isn't it?" Maz said. "And what have you been doing to pass the time? I have to say, you're looking very fit for a man of your age."

"I have been waiting for their return and training. Preparing myself physically."

"Fantastic. Sounds like we could really use you. Hey, Marshal, did you hear that?"

"I did hear that," said Tsin, who was hiding behind a pillar, her large claw sticking out like a sore thumb. "Very good."

"Very good," said Maz, turning to the warrior. "The marshal thinks you're very good. In fact, I'm willing to bet you could be one of our prize warriors. Is that the right term? Prize warriors? Something like that. Anyway, you could fight for us, is what I'm saying. And that means that you would have something to do with your time. What do you reckon?"

"The money will be restored to my people," he continued.

Maz sighed and turned to Smivil. "Smivil, where is the money and how much do we owe?"

She was amazed by how much of her time had been spent totting up bills and discussing debt. The life of a monarch really was quite far away from the opening of museums and leisure centres she had imagined. Where were her Royal Variety performances? Right now, she would give anything to sit through a mediocre turn by a gurning comedian or grinning dance troupe. If she had known how life would turn out, Maz might have taken a bit more time to enjoy the welcome parade they had put on for her when she first arrived. A giant eyeball setting a row of chickens on fire while a hamster the size of a pig twisted his ankle suddenly seemed like high culture.

"Thing is," said Smivil, "we're not sure where the money is."

"What do you mean, you're not sure where the money is?" said Maz. "You know about everything, don't you?"

"As I did just explain – in considerable detail – we

searched extensively and could not track down the funds for the service station. The money seems to be going into an account that is now closed."

"I don't get it. If the account doesn't exist, where's the money going?"

Smivil shrugged.

"That's what we don't know," he said.

"OK, so let me get this straight," said Maz, shifting in her seat, pressing her palms together. "His people built the service station. And the money from that service station goes into an account owned by his people."

"That's right."

"In a bank registered where?"

"We're not sure," said Smivil.

"We're not sure," repeated Maz. "So the money is going into a bank somewhere and is owned by his people who are now… where?"

"We don't know," said Smivil.

"Brilliant," said Maz, putting her hands flat on the table.

"Actually, I think I might know," said Kamello. Her head poking out from her hiding spot. "I believe that after they left, the Zorothians were blasted out of existence by the next batch of invaders."

"What all of them?" said Maz.

"Yes, blasted out of existence," said Kamello. "On their way out of the solar system. Poof."

"Now, that's a plot twist." Maz turned in her seat to face the warrior.

"You're the last one," said Kamello.

The alien took another step back. "It cannot be."

"That's hit you pretty hard, hasn't it?" said Maz.

The warrior looked at her through his mask and Maz really thought he might cry.

"What's your name, soldier?"

"Zono," he replied, his head hanging like a sad child.

"Hi Zono, I'm Maz. Seems like I'm not the only one having a bad week." Maz tilted her head, looking at him in sympathy. "Listen, I know what it's like to be abandoned by your family. But I also know this: you will find hope again. It's what makes us human… and Zorothian, probably. So here's an idea… how about you join us? You could put your skills to good use. Help us defend this place and maybe find some purpose. Like you say, this is your planet." She gestured at the surrounding aliens. "It's everyone's planet."

From her hiding place, Kamello made a loud retching noise.

"Ignore her," said Maz through gritted teeth. "What do you say? Want to join us?"

The warrior looked conflicted, but then nodded slowly, his shoulders slumped. "I will consider your offer."

"Good," said Maz, smiling. "In the meantime, what do you say? Let's try to find that cup of tea."

He nodded his head and Maz stood up. She was about to put an arm around him, but there was a sudden battle cry and from behind the pillar, the marshal appeared and leapt onto the Zorothian's metal back. It was quite a sight: a huge crustacean with a giant claw cutting away at a metal-clad warrior.

"What are you doing?" cried Maz. "I had it under control."

The Marshal was too busy trying to lever open the

alien's armour, using her claw like a tin opener. "I've got him!" she cried. "Have no fear, your majesty."

"Arrest this Zorothian!" said Smivil. "He threatened our Queen."

"Yeah!" said Ephew. "Get him, Bug!" He unleashed the qipoc to go and attack, but she simply scurried away under a chair.

"Imagine how cool this moment would be if we actually had a security team," said Kamello.

Denx stepped forward. "I'll do it," he grunted through the snouty part of his face.

"Everyone, just calm down," shouted Maz. "Zono is one of us now."

As she spoke the words, three things happened all at once: Zono gave a cry; everyone froze; and a laser blast rang out.

The Marshal jumped back off Zono, and the warrior stood dazed, his gun smoking.

"It just went off," he said.

"Is everyone OK?" said Maz, looking around the room.

"Excuse me?" said Smivil.

"Not now, Smivil" said Maz. "We're trying to find out if everyone's alive."

"About that," said Smivil.

Maz turned. Smivil was lying on the floor. A huge hole the size of her head ran through the centre of his body.

"I think I may have been shot," he said.

CHAPTER 19
PRESS GANG

FOR A MOMENT, time seemed to stand still as Maz stared in horror at the gaping hole in Smivil's stomach. Then, Smivil collapsed. Another slow microsecond passed and Maz's feet started working. She raced to him, sliding down onto her knees and cupping his head in her hand.

"Oh, my gosh," she said. "Medic!" She turned around desperately. "Ephew! Where's Ephew? Ephew, there you are. Fetch the doctor."

Ephew nodded and cantered off.

She turned back to Smivil. "Ephew's gone to fetch the medic. You're going to be fine."

She exchanged glances with the council. They all knew there was nothing to be done. No one survived a wound that large. The hole was as large as a dinner plate, the pale tiles of the Presley Services floor fully visible the other side. Yet somehow Smivil was still conscious. He lay there, a surprised look on his face; he blinked and opened his mouth.

"It's OK, Smivil, don't try to talk. Shh," said Maz,

putting a hand on his arm as she held onto his head with the other. "Are you feeling cold? Do you need a blanket?"

Smivil's hands went to his wound, like an injured soldier grabbing his guts in a Hollywood movie.

"That's going to take a moment to heal," he said.

But as he spoke, the hole was already beginning to shrink.

"What the...?" said Denx.

It was rare for Maz to agree with Denx, but kneeling there, watching Smivil's wound closing, she couldn't summon anything more eloquent. Within seconds, the hole was a side plate and then a saucer and then an egg cup. And, as they watched, the final section of the wound shrank to a penny before vanishing with a faint parping sound.

"Excuse me," said Smivil, turning a delicate peach colour. "That was just the air escaping."

"Isn't it always," observed Kamello.

"Are you alright?" said Maz. "We thought you were a goner there."

"I've been better," said Smivil. "I have, after all, just been shot, which was a very unpleasant experience and will give me all manner of gastric problems. But if you mean am I going to live, the answer is yes. We, Gallatian's are a resilient bunch."

"Are you immortal?" said Maz. "Like some sort of jelly bean superhero?"

"No," said Smivil. "We can certainly be killed. Crushed. Blown to smithereens–"

"Sliced up into tiny bits for someone's dinner?" suggested Kamello.

"Precisely. But flesh wounds like this tend not to trouble us for long."

"Good to know," said Maz.

"Sorry," said Zono. "The gun just went off."

"Oh, that's all right. I'm sure Smivil doesn't mind," said Maz. "You don't mind, do you, Smivil?"

"Well, actually…"

"See? He's absolutely fine about it. And the marshal is sorry, too. Aren't you, Marshal?"

"Not particularly–"

"But generally, you are. Not particularly sorry, but very definitely generally sorry. That's what you're trying to say, isn't it, Marshal?"

Maz continued to give the marshal meaningful looks, deploying a lot of eyebrow action until, Tsin grunted reluctantly. "If you say so, Your Maj."

"Great!" said Maz, smiling with a slightly unhinged air, as though through willpower alone she could stop anyone else from doing something stupid. "Now, if you just head off with the marshal here, she'll look after you, won't you, Marshal? No more trying to open you up like a tin of beans."

Maz put her arm behind the warrior alien, eager to get rid of him. "I think what we can safely do here is just take the gun away, can't we, Marshal? And then maybe, Zono, you can go along and help train the recruits. How does that sound?"

Zono nodded sadly and lifted the grille from his helmet, his purple face a picture of suppressed emotion, like a grape trying to hide a breakdown. "I haven't had a job to do with other people for a long time."

"I wonder why," said Kamello.

Maz glared at her and then smiled at the warrior. "Yes, we all know what it's like to be alone, don't we? All of us here." It struck her suddenly, "We're all orphans…"

She looked around, waiting for someone to correct her. Kamello, Tsin, Ephew, Smivil and Denx shifted uncomfortably, caught under the sudden spotlight of Maz's realisation.

"Bit on the nose if you ask me," muttered Kamello.

Maz squeezed Zono's arm pointlessly – the metal of his armour impervious to her grip. "Anyway, my point is… we'll be your family, won't we, everyone?"

"Yeah, OK," said the warrior gruffly, her voice thick with unexpressed emotion.

Kamello folded her arms. "Not sure how I feel about having another family. My last one was irritating enough."

"Well," said Maz, "If you ask me, that's perfect. What's a family without at least one person who hates being in it?"

Later, Maz went to see how Zono was settling into his new role. She discovered him alongside Marshal Tsin, sitting at a fold-out table in the middle of their damp training paddock, listening to the many excuses of the various ex-soldiers and volunteers as to why they couldn't join the army.

"I was just a chef," protested a tall alien at the front of the queue, her long fingers telegraphing distress. "I fried things."

"And I did the dishes," cried another and waved

two fists made of what looked to Maz like boiled ham. "Badly."

"Wonderful character building stuff," said Tsin with relish. "Kitchen skivvies make excellent soldiers. Used to hard, thankless work, long hours and low pay. Or, in this case, no pay."

"But we're not cut out for it!" complained the chef.

"This is true," agreed Zono. "You will almost certainly die."

"You can perish honourably for Queen and country!" agreed Tsin. "Think of that!"

"That's what I do think of," said the dishwasher, his two bottom lips wobbling as Tsin handed him his papers.

Once signed on, Ephew directed the new recruits to the assault course he had made, which consisted of a few nets on the floor in the mud and a couple of dumpsters pushed together to create a climbing wall.

"I just mucked out the stables," said a third small voice.

A tiny alien with furry eyes and a mournful face stepped forward.

"Perfect," cried Tsin, bashing the table with her heavy claw. "There's always poop to scoop in our military. I like a lad who can muck in with the mucking out."

"We will find you something equally unpleasant to do," said Zono. "You have my word as a Zorothian."

"Hear that?" said Maz with false cheer. "Isn't that great?"

Inwardly, she was wondering what the moral repercussions might be for tricking someone into the army. She had to admit, she'd had better feelings about her life choices. She would like to return to a time when her biggest moral failing had been wearing her Crocs outside the house.

"Now," said the marshal to the poor little alien, "follow Ephew over there and you can start crawling around in some mud. It'll be like the good old mucking out days."

The alien nodded sadly, took his stamped papers and handed them to Ephew, who directed him to the start of the course. "Just crawl on your tummy until the mud worms start biting and then you can scale the bins," he said helpfully.

A scrawny stick-insect alien was next in line.

"I was left behind explicitly because I was cowardly, weak, and ineffectual," he said, his antennae waving about anxiously.

"Well, we can't all be perfect," said Tsin. "Cowards often make the best warriors – always good at attracting gun fire, I find."

"Take heart," said Zono. "Cannon fodder has its uses and your death will not be in vain." He stamped the insect's form and handed it back to him. "We'll put you near someone brave and perhaps you might help to draw the sniper fire. Next."

"I was dishonourably discharged for lewdness and drunken behaviour," said a delicate alien who looked, to Maz's eye, like the middle-aged chair of a local parish council.

"Well, the good news is, I really don't care what you do in your spare time," said Tsin.

"Mainly because you will have none," said Zono, adding the alien's name to the list. "Welcome to the Dross Air Force."

Tsin and Zono seemed extremely satisfied with their new role as press-gangers. And while Maz really wanted to believe her plan would work, common sense told her it was far more likely that they were all headed for sausage mix. Looked at that way, assuming things would almost certainly end badly for everyone – no matter what choices she or anyone else made – Maz figured the two of them may as well have their fun.

From the back of the queue came a voice: "I've got no arms or legs," it said. "I was injured in the line of duty, given a medal for bravery, and honourably discharged."

"No matter," said Zono, searching out the voice in the queue. "We can get you fitted up with prosthetics, can't we, Marshal?"

"Oh, I'm not sure we have that many mechanoid pieces," said Tsin. "But maybe Denx and his bugs can find you some wheels. And for the hands, perhaps a couple of gloves filled with sand."

Maz took back the thought she'd just had.

"You know what?" she said. "I think we might have just bulldozed waaay past the place where I draw the line. I'll admit my morals have got a little woolly here recently, but even I'm not ready to send someone into battle with hands made of sand."

"It would add some grit to Ctan's dinner," said Tsin. "Imagine how annoying that would be."

"Even so…" said Maz.

"Fine," said the marshal, with a disappointed sigh. "You can go."

Under her breath, she said to Zono, "Grab that one later." Zono nodded.

"Do not do that, Zono," said Maz.

The next recruit approached, a series of spheres all spinning around each other like soap bubbles caught in an embrace.

"I was scheduled to be executed for desertion when my people left," the bubbles gurgled. "And if you don't mind, I'd probably prefer that to fighting in your doomed venture."

"Wouldn't we all," chuckled the marshal. "Wouldn't we all." She stamped the form and pushed it into one of the bubbles. "Next."

A short time afterwards, the curator and the marshal caught up with Maz while she was taking Bug for a stroll.

"We've got it," Kamello said.

"Got what?" asked Maz, assuming there was some other drama unravelling before her. "Don't tell me there's another disease going around. We can't all have a tickly cough."

"We've got the plan," said Kamello. "We know what we should do to evade capture."

"Fantastic," said Maz. "Talk me through it."

"We'll do a mix of the Jalatarian Advance and the Goffijn Shove."

"With a bit of the Palvaphoon Wiggle thrown in for the hell of it," said the marshal.

"Great news," said Maz. "Sounds terrifying. Especially that bit about shoving. I look forward to your explaining the whole thing. I was just going to see how the fleet was coming along. Why don't you join me, then you can tell me all about it?"

CHAPTER 20
QUINTON'S HEART

QUINTON FELT dread seep into his heart.

Impossible, of course, since Quinton didn't have a heart. He wasn't supposed to have feelings either. Yet here he was.

"What do you mean the alien has defected to the side of the Dross?" said Lord Ctan Thunderbeak, mighty warlord of the Yendoi, the primary planet in the Sinovian Prelode. He was enjoying a warm bath in his royal quarters, surrounded by ceiling-high tanks full of krill and tiny fish that lit the room with an iridescent glow. "How could this have happened?"

"They were nice to him?" offered an adviser who was standing quivering before him. He was a large Yendoi with plump golden top tentacles waving out from his mantle. His eyes were averted to the ceiling in order not to embarrass either his lord or himself.

Quinton assumed this was the new chief adviser, although he had lost track now. They lasted so little time, Quinton rarely used up precious memory to learn their names. This one, however, had taken the step of wearing a badge with his name on. "Hi, I'm Joubini," the badge read. "Chief Adviser."

"What do you mean, they were nice to him?" said Lord Thunderbeak. "We were nice to him. Was I not nice to him, Quinton?"

"I believe you could not have been nicer," said Quinton.

"There you go," said Thunderbeak, splashing a tentacle into the bathtub. "And if Quinton says it, it must be true, because Quinton cannot lie, can you, Quinton?"

"I was fitted with an inhibitor at my construction," said Quinton.

He didn't mention what had happened to him after his construction. Still, he was careful with how he spoke, always trying to keep to the spirit of his foundational directives. It was true; Ctan really couldn't have been nicer. It wasn't in his nature.

"I offered not to eat him in return for killing this queen of theirs. What could be nicer than that? What say you?" He eyeballed Joubini. "How could I have been nicer?"

"Perhaps we could have offered him more of an incentive," suggested the Joubini. "Maybe money, or a title. Land perhaps."

"How should I kill this one, Quinton?" said Ctan, enjoying watching as the new chief adviser blanched and his once-golden tentacles stilled.

The dread in Quinton's non-existent heart travelled to his non-existent stomach, and he felt amazed that sentient beings could survive feeling so much – could go through every day with such an inconvenient surfeit of internal guff. These peculiar new empathetic electrical impulses running through his circuitry were making it hard for him to function. He imagined this was what nerves felt like.

"You should not," was all he could manage.

"Please, my liege Lord," stammered the chief adviser, "have mercy."

"What do you mean, I should not?" said Ctan. The small hair-like tentacles on his mantle stilled. His skin flashed red. Quinton knew he was in danger. He could not help himself.

"If you continue eradicating your advisers at the current rate, you will have no one intelligent enough to take on the role by the end of the year," he said.

Ctan's top tentacles stirred into life and his skin became pebble-dash grey. His interest had been piqued. "Is this so? What has happened to the Yendoi education system that I have so few capable people around me?" He sighed. "Sometimes I think, Quinton, that you are the only one near me who truly understands what it is I want."

Quinton whirred, but remained silent.

"My beloved understood me, of course, but she couldn't live the life I had chosen," continued Ctan. "I am still so sad we have to kill her."

He began inspecting his lower tentacles, as though checking his nails for dirt. Quinton felt a sudden electrical pulse of anger shoot through his system. It was true, the high mistress of the Yendoi, the lady Tula had understood her lord very well. And it was true she had not wanted to live the life Ctan had chosen for them. But not because she rejected a life of leadership – she did not seek glory for the sake of it, but she understood the concept of serving her people. She had simply been repulsed by what her partner had become and had rejected him and everything he hungered for.

But she was safe, for the time being, and Quinton could not let his new emotions jeopardise that. For her sake, and for the one she would leave behind.

"You're the only one who can see my vision in its entirety, who can grasp what it is I am trying to achieve here," said Lord Thunderbeak, holding out a tentacle for a towel.

"It is in my programming, Lord," said Quinton.

"If only we could all have your programming," said Ctan.

"Yes, my Lord," said Quinton.

The Yendoi adviser Joubini seized his moment.

"We are in the midst of wiring all the new Preparators for the invasion, your Lordship," he said. "Might I continue my work?"

Lord Thunderbeak slipped out of his bath, and Quinton shielded his eyes from the sight.

"Yes, yes," sighed Ctan, towelling off his tentacles. "Carry on."

And Joubini hurried off, his skin strobing in a flurry of emotional display.

"Whatever is the universe coming to when a warlord can't kill his own advisers?" said Ctan.

"I really don't know, Your Lordship," said Quinton.

But thanks to the upgrade he'd been given, it was starting to feel as though he did. And with that feeling came a realisation.

He needed to do something.

CHAPTER 21
READYING THE FLEET

"THAT ALL SOUNDS SO SIMPLE," said Maz when Kamello finished outlining the plan.

"Yup," agreed Kamello. "All we need to do is make sure the fleet is ready and the troops are ready."

"Not to mention the really hefty shove," added the marshal.

"Well, it wouldn't be the Goffijn Shove without the shove, would it?" agreed Maz.

"What's this?" said Denx.

But Maz didn't answer. She was too distracted. They had arrived at the mechanics yard and before them, in all its glory, was the fleet of fixed-up spaceships that Denx had been working on.

"Wow," said Maz, admiring the array of shiny ships.

Well, in her memory she would recall it as shiny, but actually, the glamour was purely there thanks to the drizzle of Dross, which tended to cover the land in a haze of moisture for most of the year. Still, it was pretty impressive… or at least it would be impressive if all the ships were new, rather than covered in rust and slightly bent out of shape. And if they all looked the same, instead of like the forecourt at Honest John's second-hand car dealership. But, she thought, beggars can't be choosers, and regardless of any failings she felt a pride swelling in her. This was her first ever fleet of spacecraft, after all. Even if, by fleet, she meant just twelve slightly sorry-looking vehicles, one of which looked like it might fall apart before it got within sniffing distance of the upper atmosphere.

Some enterprising soul, she noted, had even painted 'Royal Air Force of Dross' on the side of the ships, which made it look almost legit. Sure, whoever it was had evidently run out of paint at some point, since a few were done with what was left on the brush, the words fading to nothing on the final vessel. And, true, whoever it was had spelled both 'Dross' and 'Air' wrong, and 'Royal' had clearly been added as an afterthought, the "A" and "L" wandering up the side of the craft as room ran out.

But still, Maz told herself for the fourteenth time, it's better than what we had before, and that's what counts.

Everyone was looking at her, at which point Maz realised all of those things she thought she had been thinking she had actually been saying out loud.

"Really excellent work," she finished, giving a thumbs up. A clutch of Carabid beetle aliens stood on the rim of one of the ships, their chests swelling.

"We have taken the Scrap and made it into bigger Scrap," they said.

"You really have," Maz said. "I'm genuinely amazed by how much you've achieved, and I'm not just saying that to cover for the things I said earlier about Honest John's car dealership."

Denx grunted with reluctant pride. "Yeah, even I have to admit they are pretty fast learners."

"See, I told you it would all work out." She gave him a gentle nudge with the side of her arm. "Now we have this beautiful fleet of ships, and we have some troops who actually can fight – or at least can stand up straight so long as they've had their cough medicine – and we have a plan. Can you believe it? I can't."

"I can," said Kamello, "because I am able to process information. Unlike some people, apparently."

"I too can update my understanding based on readily available data," said Zono.

"Well, fiddle-de-dee, aren't you both marvellous?" said Maz. "Whatever! I think you've all done a brilliant job. Look how far we've come in a few days. Think what we can achieve in future!"

"I thought you wanted to go home," said Ephew. "Haven't you been begging Smivil to organise a return flight?"

"Well, yes. Obviously, I have to go home after this. I meant, think what 'you' can achieve, not 'we.'" Maz shifted uncomfortably. "Obviously."

"The Yendoi will be here in a day," said Smivil, keen to get back to business.

It had taken Maz a while to work out how long a day was here on Dross. She had been sleeping erratically, tossing and turning on her hotel mattress, wondering how Jim would be coping without her, thinking about his affair with Belinda, and – most of all – the hundred quid Belinda had won on the lottery, and when she woke, it was either so early the mist was still snuggled on the grass, or so late the hotel restaurant was serving the lunch menu. So, it came as a surprise to learn the days were, almost to the minute, the same length as the ones on Earth.

"Amazing what suppressed trauma will do to someone's sleep patterns, isn't it?" Kamello had said when Maz expressed her surprise. "The nervous breakdown is right around the corner."

"Is that for the childhood abandonment or the adult abduction?" Maz had asked.

"Take your pick," replied Kamello.

And so a day really did mean a day, which meant they had nearly twenty-four hours to get everything ready.

"How many troops can we carry across these twelve ships?" Maz asked.

"Enough," said Tsin. "Nearly all of them."

"And does everyone know what they're doing?"

The plan almost felt too good to be true.

"Aye," said Tsin. "And some of them even managed to get over the bins on the assault course."

"It was beautiful," said Ephew. "I'm not sure I've ever been happier than I was seeing them scale that dumpster for the first time."

Zono nodded. "The dog human speaks the truth. The troops are ready to meet their maker."

"Fantastic," said Maz. She looked at her council and felt a strange swelling feeling in her heart. And then a thought struck her. "You know what? I think we're ready." She turned to the marshal. "Marshal Tsin, gather the troops. It's time for a team talk."

Maz stood on the base of the statue. Elvis Presley loomed over her, twenty feet of gold, hip-swinging sex appeal. A tribute to a man who had briefly visited this planet in the middle of what was, almost undoubtedly, an unspeakably stressful alien abduction. It seemed fitting to stand next to her fellow abductee – the king to her queen – even if she did have to occasionally grab his leg to stop herself falling off. And really, she had to stand here: there was nowhere else appropriate. Maz had knocked down the better part of the Visitor Centre with Black Beauty, and the training paddock was currently both too muddy and too drizzly.

And so they stood in the Presley Services. All the troops assembled in what could almost be called a line if you squinted and tilted your head to the side… And if you didn't know what a line was. Maz was also thrilled to see some of the service station staff and local inhabitants watching on.

Here they were. Her people. Of every colour, every shape, every species. It reminded Maz of her arrival at the service station, when the sight of the aliens had overwhelmed her with the sheer diversity of faces and designs. Evolution, thought Maz, is a funny old business.

"Aren't they a sight for sore eyes?" said Tsin, standing by the base of the plinth. "Some of these soldiers can even fight, would you believe?"

"You say that like it's a surprise," said Kamello.

"It is," said Zono. "Many of these beings would have been terminated on my planet for being craven and inept. But they have not yet soiled their undergarments, which by Dross standards makes them almost competent."

"No judgement here," said Maz.

"I wouldn't be so sure about that," said Ephew. "There's a scent coming from that little dude with the twisted ankle that's making it hard for me to resist pressing my nose against his buttocks."

"OK, and on that note, I think we'll crack on," said Maz. "Time to get some silence."

She gave a nod, and the brass section from the welcome parade attempted a rousing flourish. It sounded like a pondful of ducks were being strangled in unison. Still, it did at least have the desired effect, since everyone immediately stopped talking and placed their hands over whatever they used for ears.

And in that involuntary silence, Maz began her speech.

"When I was a child, one of my foster homes showed us a very old film called 'Independence Day'… Has anyone here seen that?"

She looked around and was glad to see blank looks. This was good news, since she intended to plagiarise the President's rousing soapbox speech at the end of the film in its entirety. But then Kamello put up a hand with all the energy of a reluctant teenager admitting she was the one who wrote 'willies' on the toilet door.

"We've all seen it. It was one of the films I showed as part of our Earth cultural enrichment season at the Visitor Centre cinema."

"Right. Good," said Maz. "In that case, forget I mentioned it."

She had a brief moment of panic, wondering what she would say next, but then the words seemed to find her, helped in part by a leaflet about the history of her home town that she had once read in a dentist's waiting room and which, for some reason, had stayed with her ever since. She took a breath and tried to look queenly.

"I grew up in a place that is regularly named as one of Britain's worst towns. It's called Telford. Created as a new town in the 1960s, it was built on the scars of the Shropshire coalfields in the shadow of the Wreakin hill, surrounded by an area of outstanding natural beauty, with good links to Wolverhampton and Birmingham via the M54 motorway. It is the birthplace of the industrial revolution, when, in 1777, a man named Abraham Darby III built Iron Bridge across the River Severn – the world's first cast iron brid–"

She caught sight of Denx – who was frowning so hard she thought his eyebrows might fuse – and abruptly stopped speaking. What the hell was she talking about? Think Maz, she thought.

"What am I talking about?" she said out loud, and then, panicking, repeated it as though it had been a rhetorical question. "What am I talking about? I'm talking about knowing what it's like to live in a place that everyone looks down on. I know what it's like to have people from Shrewsbury mocking us. Acting all high and mighty because they've got a castle and a town centre and those amazing medieval buildings that look like they're going to fall dow–"

She caught Denx's eye again, and he shook his head.

"And, let's not forget," she said, changing tack. "I grew up in care. No one wanted me. I was a naughty kid. Some might say I was a bad kid. People said it all the time, in fact. Miss Hudson said I'd never amount to anything, so it shows what she knows. Look at me now, ha! I'm a bloody queen, mate!" She coughed and regained her thread. "The point is, I know what it means to be dismissed and mocked. I know how it feels to be treated like a third-class citizen.

"And yes, Dross might be a crap hole, but it's our crap hole. And all the boring people you love live here. We don't want to see them being popped into the freezers of some superior race just because they're better at meal planning than us.

"You might think you're the dregs of humanity – or alienity, or whatever it is – but you're not: you're survivors. You have survived in the most invaded planet in the known galaxies with your sense of humour intact…" she glanced at Smivil. "Some of you, anyway.

"You," she said, looking over at the service station workers who were lined up in front of the nearest service hatch. "You can work a night shift in a windowless roadside warehouse and not lose the will to live. Just think what you could achieve if you could be bothered – and if you had enough vitamin D. Think what you could do if someone just gave you the chance."

And now she cast her gaze out, trying to make eye contact with everyone in turn.

"In fact, you remind me of a lot of the kids in care in my country."

"Are they also chopped into small pieces and eaten?" asked Ephew.

"Not quite," said Maz. "But they ARE badly treated, ordered around by different people who all think they know best, discarded and left to fend for themselves in a world that doesn't see their value." Maz thought about it some more, warming to her subject. "Or, in your case, in a galaxy that doesn't see your value."

A thought struck her.

"You're the dregs. You're what was left behind. That's what people tell you, isn't it?"

Some of the beings looked quite uncomfortable here.

"I'm not sure anyone has said that to my face," said Taridan, the small beetle.

"I have," said Caroline, raising a hand. "I have told you that."

"She has," agreed Matthew. "I have heard her say it."

"But no!" cried Maz, banging her fist into her hand and nearly falling off Elvis's plinth. "You think you are the ones who were left behind. The ones that no-one wanted. But you aren't what was left behind. You're the ones who were strong enough to stay. And by staying, you brought your own special skills and abilities and you made this planet better."

"Denial and self-delusion are under-rated as coping mechanisms," said Kamello.

Maz continued. "You aren't the dregs…not at all. You're the DROSS! Every single one of you. And you know what Dross does, don't you?" She paused for dramatic effect, ignoring the small voice in the crowd that said, 'Does it go down the lavatory?' and continuing with the same passionate fervour. "It rises to the surface."

There was a pause while Maz waited for some applause that didn't come.

"Isn't that scum?" said Caroline in the silence.

"Yes, I believe you are right," agreed Taridan. She called up to Maz. "Queen of the large folk, we believe you are speaking of scum."

"Yes," agreed the unison voices of the Carabid. "Scum rises. Maybe we are scum."

"And that's what we're going to do," continued Maz, her voice getting louder and slightly shriller. "We're going to rise to the top. Because all of us have been chewed up and spat out too many times before. We're not going to be anyone else's dinner. If they imagine they can just waltz in here and order us like something off the menu, they've got a horrible surprise coming. We won't be anyone's main course. We're going to give them HELL! And that's just for starters."

"Is she doing motivational cooking puns now?" said Marshal Tsin.

"Oh dear gods," said Kamello. "Make it stop."

Maz decided it was time for her big finish.

"So let's get out there and ram this one down their throats: we're not going to be anyone's dinner. We're Dross and we always rise to the top."

"Yeah!" whooped Ephew, applauding alone in a silent room. "Or sink to the bottom, am I right?"

Maz looked around at the slightly bored-looking audience and sighed. "OK, everyone, you can go now," she said.

"That went well," observed Kamello as the Dross filed out.

"Yes," agreed Smivil, "I really think some people might have followed at least some of it."

"Glad to hear it," said the marshal, "because I have to say, I had not a clue."

"They are wrong in what they say," said the elfin tones of Sammiel. "I believe you have inspired them, even if you also bored them. Too long they have dwelt in self-doubt and shame about their pitiful failures. You reminded them that there is always someone out there worse off. They will go away and think about what you have said."

"Thanks," said Maz.

"Especially," said Ephew, "that bit about the M54."

The following day, the troops were assembled at Denx's garage. The council was there too, ready to see off the bold heroes for phase one of Operation *Let's Not Be Dinner*. Behind them, the fleet of twelve ships were ready and waiting to take the Dross army into the skies.

"I'm proud of them," said Marshal Tsin. "I'll be sorry to see them go."

"Wait," said Maz. "You're not going with them?"

Tsin laughed. "Oh no! What do you take me for? I'm not a total idiot. No, no, the leader of the army stays at home and keeps an eye on things. Makes sure everything's going smoothly, you know."

"But who is leading them?" said Maz.

"Zono here," said the crustacean. "He's my new sergeant."

"Congratulations sergeant Zono!" said Maz. "Wait, is Zono your first name or your last?"

"Yes," replied the sergeant.

"And how are you feeling leading your troops on this mission?" said Maz.

"It will be a privilege to witness their upcoming demise," said Zono.

"Great," said Maz.

"What is the plan, anyway?" said Denx. "You haven't told us."

"That's on a need to know basis," barked the marshal. "And you don't–"

"–need to know? Yeah, I get it," said Denx. "I'm just the dumb guy with the wrench, right?"

"That's certainly one way to describe you," said Maz.

"It is what we call him," came the unison voices of the Carabid, who were standing on a raised platform they had built for themselves out of scrap. Denx glowered at them, his face turning slightly hoggy.

Maz looked at the fleet of vehicles and inhaled the damp, slightly foetid morning air.

"You know," she said. "I really think this is going to work."

Later, Maz would look back at this moment as a defining point in her time on Dross; a more innocent time, when she really believed things were possible; a time when she didn't appreciate just how bad things could get on a planet that seemed to be the universe's cosmic whipping boy – when she really believed their plan might actually work.

Because, right at the moment she said those words, she got an object lesson in failure.

A large rumbling sound followed closely behind a tremor that sent Maz and the council reeling backwards, staggering as the ground shivered and quaked. At the epicentre, a hole began to form as the ground collapsed. Within seconds the entire fleet had disappeared, sucked into the earth in a chaos of dust and soil and rubble.

"What the fudge just happened?" said Maz, lost in a cloud of dust and dirt.

"Just a sinkhole," said Denx. "Is everyone alive?"

In the dusty gloom, everyone affirmed their aliveness.

"A sinkhole? A SINKHOLE?" cried Maz, staring down, searching for sight of anything. "WHY ON DROSS IS THERE A SINKHOLE HERE?"

"It's a common issue," said Smivil. "We've raised it at committee meetings a number of times, but nothing has been done."

"Because no one is actually in charge," said Kamello. "And the committee has no power."

"Maybe this might have been worth mentioning?" said Maz as the cloud of dust and dirt drifted about her.

Kamello shrugged. "Easy to say in hindsight."

"It was in the presentation," said Smivil, clearly a little put out. "Was no one paying attention."

"Potholes! You said it was a pothole problem."

Smivil shuffled uncomfortably. "What's a sinkhole if not a large pothole?"

The sinkhole was deep and vast, but through the murky gloom Maz could just make out the wreckages of her fleet at the bottom. Gazing into this abyss, Maz had the opportunity to contemplate where life had brought her. No matter how often she tried to come to terms with the last few weeks, she really couldn't get beyond the bit where she had been pressed through the anus of an ancient spacecraft to be greeted by a couple of elderly lizards. Kamello was right: her mind seemed to be incapable of processing any further information. And so, as the detritus floated about her, she simply began to laugh.

"Err," said Ephew, glancing around in the hope that someone was going to do something. "Is she meant to be doing that?"

"Her behaviour is abnormal," assessed Zono. "I suggest we put her out of her misery."

He raised his gun but Tsin put out a claw and lowered the weapon, with a shake of her head and a signal to be quiet.

"Give her a minute," she said. "But standby for orders."

"Hey," said Kamello. "Something funny, oh Queen? Care to share the joke?"

Maz wasn't listening, however. "Brilliant," she said. "Absolutely marvellous. Got anything else for me?" She turned to the sky. "Anything else you'd like to throw my way? Or is that your best shot? Because really, COME ON! I can take it."

Nothing happened. The motes of dust floated gently through the air, settling on everything and everyone around.

"No?" said Maz to the sky. "Nothing? You've really got nothing else to give?"

"Your majesty," came Smivil's voice from somewhere in the brown haze. "We have a problem."

He emerged from a cloud and Maz wagged a finger at the sky. "I knew it! You rascal you." She turned back to Smivil, who was waving his tablet. "What new nightmare have you got for me, Smivil?"

"We have a call from Lord Ctan Thunderbeak."

"Super!" she said, rubbing her hands together. "Patch him through, or whatever it is you do. Let's speak to the ugly calamari."

"He's already connected," said Smivil, holding the tablet up so Maz could see the Yendoi alien's face peering out at her like a creep at a window.

"Marvellous. How are you, Mr Thunderbeak?" she

said, drunk on failure. "Tell me, have you ever heard of salt and pepper squid? It's really delicious. For some reason, I always think of it when I see you. I miss Chinese takeaway." She glanced around for Ephew. "Ephew, do we have that here? Chinese food? I could really go for some chilli beef right now."

"The neggle has nearly bleated, and yet we have not had your surrender," said Lord Thunderbeak.

"Yeah, I wasn't entirely clear what time that actually is. What is a neggle, anyway, and why is it bleating?"

"Don't think we haven't noticed that you are preparing your troops," said the warlord. "Please do not imagine for one second that you can fight us."

"You're right," said Maz. "I definitely can't imagine that. Not any more anyway."

It was clear from his demeanour that he had a whole speech planned.

"What was that?" he said, wrong-footed.

"You're right," she said. "You're absolutely right. We can't do it. We can't fight you. I'm sorry. I don't know what I was thinking. I thought I could help these people, but I really can't. I still don't even know whether to call them people or not. Is a person only human or what? I honestly don't know. I'm not sure what I thought would happen here. It was a silly idea and frankly, I'm embarrassed. So I surrender. We surrender. Please don't hurt us too badly. And if you wouldn't mind, I'd really appreciate you maybe avoiding Telford when it comes to destroying everyone on Earth. But you know, that's up to you. I won't be around to stop you."

"Right," said Lord Thunderbeak, slightly deflated. "Good. Glad we've got that sorted." He rallied, regaining his usual oily self-satisfaction. "And because you have been reasonable, I will show lenience. I will kill you slightly more swiftly than I intended. In fact, I might use your meat to try out one of my new recipes. Something with a bit more spice."

"Thank you so much. I'd like that. I can recommend chilli beef."

"Good. Well, I'm glad I can be of service to you. We will expect you here in twenty-three of your Dross hours for your official surrender. In the meantime, don't try to evacuate anyone. We assure you that any ships caught trying to flee the planet will be treated with extreme prejudice."

"Right you are," said Maz. "Wouldn't want you to lose any dinners, would we? I'll have everyone lined up and ready for the chop. How about that?"

Thunderbeak glanced sideways as though hoping for guidance from someone off camera. "That sounds marvellous," he said. "I look forward to eating you all."

He made a strange gurgling laugh, and the call disconnected.

"You're all staring at me again," said Maz, addressing a sea of alien eyeballs. "Always with the staring."

"Your majesty, I think the sinkhole might have affected my hearing," said Smivil, "because… well… Did you just surrender?"

"I certainly did. Yes. What choice did I have? All our ships have been destroyed. They're all in a bloody great hole in the ground, in case you hadn't noticed. Can't see us digging all those out in the next few hours, can you?"

Smivil muttered something about how he supposed not.

"Wow," said Kamello. "She's completely cracked, hasn't she?"

"Where is Denx?" said Maz, swinging her whole body around to look, which only added to her manic appearance.

"He has gone," came Sammiel's voice in the haze. She approached and Maz had a moment to wonder how she could be so immaculate in all this dust. "He is upset about the loss of the fleet."

"Aren't we all, but you don't see me sulking, do you?" said Maz. "I'm perfectly fine!"

A small voice told her she might be losing her grip on reality.

"Yes, thank you, Taridan," she said, trying to locate the small voice through the gloom. "Your feedback has been noted."

"I think maybe your brain is becoming broken. Just like the trash," Taridan continued.

"I agree," said Caroline. "We will soon be able to harvest your organs like machine parts."

"Sammiel," said Maz. "Can you ask Denx to do what he can to find a working ship? Anything will do at this stage."

"Certainly," said Sammiel. "Although I should say, I agree with the small shiny beings."

"We are not small! Giant idiot fairy," the Carabid chimed.

"Smivil," said Maz, wheeling around, "you put together the surrender document." She swung round to Sammiel. "Sammiel, you oversee the retrieval of the vehicles, and Tsin…"

Maz paused. As the huge dust cloud fully settled, something unusual had taken her eye down in the sinkhole.

"Tsin, you Kamello and Zono, you come with me."

"Where are we going, soft shell?" said Tsin. "Because if you ask me, you could do with a lie down. Maybe a flannel on the forehead in a dark room. I've seen people's minds crack in war before and it's not a pretty sight."

"We're going in there," said Maz, pointing downwards.

The council edged forwards and followed her finger, peering down into the hole. There, beside the broken spaceships and sunken earth, was a rusty metal wall and an even rustier metal door. A tiny bulkhead lamp was glowing dimly on its front.

"We're going to find out where that leads to," she said.

CHAPTER 22
BUGS

THE GRUB-LIKE ALIENS living below ground came to Dross thousands of years ago. So long ago, in fact, that no one, including the grubs, remembered what planet they were from, nor where to find it. They called themselves the Vermies, though they couldn't say if that was their tribe, their nationality, their species, or a name derived from the planet they once called home.

They made their home in vast underground caverns that crisscrossed the planet's crust, dug from the clay soil, foraging for dead wood among the leaf litter of the vast forests, coming to the surface only rarely to trade their silks and sweet saps before returning to their world underground.

But the years passed, and the grubs grew tired of the damp, cold planet. They resented the constant onslaught of the invading aliens who seemed to alight from the sky every hundred years or so (and more regularly, as space travel improved and distances between worlds shrank). And so, they began building their spacecraft, relearning skills they had forgotten centuries ago, regaining their mastery of interstellar flight. And when it came time to leave, they were ruthless.

"So, you see, this," finished the giant grub, peering down at Maz and the council, "is how I camest to be forsaken by my own people."

Maz, Zono, Tsin and Kamello were all standing in the Queen Lucan's earthen chamber, lit by the glow of a thousand tiny fire bugs – just like the one that had alerted Maz to the presence of the door. For the first half of the story, Maz had been trying not to stare at the giant grub-queen's huge leathery abdomen, which was spitting out slick white eggs in regular succession, nor her flat brown ant-like face with its round dark mouth filled with sharp teeth. And she had been briefly distracted by the smaller grub-like creatures that tended to the Queen's eggs, hauling off the leathery sacks to some nursery chamber elsewhere. But Queen Lucan was a natural storyteller and, despite the strangeness of her appearance and her haughty, antique way of speaking, Maz was soon drawn into her tale.

"I don't get it. Why are you still here?" she asked.

"For they did abandon their great Queen, those ingrate fools," said the Queen, reclining on her large bed-like couch covered in sumptuous fabrics. "And those base wretches raised a new queen – a prattling milksop upstart, a wretched cockalorum, a witless bantling – and took with them all the provisions and chattels, the most mettlesome warriors and stoutest labourers. Their great Queen was forsook. Unfed, uncared for. Left with naught but the colony's most feckless and drone-witted."

"Sounds awful," said Maz. "I mean, I only got about half of it, but I'm going from the vibes that it was bad."

"Lest our enfeebled colony perish for lack of victuals, we set them all to slumber, using a special secretion from our netherage, to await more salubrious times, and, once done, did place ourself into the same winter repose as our subjects, that we should pass our days in blameless stupor."

"What's she on about?" said Marshal Tsin.

"That secretion would be useful for the twins' bedtimes," said Maz. "Is there a recipe, or…?"

"So, how come you're awake now?" said Kamello. "Things are still the same here. Same crummy weather, same idiot population."

"Same endless invasions," added Tsin.

"I did discern a voice through the ether," said Queen Lucan. "The singing of a peerless paragon."

"Singing?" said Maz. "Has anyone been singing?" She turned to the others.

"That'll have been the human, Presley," said Kamello. "There was a concert here when he passed through."

"And then came the stench," said the Queen.

Kamello nodded. "Ah yes, the Great Stink." She leaned towards Maz. "No one collected the bins for months. There was a dispute with the contracts."

"And so," said the Queen, champing her mandibles and squeezing out another egg, "We awakened and commenced our preparations. Biding our time. Waiting to increase our company so that we may once more take dominion. Then we shall rule as rightful Empress."

"And then what?" said Maz, raising an eyebrow. "Seriously, what is this obsession with ruling a planet? Haven't you people ever heard of box sets? Who's got the time to rule an entire planet when there are, like, twenty seasons of *Grey's Anatomy* to watch? I know what I'd rather be doing. Answer me this: why did your people really leave you here? Bad weather? Lack of population to devour? Endless battles? All of the above, right? And how are things going to be better now? Can you really be bothered with the hassle at your age? On our planet, Queen Elizabeth II worked right up until she died, and for what? So she could spend her days asking people if they'd come far, and accepting ceremonial salad bowls from countries her ancestors once oppressed.

"I mean, no offence," Maz continued, "but just look at the size of your thorax. Who needs the stress of trying to haul that bootie from one end of the planet to the other just so you can appear at the grand opening of a leisure centre? Besides, we're about to be invaded again, which will mean your people will soon be a high protein snack." She waved a hand. "So, I'm sorry to say it, but all that waiting was for nothing."

Maz finished her rant, and a hush fell over the room. Everyone was waiting to see what Queen Lucan would say.

"What is a 'boxed-set'?" she said.

An hour later, the high ruler of the Vermies was happily ensconced in the first season of *The Good Wife*.

"All those years," she said, peering at Maz's phone. "Why did no one tell us about the 'boxed-set'?"

"See?" said Maz. "Isn't this a better option? Far better than invading or waging war. I know what I'd rather be doing. I've got the entire first season downloaded."

Maz watched a few episodes with her, concluding that kicking back on a daybed with a fellow queen counted as both some much needed R&R – as well as important diplomatic outreach. Once she had cemented their friendship by introducing her to *A Bug's Life*, she decided to broach a peace accord.

"Any chance you could not invade us?" she said.

The Queen inclined her large head, an agreement with caveats. "We shall wait until we have seen everything on your tiny light box, or until you are all deceased, whichever comes first."

"Great," said Maz. "Now, about that. Any chance you could join us in our battle against these oppressors?"

"Like the bugs helping the ants?" said the Queen.

"Just like that!" agreed Maz.

"Nay," said the Queen. "We shall not send our subjects into the maw of peril. We have waited too long to risk losing everything. We shall instead wait for your populace to be annihilated, and then we shall reclaim our rightful place as Queen."

Maz felt overcome with a sudden sadness. Through all of this she had clung to a crazy kind of optimism: that all this was too insane to actually end this way; that aggressors don't invade and start cooking their captives; that she and the council would somehow, against the odds, save everyone, and she would return home and get back to her normal life.

"OK, final request," she said. "How about you take the civilians down to your tunnels? Just the weak and the young?"

"Hush," said the grub Queen staring at the phone, "you interrupt a vital moment."

Maz nodded in sad acceptance, put her hands to her knees, and rose from Queen Lucan's couch. "Sounds like you've made your decision," she said. "You will not come to our aid. I understand. But before I go…"

The grub queen glanced up. "Say your piece so that we may return to our programme. But we warn you, we shall not change our mind."

"I'm going to leave you to it," said Maz. "But I'll just give you one more thing to watch. It's called *Star Wars*. I think you'll love it. You remind me of one of the characters."

"Oh?" said Queen Lucan. "Tell us."

Maz took the phone and searched for the film.

"His name is Lando," she said, "and he wants to do what is right by his people. He doesn't want to get involved. He wants to keep them safe."

"He sounds eminently sensible," said the queen.

"I suppose he is," said Maz. "Except he realises something."

"Is this where our lesson begins?" said the queen.

"He realises," said Maz, "that if his friends lose, everyone loses."

She pressed play and handed the phone back. "Excuse me, I need to get back to my subjects."

CHAPTER 23
GRAND DAY OUT

"ANY LUCK FINDING A SHIP?" said Maz.

Denx, deep into organising the recovery of his vehicles from the giant sinkhole, took a moment to respond. They had been working tirelessly, Denx in full hog mode to make the most of his brute strength (and because he was furious); the little Carabid scuttling here and there, carrying what they could manage with their surprisingly strong bodies, constructing small cranes and winches for things they could not. They had managed to drag out a number of ships, and yet Maz didn't hold out much hope. The ships they had salvaged looked in a bad way and the whole place was closer to the Carabid scrapyard than to a garage forecourt – not helped by the giant crater that now split the area in two.

Denx slung a greasy cloth over his shoulder like something out of a big book of manly clichés. "Yes," he said in his usual weary way, his face becoming more human. "I got you something."

Maz followed his gaze over to the far end of the

yard, where, on the other side of the sinkhole, Vedna and Roydrick Pollup were waving cheerfully. They were standing next to the Lovely Cheryl, their ancient space tourer.

"Coo-ee!" said Vedna.

"That?" said Maz. "But Lovely Cheryl almost killed everyone aboard last time I was in it."

Denx gave her a long, level look. "That's because someone crashed it."

"That wasn't me! I didn't touch the wheels."

"If you say so."

"Seriously, is it even actually space-worthy? People on Earth saw ones just like that flying around the skies in the fifties."

"It's a classic," said Denx.

"The Reliant Robin is a classic, but it doesn't mean you'd want to drive it into a battle. Or at all, frankly."

"She will get you there." He hesitated."Probably."

"Well, I'm reassured, thanks. And what about the return journey?"

He scuffed some gravel with his feet. "Should be OK."

"You will not be coming back, anyway," called up one of the Carabid. "The squidgy-limbed beings will have devoured you by then."

Maz squinted down and saw that it was Taridan. That figured.

"I mean, she's got a point," said Denx.

"Fine," sighed Maz. "But if I die on my way to being killed and eaten, then I'm going to be extremely cheesed off."

"Fair enough."

"Coo-ee, hen!" called Vedna. "Are you coming over or not?"

"While we're young," said Roydrick. "I've seen skin shed quicker."

Maz realised she was strangely happy to see the elderly lizard couple.

"Coming!" she called.

After a mere twenty minutes of edging around the massive hole, climbing over half-swallowed space craft and fallen garage forecourt, Maz made it to the other side, where she found herself gathered into a leathery embrace.

"Why didn't you leave while you still had the chance?" she asked, holding Vedna's arms affectionately (while successfully resisting the urge to brush away the skin flakes that had stuck to her jumper).

"We didn't have anywhere to go," Roydrick said, chuckling.

"I know we're not from Dross," said Vedna, "but we've been here so long waiting for Denx to fix our extreme-distance engine…"

"And then someone crashed our Lovely Cheryl," added Roydrick cheerfully.

"I hope you're not implying that was me," said Maz.

"…That we've come to think of the lodge as home."

Maz briefly wondered if she could ever think of the service station hotel as home.

"So what you're saying is that you – my kidnappers – have been held hostage here against your will and now you've become institutionalised?" said Maz. "I think I know how that feels."

"Och, you are a hoot, hen," said Vedna, flapping the

back of her hand towards Maz's stomach. "You should be on the TV."

Maz had seen Dross TV and she knew that was possibly the weakest compliment anyone could pay another person. She had seen dead fish with more personality than the people working in the Dross entertainment industry.

"Thanks," she said.

"And we know what we're talking about. We've paid for the extra channels in our hotel room," said Roydrick, winking.

"I'd give anything not to have heard that," said Maz, faintly.

"We've got Britbox now," said Vedna. "Roydrick loves a cosy crime. Don't you, Roy?"

"You remind me of the vicar who solves the murders," said Roydrick.

"I remind you of an old man in a cassock?" said Maz.

"Och, don't take offence, dearie," said Roydrick. "You all look the same to us."

"Are you excited about our little adventure, hen?" said Vedna.

"What, the one where I fly to an alien vessel and surrender my life?"

"That's the one! Not every day you get to do that, is it?"

"I'm looking forward to seeing the Yendoi frigate," said Roydrick, rubbing his hands together and sloughing off a snowfall of skin. "I've heard very good things about the propulsion engine."

"I think it's over-engineered," said Denx, who had somehow made it across the void without a sound. He backed up his opinion with some technical guff that Maz struggled to recognise as English, let alone understand.

Roydrick chuckled. "A traditionalist, eh? I wouldn't have expected that from you."

A few more minutes passed while the two aliens debated the relative merits of a Yendoi frigate versus a Yendoi destroyer, with the Carabid chiming in with their own united chorus of views. Maz wondered if it was too late to pop for a last wee. But Kamello and Smivil were approaching via the main path from the Visitor Centre and Royal Lodge respectively. At the same time, Zono of the Zorothians, Ephew and Marshal Tsin appeared from the training paddock on the far side. They had to traverse the giant sinkhole as Maz had done. For Zono in his heavy metal armour, and Tsin with her large shelled body, moving around the edge of a steep precipice was not easy.

"I tell you what," said the marshal, shuffling her articulated rear cautiously past a recent smaller landslide. "This is a right pain in the tail."

"I think it's fun!" said Ephew, with his usual Labrador enthusiasm, bouncing Bug in his arms, before slipping on a piece of loose soil that crumbled away down into the vast hole. Zono caught him before he fell to his death.

"Thanks dude," Ephew said. "That would have been a bummer."

"To die in such a manner would have been humiliating for your family. Not to mention an inconvenience for the rest of us."

"Kind of you to say," said Ephew. A flash of sadness

crossed his face. "But I don't have a family, other than Bug here."

Maz thought of his father experimenting on him, this cheerful innocent creature, and shuddered.

And so, more time passed, and the sun got slightly lower in the sky, and Maz's need to wee increased.

"Pop and use our bathroom if you like," said Vedna.

Maz hesitated.

"It's OK," said Denx. "We have a toilet."

He gestured to the garage entrance. "It's through the office. Just don't leave the sucker in the pan. Sammiel hates that."

"I hope to never find out what that means," said Maz.

"While she is evacuating her water sacks, we shall do the final checks of the Scrap," called Taridan, carrying a bolt that was the size of her body. "This looks like it has fallen off somewhere."

"OK, good," said Maz. "Definitely pop that back in before we launch into outer space."

She darted off. Denx had vanished when she returned.

"Where does he get to? He's like the Invisible Man or something. Wait," she glanced around. "That's not it, is it? He's not actually just turning invisible. Is it like the opposite of when he goes feral or something?"

"He is coming," said Sammiel, who was standing near to Kamello. She was one of the few people who looked at the small curator eye to eye – if you ignored the one on top of Kamello's head. "We go everywhere together," she added.

Maz tried to hide a pang of envy. "Of course, I forget how close you two are."

Kamello rolled all of her eyes. "You have no idea."

"We need to be on our way," said Smivil, tapping his tablet. "If we are to make it to our new alien overlord's vessel at a reasonable hour."

"Let's do this," said Kamello. "Time to make the previous few days of our lives even more pointless than the rest of our sorry existences."

"Thanks, as always, for the pep talk," said Maz.

"No problem. You certainly made us all hope for something better for a moment. I guess we should be grateful for that. Even if you did turn out to be a massive let down."

"Good to know," said Maz.

Kamello headed onto the ship.

"It was fun while it lasted," said the marshal.

"We should probably settle your bill," said Smivil. "You have incurred considerable debts, not to mention the interest on the money your family owed."

Maz put a hand on his back and guided him towards the ramp. "How about we sort that out en route? Give us something fun to do."

They began boarding. Ephew and Maz were the last, but half way up the ramp, Ephew stopped, his dog-like ears twitching. Maz stopped too and heard what she could only describe as a galumphing sound. They scanned the area and saw one of Queen Lucan's grub aliens lolloping towards them like a walrus on a beach.

Tsin poked her head out of the tourer's door and spotted the approaching Vermie.

"Alright cockle? Quick as you like," she called to him. "We haven't got all day, you know. Get a wiggle on." She turned back to Maz. "Same to you, soft shell.

You need to shake a leg if you don't want to incur the wrath of the mad octopus."

Zono appeared in the doorway. He took a gun from his arsenal and pointed it at the grub.

"What are you doing?" hissed Maz.

"Protecting my Queen from an enemy."

"They're not enemies... Well, not currently. Not yet. Put it down before you start a diplomatic crisis."

Zono ignored her for a few seconds and then reluctantly lowered his weapon.

"I will not shoot the giant worm," he said. "Though it would please me very much."

"You know, I'm really glad you're on our side," said Maz.

The grub approached, slouching slowly towards them with rasping breath. Evidently, he was unused to hauling his bulk this far. After centuries spent underground, the Vermies were out of shape.

"Is he alright, do you think?" said Maz, watching as he stopped to lean against a recently recovered spaceship. "Are you OK?" she called. She watched him breathing heavily for a moment longer and decided she couldn't bear the wait. "I tell you what. We'll come to you."

She trotted down the pathway and met the alien near the ruined wall of the Visitor Centre, which was still very much a building site. The whole area had changed unrecognisably since Maz had arrived. One ruined building, thanks to her, and one giant sinkhole filled with dead spaceships, thanks to the wheezing alien before her.

"Many thanks, mistress," puffed the Vermie. "I come with a missive from our great Queen."

The alien hunched over, winded, trying to regain his breath, and Maz could feel Zono growing tense with impatience.

"You want to try doing a few burpees," said Tsin, eying the breathless messenger.

"I concur," said the Zorothian. "I suggest total body reconditioning."

"How can I help?" Maz said to the grub, hoping to hurry him up before the marshal and the Zorothian started building a full exercise regime for the poor soul.

Slowly, he reared up and withdrew a note from a fold of pale skin. Maz tried not to pull a face.

"Thank you," she said, taking the note gingerly between pinched fingers. She opened it and read:

"Child, we have decided to take in your feeble and your callow. You may send them with this drone slave we have supplied."

Maz had never felt relief like it.

"Was it *Star Wars*?" she said.

The alien nodded. "Her Majesty is very taken with the tale from long ago."

"Thank you, Lando," said Maz, grateful to the playboy for persuading Queen Lucan where she couldn't. "And will she join the resistance, as Lando did?"

"No," he puffed. "Majesty said, 'We were not born yesterday,' and that Lando's change of heart was, 'the actions of a drone-witted ninny'."

The drone flushed, a little embarrassed at the insult to his kind, and Maz gave him an apologetic smile. But she didn't have time for his feelings, no matter how heartless that was. She thought again of her descent into despotism, but decided to park her moral crisis until after the surrender. Instead, she felt a cold grip of icy resolve seize her. The fight wasn't over yet. She turned to Zono.

"Change of plan. Tell Ephew to lead our civilians to the tunnels."

"Yes, sir," said Zono, giving the Dross salute.

"Then I have a job for you," Maz said. She beckoned the lobster. "Marshal, you're going to want to hear this."

Vedna was waiting when Maz walked back up Lovely Cheryl's ramp with the marshal.

"This time, you can come in through the entrance," said the lizard.

Maz shuddered at the memory of the sky anus. "What a treat."

Inside, the tourer was just as cluttered and grotty as she remembered.

"I know what you're wondering," said Vedna, chuckling, "and the answer is yes. Yes, we did tidy especially for you."

"I'm honoured," said Maz.

"What's that smell?" said Kamello followed by "Ow!" when Maz elbowed her in what was meant to be her ribs, but, thanks to the height difference, turned out to be her face.

Maz sat down on one of the brown banquettes that lined one corner of the living space. It was strange to be back in the place where she had begun. She gave the bench an affectionate pat.

"It's sticky," she said.

"It's original," said Vedna proudly.

"Is it meant to be sticky?"

"I'll drive!" said Vedna.

"And so will I," said Roydrick,

"Oh good," said Maz.

"Time to hand them our arses on a platter," said Denx, appearing by Maz's shoulder.

"I mean, literally," said Kamello.

Within an hour, they were approaching the hold of the Yendoi frigate.

"Should have taken ten minutes," muttered Denx.

"Roydrick got a bit lost," said Vedna, calling in from the cockpit, the steering wheel in her hand veering alarmingly to the right.

"No, I did not," yelled Roydrick over his shoulder for everyone's benefit and turning the steering wheel to the left. "You were the one driving."

"I was not! I was having a nap. You said you wanted to drive the last bit."

"Lies!" Roydrick said. "Bloody lies."

Maz wasn't really listening. She had gone to the small window and pushed aside the doily and was now trying to get her head around the sight of a ship the size of Wembley Stadium floating in space. It really was the stuff of dreams. Like a gigantic metal whale powering through space, at once imposing and graceful. There were huge cannon dotted over its shiny carcass, multiple pods and docking bays, as well as countless viewing platforms with thin letterbox windows. If only the people on board weren't a bunch of psychotic cannibals, she thought, this would be the best thing that had ever happened to her. Although, given her life so far, it still wasn't exactly the worst. After all, at least she finally got to really experience something – even if that something concluded with butchery by a high-tech food processor.

"Impressive, isn't it?" said Kamello.

The curator was perched on the sticky banquette, her feet not touching the floor.

"Don't tell me Kamello Koturnix, queen of snark, is actually awed by something?"

Kamello shrugged.

"Despite our heritage, many of us have only been into space a handful of times," she said. "We came to Dross and then we stayed there. I haven't seen much beyond the four walls of the Visitor Centre. Or," she added, "three walls now, thanks to you."

"How do you know so much about my planet, then?" said Maz, ignoring the mention of the Visitor Centre fiasco. After all, how many times could one person apologise? But Kamello didn't get to explain her knowledge of Earth because they were all knocked sprawling by a sudden impact.

"Brace for landing!" said Vedna cheerily as the caravan thudded down onto the frigate's hold. Maz felt her stomach flip as Lovely Cheryl bounced gently upwards away from the floor, then careered back towards the deck, landing again with an even bigger thud.

"There we are," said Roydrick with the sort of satisfaction you'd expect to hear from someone who had just completed a particularly fiendish parallel park.

"Textbook," said Kamello.

"I thought so," said Vedna. "You have me to thank for that."

"Ooh, what a lie!" exclaimed Roydrick.

Once she had got up off the floor, Maz returned to the doily window and peered out.

There it was. The kind of spaceship hold she had always imagined. Clean, metallic, white. And enormous. Vast, in fact. Spreading out for what felt like miles. A cavern filled with technology that would set a human mind spinning. And aliens as far as the eye could see. If she hadn't been about to surrender her life to a giant octopus, she would have been really excited.

Denx joined her at the small window and they watched as a gleaming white robot wheeled towards them. It looked, to Maz's untrained eye, like a normal robot. Except for one thing. Or, more precisely, two things.

"Weird arms," she said.

"Yep," agreed Denx. "Seems to be some sort of assistance droid mixed with a battle droid. I've never seen anything like it before."

The robot approached, wheeling up to the ship, stopping right near where Maz was peering out. She felt the robot's eyes on her and had a strange sensation, as though she was looking into the eyes of an intelligent being.

"Do the robots have sentience here yet?" she asked.

"What are you talking about? No, of course not."

"On Earth, we have these little robot vacuum cleaners. They don't have sentience either, but they sing the saddest little songs. I've always had the feeling they were trying to tell us something."

"That their battery is low, presumably."

"Yeah, you're right, I'm just being silly."

Nevertheless, she couldn't help lifting a hand and

waving at the robot. It looked so tiny and forlorn there in the landing bay with its massive arms.

Behind the robot, a vehicle approached. Shaped like half a mussel shell, it floated towards them, its base hovering above the floor.

"Amazing," said Maz.

"Magnets," said Denx.

"They're basically the same as magic, I always think."

"What, magnets?" Denx grunted and almost smiled. "Me too."

Two cephalopod aliens sprawled out of each side of the vehicle like underset jellies, their tentacles almost skimming the floor.

"You will emerge with your limbs far away from your bodies," said the larger Yendoi. He was speaking into a microphone of some sort and they could hear his voice clearly from within Lovely Cheryl.

"Sounds like we had better go and say 'hi'," Roydrick said.

"You stay here," said Maz. "This has nothing to do with you."

"You will all come out," said the Yendoi as though he could hear them.

Reluctantly, Maz offered Roydrick an arm while Denx took Vedna, and they escorted the Pollups down the ramp.

She looked up at the surrounding hold. "See, this is what I'm talking about," she said. "This is what space is. Have you Dross ever watched any futuristic dramas? These people clearly have. This is what the Presley Service Station should look like."

"The service station was the very latest in architectural design," said Smivil, a hurt tone in his voice. "It was inspired by the buildings on your home planet, in honour of your king of rock and roll – and as tribute to your own adoptive home."

"So it's my fault, is it? Great to hear."

"I quite like it," said Kamello. "It's the Dross aesthetic: beige underwhelm."

"You will come with me," said the butch-armed service robot, lights flickering across his round head. He approached and spoke with a strangely human quality, as though he was really hoping she would comply.

"Hi yer," Maz said, putting out a hand. "I'm Maz. What's your name?"

"It's a robot; it doesn't have a name," said Denx.

Kamello masked a smile.

"I have been named Quinton," said the robot. "I am here to disable your vessel and welcome you aboard."

Maz gave Denx and Kamello a triumphant smile and turned back to the robot. "Great to meet you, Quinton. So come on then: take me to your leader."

Quinton scanned the ship, discovered the energy port located on of the lower panels, and stuck a magnetic device to its metal shell. The lights in the ship dimmed.

"What have you done to my Lovely Cheryl?" said Vedna.

"I have ensured your vessel will not function how it did," Quinton replied.

"Great," growled Denx. "Finally fixed her, and this is what you do."

Maz turned her attention to the Yendoi in the vehicle.

"Hello," she said.

They looked uncomfortable and didn't catch her eye.

"The Yendoi prefer not to speak to their food," said Quinton.

"Why's that?" said Maz, and then the penny dropped. "Oh, I see. It's like naming the cow you're about to eat." She leaned forwards. "You don't want to get attached, is that right? I understand. Don't worry about it. We won't make you feel bad about eating us, will we?"

She turned to her council.

"Not at all," said Kamello. "I won't mention my wife and twenty children."

"I had a Sudoku I hadn't finished," said Smivil. "I won't say how disappointing this is."

"And I won't talk about the many beings that rely on me for a living," said Denx. "Nor how I really hoped that someday I could see the sea."

Maz put a hand on Denx's arm. "And we mustn't talk about how we have fallen deeply in love and hoped to start a family."

Denx glanced at her in surprise, and Maz immediately regretted her joke. She removed her hand quickly and turned to the Yendoi. "We were just kidding…"

"I wasn't," said Smivil quietly.

"He already has a significant other," finished Maz. She waved a finger around the room, ready to point Sammiel out, but Denx frowned and shook his head slightly. She dropped her finger. "Who apparently didn't come with us." She put a hand over her mouth and said quietly. "She really is a fairy, isn't she?"

Their guilt-tripping had done the job. The Yendoi turned away, their skin changing from bold colours to pale greys as though they were hoping to blend in with their surroundings.

"We can still see you, you know," Maz said. "But nice try." She turned to Quinton. "So, should we just follow you, or…?"

Quinton's lights flashed as though he was embarrassed. "You will climb into this," he said.

Awkwardly, he lifted up a massive arm and gestured towards a small trailer behind the Yendoi vehicle.

"Like lambs to the slaughter, eh?" said Maz. "Come on then, team." She turned to her council.

Quinton opened the rear of the trailer and Smivil's large slug foot split in half so he could step onto it. Kamello was next, and she clambered on, struggling with the height of the step.

"Haven't you people heard of accessibility?" she said.

Standing near Maz, Sammiel piped up. "I agree, this is not easy for us smaller folk."

"Where did you spring from?" Maz said, and Sammiel gave her a quizzical look.

"Same for us, dearie," said Vedna cheerfully. "I'm not sure how you expect my husband and me to clamber into that."

"Not with my lumbago," agreed Roydrick cheerfully. "We're not as young as we were, you know."

Maz saw an opportunity to make the Yendoi squirm some more and took it.

"They don't care about our unhappiness, do you fellas? It's all about getting the meat into the wagon. Am I right? Nothing farm-assured about this particular plate of food."

She pointed at herself with both thumbs, and the Yendoi averted their eyes, unhappy with this whole mission.

"Fine," the larger one eventually barked. He had gold tentacles on his mantle, which seemed to squirm with visible embarrassment, and he was wearing a name tag. "The infirm can remain here. But they will be watched at all times."

"That's very good of you, hen," said Vedna. "We've brought a picnic, so we'll enjoy that while we're waiting."

"Yeah, thanks, Joubini," said Maz, reading his name badge. "Chief adviser, eh? Good for you!"

Joubini looked away, his skin flushing rouge, his golden tentacles stilling.

Maz and the rest of the council filed obediently onto the trailer, waving to the Pollups as the vehicle took them from the hangar.

"It's nice that they've decided to turn this into a day out," said Maz, watching the Pollups shrink into the distance, her hand raised in a farewell as the vehicle sped away.

The journey took a good ten minutes, through long corridors and vaulted atriums, up many floors and past countless Yendoi who stopped to stare as the trailer passed, some of them flashing darker and waving their tentacles in delight, others more sober, blushing a shade of pink that looked to Maz like embarrassment or fading to a pale white, trying to go unnoticed. Beside her, Quinton made a whirring noise.

"Are those your real arms, Quinton?" said Maz. "Because I have to say you should maybe stop skipping leg day."

Quinton's lights flashed in his visor and Maz thought he seemed a little down.

"No offence. They're excellent arms," she added. "I'd love to see what you can bench press."

She decided to change the subject.

"What's it like working for the Yendoi? I imagine it's a bit of a drag."

"I cannot answer that question," said Quinton in a tone Maz would have called sad and desperate if Denx hadn't just insisted that robots didn't have emotions.

"Why?" said Maz. "Did you sign an NDA or something? Non-disclosure agreement. I expect you did. I even had to sign one at the part-baked bread company and the most secret thing we ever discussed was whether we could get away with an even cheaper flour." She paused. "I supposed I just broke the NDA there, didn't I? Let's hope the lawyers didn't hear me."

"Your secret is safe with me," said Quinton, his visor lights flashing. "I have not signed an NDA, but I was programmed not to lie and I was programmed not to bring harm to the reputation of the Yendoi."

"Ah, gotcha," said Maz with a wink. "The NDA was built in."

"Yes," said Quinton. "I suppose it was."

His lights went out and the whirring sound stopped for a moment and Maz wondered if he had run out of battery.

"You OK?" she said.

Silently his lights flashed on again and he turned his head to hers with a clicking sound.

"I cannot answer that question," he said.

"NDA on your feelings, too, is there?" Maz said.

"I do not know what OK is," he answered. "I have never felt it before."

Silently, Maz put a hand on Quinton's shoulder, where his massive arm met his normal body.

"I hear that," she said with a sympathetic sigh. "I'm beginning to think I haven't either."

Along they went until, finally, they pulled up outside the private quarters of Lord Ctan Thunderbeak, mighty warlord of the Yendoi of the Sinovian Prelode. Their escorts clambered out, their main tentacles flopping onto the cool floor while their mops of smaller tentacles on their mantles waved around like little grasping hands.

"You will follow them," said Quinton, gesturing with his big hand. "Please go in now."

"Right you are," said Maz, not wanting to make him any sadder. "Let's get this surrender under way, shall we?"

CHAPTER 24
SURRENDER

LORD THUNDERBEAK'S private quarters were dark. Where the rest of the frigate had been filled with white light, Ctan's space could safely be described as gloomy. Red lights mingled with the occasional orange glow to create the sort of effect you'd expect in the ambient room of a nightclub or, Maz thought, an evil aquarium. She looked around for light switches.

"A bit dark in here, isn't it?" she said, squinting at the leader. "I don't mean to sound like an old person, but is there any chance we could put the Big Light on?"

"You couldn't get much reading done in here," agreed Kamello.

"Where's the light switch, Quinton?" asked Maz.

"Here," replied Quinton, pointing to an array of switches.

"Silence!" cried one of the Yendoi.

A ring of advisers were surrounding Maz and her council like teens watching a fight. Behind them, at regular intervals along the walls, Thunderbeak's personal bodyguards provided exactly the right sort of menacing ambience.

"No, no," said Lord Thunderbeak, staying the adviser's outrage with a gesture of a tentacle. Maz noticed they were lacquered at the tips with some kind of coloured varnish.

"Nice manicure," she observed. "Nice earrings too," she added, admiring the circles of gold that ran up the flaps on the side of his head. "At least, I assume they're earrings."

"Thank you," he replied. "I do like to make an effort. Especially when I'm meeting my dinner for the first time. Or should that be eating?"

He looked delighted with his joke, searching the surrounding faces for amusement. His entourage obediently chattered their beaks and flashed colourful strobes to show their pleasure.

"Very funny," said Maz. "The world of light entertainment is the worse for your absence. So what's the plan, Thunderbeak? When's the big cook out?"

"Oh, no rush," replied the warlord. "We can get to know one another a little first."

He manoeuvred his soft body over to a nearby desk and perched on the edge, a company CEO trying to pretend not to be an uptight weirdo.

"You want to get to know me a little?" said Maz with a shiver. You're not gonna make me wear some dress you've had in storage, are you? Something your mother owned, or your ex-wife, or sister, or something?"

"No," said Thunderbeak, blanching and waving away an approaching assistant holding fabric. "Nothing like that. That's ridiculous." He coughed. "But it would be nice to find out a little more about the origin of my meal, the provenance. Tell me, where are you from?"

"I'm from a place called Telford."

"And what is this… Tell-ford like?"

"It is what we describe in the UK as a new town. It was built in the 1960s when people were really into the concept of roundabouts."

"Roundabouts?" said Thunderbeak.

"Small circles of hell that allow drivers to argue more efficiently about whose turn it is to go."

"Wonderful," said Thunderbeak, flapping his tentacles together in delight. "What a marvellously primitive species you are. I always find those are the tastiest."

"It's true. We are pretty primitive. Although we have moved beyond cannibalism."

"Oh," said Thunderbeak lightly, "but this isn't cannibalism. You eat lesser beings on your planet, too, don't you?"

"Yeah, but," Maz began.

"Thought so," cut in Thunderbeak. "This is no different. It's not cannibalism, it is simply good organisation."

"What is your obsession with organisation?"

"I just like to have everything ready, that's all. I'm a single parent and I find the best way to stay on top of my week is to prepare the meals in advance during the weekends. If everyone on my planet can be that organised, just think what we will achieve."

"Single parent?" Maz was surprised.

"Yes. My wife is – alas – departed," said Lord Thunderbeak.

"You didn't eat her, did you?" said Maz, smiling.

Her smile dropped suddenly as she looked at the skin of the Yendoi surrounding their lord. It was flashing in a complex pattern that even Maz could read as, "danger." The lights in Quinton's visor also seemed to strobe in some meaningful pattern.

"No, I did not," said Lord Thunderbeak stiffly.

There was a tense silence, but then the Yendoi warlord broke into a smile. Maz wasn't sure how she knew he was smiling since he didn't really have any lips. Perhaps within that common language, she had already gained an understanding of the many and varied types of alien body language. But whatever it was, she could feel the smile emanating from him somehow. And she could tell it wasn't the good sort.

"Tell me about your child," said Maz. Then she hesitated, trying to remember how octopuses have babies on Earth and wondering if it was the same with the cephalopod-like aliens. "Or do you have more than one?"

"No, no. Just the one, for my sins." He raised his tentacles up to the heavens, and Maz felt a genuine warmth. "She is my little angel," he said.

"I'd love to meet her," said Maz and realised she meant it. She hadn't seen many baby aliens before.

"Of course, of course. My house is your house, for the time being at least. Quinton, fetch the child."

Quinton didn't move, and Maz could almost taste the subtext in the air: something was happening that she didn't fully understand.

"Or perhaps another time," said Thunderbeak, turning away with studied casualness. "She's a little tied up right now."

"The doesn't sound at all sinister," muttered Kamello.

"You know what these children can be like," continued the Yendoi leader. "I think it's best we crack on with your surrender. After all, it's getting quite late, and I would really like to have you all packaged up and popped in the freezer before the end of the day."

"Efficiency is important," agreed Smivil.

"Sure, I understand," said Maz, taking a few steps backwards. "No problem. In that case, let's get it done, shall we? How should I do this?"

Quinton wheeled over and handed her a tablet. She peered at it. It just said "I, Marion Star, surrender on behalf of Dross." This didn't seem grand enough to Maz, so she decided to busk it.

"I, Marion Star, queen of Dross, defender of the Presley Service Station, empress of the Visitor Centre, patron of the Royal Lodge, overseer of the Scrap Heap…"

"None of those are your titles," interrupted Smivil.

Maz ignored him. "…do hereby surrender. On behalf of the Dross, my adopted peoples."

"Fantastic," said Lord Thunderbeak. "Did everyone hear that?" he said, turning to the troops. "Let's give her a round of applause."

The applause was deafening – all those tentacles slapping together like those inflatable thunder sticks at a sports stadium – and Maz wondered if it was possible to have a weirder reason for losing your hearing than suffering a standing ovation from a consortium of cephalopods. Then, Thunderbeak lifted two limbs and, just like that, there was silence.

"Send out the Preparators," he cried. "Let the invasion begin."

The Yendoi sprang to life, barking orders in their own language. All around the dark room, black monitors – like phone screens in night mode – were woken as the Yendoi began swiping and prodding at them with their tentacles. In the middle of the room, an image appeared, rendered in 3D.

The Presley Services.

Maz couldn't believe what she was seeing.

"What's this," she said.

While they had been travelling to surrender, their alien captors had landed on the planet. The car park was filled with the Yendoi attack fleet, the service station surrounded by troops and huge Preparator machines.

"Heavenly Grud," said Kamello.

Maz felt her heart sink. She had spent a lifetime suffering bullies like Thunderbeak, and now everyone would pay the ultimate price for her failure. But while she still drew breath, she had no intention of letting him see how desperate she felt.

"I want you to witness this first hand," said Lord Thunderbeak. "Let us head to the landing pod."

"What, really? Is that all the way back at the docking bay?" Maz said, "Because if so, for someone obsessed with efficiency, this is a pretty huge waste of time. Smivil here would have organised a better itinerary."

Smivil bowed. "It is true, there are some inefficiencies in the workflow here."

Thunderbeak darkened. "On second thoughts, perhaps we should save time and get the ball rolling. I wouldn't want to waste any more of your time, after all."

"No," said Maz hastily, "it's fine. We can go back to the bay and travel back to Dross. We're not in any hurry, are we gang?"

But Thunderbeak raised a tentacle and dropped it dramatically, like a Roman Emperor signalling the start of a gladiatorial contest. The doors to the Presley Services opened, and a queue of aliens shuffled out into the open, poked from behind with what seemed to be the equivalent of cattle prods. They were directed towards the bladed machines.

"Nice work," said Kamello. "Always helps to enrage a despot, I find. If history has taught us nothing else, it's that psychopaths respond really well to personal criticisms."

But Maz was oblivious to Kamello's torrent of sarcasm: she was distracted by something happening on-screen. From among the throng of Dross, Zono appeared. Kamello squinted at the screen, all three eyes peering at Zono.

"What is he doing?" she said, as he charged into the fray, waving one of his weapons.

"Dross!" he shouted. "Attack!"

"Yes!" said Maz.

It was her plan in action. It was actually happening!

One by one, the Dross pulled out a weapon. From gun to gardening implement, from wrench to rocket launcher, everyone was armed with whatever they had managed to conjure up at short notice.

"There are more of us than you," said Maz, turning to Thunderbeak triumphantly. "Surrender now, and I will allow you to leave our planet and take your people – and your daughter – with you safely."

"Oh gee, you got me," said Thunderbeak.

And Maz was too triumphant to notice the tone of sarcasm. She held on to Smivil, squeezing the soft-bodied alien like someone grasping an executive stress toy.

"We did it!" she cried. "We actually did it!"

"Maz," said Denx in a warning tone.

Maz didn't hear.

"Thunderbeak," she said, "order your troops to retreat."

"Oh, I'm afraid that's not going to happen," Thunderbeak replied. He looked at her almost sympathetically. "Oh dear. Did you really think you were going to beat us? What a bizarre, little deluded world you must inhabit."

Ctan made a clicking sound, and Joubini stepped forward. The warlord gave an order in his alien tongue, skin colours providing additional meaning, and the Yendoi advisor flashed a command into a screen. Maz saw the alien captors down on Dross become enshrouded in rippling defence shields. From the surrounding ships, a hundred more aliens advanced until the area was completely overrun by cephalopods.

"What the?" said Denx.

"Oh dear," said Smivil.

The Dross were vastly outnumbered. Even the hot-headed Zono wasn't stupid enough to fire. The plan was over as quickly as it had started. Maz clenched a fist and felt Kamello hold her wrist to stop her from running forward and punching the smug warlord in the eyeball.

"Do you think we haven't encountered resistance before?" Lord Thunderbeak sighed. "I have to say, I'm disappointed. Was this really the best you could do?"

The warlord turned from Maz and spoke to Joubini.

"Tell them there is no need to stun the meat before processing it. Put them in alive."

"Now, come on," said Denx, turning more feral.

Maz pulled herself from Kamello's grasp and put her hands up.

"Please," she begged Thunderbeak, "Don't hurt them. Not yet anyway. I'm sorry. That was all my fault. It was nothing to do with them. If you want to mince someone painfully, do it to me and leave them."

"How very sweet you are," said Thunderbeak. "So thoughtful." His voice became sorrowful. "I can't deny I'm disappointed that it's come to this. But you see, you threatened my daughter. And, I suppose, the meat will taste all the better for having been hard won… if that is what we can call it."

Maz reached her hands up even higher.

"Everyone ready?" she mumbled.

"For what?" said Smivil.

Maz began backing up towards the wall, a look of anguish on her face. "I'm sorry. I surrender. We all do. Just please…"

She reached over to the wall and the light switches and slid her palm up all of them. The room fell into darkness.

"RUN!"

Ctan Thunderbeak roared and lights flashed from his photophores, creating beams of illumination that blinded everyone in their path. Quinton turned up the brightness on his visor lights, and he headed to the switch. He hesitated.

"Turn the lights on," screeched Thunderbeak, still strobing with bioluminescence.

Quinton waited another millisecond before he did as he was told, turning on the big light too so that the Yendoi were blinded even more

"Where are they?" shrieked the warlord, looking around desperately.

"They escaped," said Quinton.

And for the first time, he realised he felt OK.

"What are you doing?" cried Smivil, following as best he could with his large slug foot (which, Maz thought, was surprisingly fast). They raced towards the clamshell vehicle and began clambering in.

"We're escaping," she said, "obviously. He's going to kill us all, anyway. The least I can do is make it harder for him."

"But we're trapped," said Smivil.

"Well, so are they," Maz said. "Watch this." She charged back to the door and kicked the electric panel on the wall. Sparks flew. "They won't be able to follow us now."

Denx stared at her. "What are you talking about?"

As he spoke, the doors slid part-way open and Thunderbeak's guards pushed their tentacles through the gap and began leaking out like wrathful gunk.

"I thought I'd disabled it," Maz said. "That's how it works in films."

"If we get out of this alive," Denx said. "Which we

won't. We really need to have a conversation about your obsession with films."

He went to the panel and fiddled with it for a second. The doors shut with a shushing sound, slicing off a guard's tentacles, which wriggled and writhed on the floor by Denx's feet.

"Now they're locked in," he said, staring at her balefully. He was entirely Warthog, and Maz could see puffs of steam emanating from his nostrils.

"Like you've got your own microclimate," said Maz in momentary wonder.

Still huffing, he picked her up and put her onto the vehicle before jumping on himself just as Kamello pulled away.

"You sure you want to die looking like that?" Maz asked him as they sped away. "It's certainly a choice."

He ignored her, and Maz turned her attention to Kamello, who was weaving around a lot of surprised-looking Yendoi. Suddenly, an alarm started up, filling the frigate with warning sounds. A voice over the speakers rang out. Ctan was speaking to his people.

"Stop them," he commanded. "Or be deep-fried for supper!"

Some of the Yendoi sprang into life, their tentacles reaching out to grasp at Maz and the Dross as they passed. Others climbed onto their own clamshell vehicles and began pursuing, albeit at a safe distance. Maz was struck by how lacklustre their efforts seemed to be.

"They're not trying very hard to capture us," she said.

"I agree," said Sammiel. "They seem reluctant to get close."

"The real troops are down on Dross or trapped in

the room with Thunderbeak," said Smivil. "These are more likely to be civil servants and admin staff. It's not really their forte."

"It's like having a ship full of Smivils," shouted Kamello over her shoulder, her long eyebrows whipping in the wind like ribbons on a kite.

After a long and protracted journey through a ship with miles of corridors, they reached the parking bay and pulled up at the Lovely Cheryl. Outside, Vedna and Roydrick dozed on two fold-up chairs, half-eaten sandwiches clutched in their hands. It looked like the scene of a picnic – albeit one in an aircraft hangar. The lizard aliens woke with a start.

"Och, that was quick," said Vedna cheerfully, stuffing the last bit of her sandwich in her wide mouth and dusting off her legs as she stood. "Are we off?"

Roydrick was still chewing when Vedna started trying to fold up his seat. "All right now, Ved, don't rush me or I'll choke," he said.

"We've got to go," said Maz. "Right now."

She started helping the Pollups to clear up.

"Leave all that," she said, watching Vedna try to retrieve a fallen napkin while Roydrick swept up some crumbs with his foot.

"I can't leave the chairs," said Vedna, hoisting the folded chairs up like luggage.

"Come on!" shouted Kamello, glancing at the hangar entrance as the Yendoi guard speeded in on their clamshells.

Denx grabbed the chairs from Venda and flung them away.

"Oh!" Vedna cried, ready to chase after them. "Those were my auntie's."

The Yendoi were closing in, covering the large distance of the hangar at surprising speed.

Maz took Vedna and Roydrick by the elbows and ushered them up the ramp to the Lovely Cheryl.

"I'll drive," said Roydrick and Vedna at the same time.

"No," said Denx, Kamello and Maz at the same time.

"I'll drive," said Denx.

He headed for the cockpit while Maz and Kamello helped the Pollups to settle on their sticky banquette next to Smivil. Denx switched on the power converters. Lovely Cheryl spluttered into life, chugged briefly, huffed once, and then fell silent.

Denx slammed the console.

"What's wrong?" said Maz. Through the doily window, the Yendoi troops were spreading out, preparing to surround the Lovely Cheryl on all sides.

"It's disabled," he roared, hog bristles sprouting from his cheeks. "The damn robot put the inhibitor on."

Through the cockpit screen, they could see the docking bay door began to close.

"We need to hurry," said Kamello.

"Oh dear," said Smivil, deforming his own hands as he kneaded them in worry.

"An act of senseless bravery is needed," called Sammiel from the cockpit. "Maz, you must do something pointless but heroic. It is the only way."

"Right!" proclaimed Maz. "Leave this to me."

She leapt to the door and poked her head out. The hangar bay was lit with flashes of laser blasts from the Yendoi troops and Maz ducked back inside before a bolt took her head off.

Lord Thunderbeak's voice boomed over the intercom.

"Do not kill the Queen. I want to slow roast her alive!" Maz felt strangely secure upon hearing those words. "But feel free to maim her beyond recognition," he added.

This was less reassuring. Still, she had to do something. She got on her stomach and carefully reached up to open the door again. This time she crawled carefully forward and, risking gun fire, leaned around and under. Just out of reach, the inhibitor sat silent and grey, dimming the Lovely Cheryl's lights and leaving them stuck here like apples in a barrel.

She leaned out as far as she could and tried to reach the box off, but she couldn't get close. The rim of the saucer jutted out too far, making the garage below just out of reach.

"I can't get it off," she called, as though Denx could hear her through the front window of the tourer.

She looked up and saw the Yendoi guard closing in on the Lovely Cheryl. To her right the doors of the docking bay were nearly closed. A laser shot sent her scrabbling back inside the ship. She shut the door and lay on the floor, the others looking at her hopefully. She shook her head.

"I couldn't reach it. It's too close to the bottom."

"Well," said Vedna. "There is another way out."

Maz took a moment to contemplate the puckered flanges. She was in the garage below the living quarters, crouching around the hole where, not too long ago, she had experienced a kind of reverse rebirth through what turned out to be the waste disposal chute. Kamello, Smivil and the Pollups stood over her, expectantly.

"Hurry up!" called Denx from above, as though they had all forgotten the warriors gathering outside.

"My life really is just dealing with one arsehole after another," Maz said. "If I die, please don't tell anyone this is how it happened."

"I absolutely will," said Kamello. "This is going right in the records."

Maz nodded in grim acceptance, took a deep gulp of air like a sea diver and plunged head first into the hole.

She emerged with a gasp and began orientating herself. There it was! The device was almost within reach. She edged out a little more and felt her body begin to slide along the garage floor. Her fingers brushed the inhibitor, but she couldn't get enough of a purchase to lift the unit.

She edged out of the hole a little further. Soon her whole body would be in the chute, but still she couldn't quite reach the unit. By now only her feet were hooked over the garage floor and she wished she had thought to tie something around her waist to keep her from falling out of the hole.

With weary resignation, she unhooked her feet and let the rest of her body slide downwards and into the hole. She could hear muffled cries from above, presumably the others realising that she was going to fall out. But she didn't have time to think. Desperately, she grasped at the inhibitor, trying to gain a purchase.

It was stuck fast.

By now the Yendoi troops had spotted her and were approaching the underside of the vehicle, their weapons pointed at her. Maim her beyond recognition, Thunderbeak had told them, and yet they still hesitated to shoot. Perhaps it was hard to avoid killing with weapons like that. Instead, some of them had lowered their weapons and now they began reaching up to her with their long tentacles, ready to pluck her from the grasping flanges.

She tried again to free the unit, twisting and pulling to no avail.

"Think, Maz," she told herself.

She began investigating the device, trying to find a release mechanism or an off switch. There were a selection of buttons on one edge and she tried to work out what they meant, squinting at the foreign symbols as though it might help her decipher the language. She had a fleeting regret that she hadn't taken that speed learning course, but then she was distracted by a long tentacle that reached up and began coiling around her arm. Another grasped her around the waist and, with her free arm, she smashed the tentacles as hard as she could, shocking the soldier into letting go, and briefly freeing her arm. But it didn't last. Another tentacle soon had her in its grasp, and she experienced a jolt of panic as the tentacles began tugging her towards the ground.

She was being pulled out of the chute, her body sliding slowly out. She reached out with her free arm, desperately trying to pull herself back towards the inhibitor. Her legs emerged from the chute and she knew she didn't have much longer before her whole body was free of its grip. But then she felt a tugging from above.

Someone was holding onto her feet.

"We've got you, hen," came the muffled cry from Venda in the store room above.

"Ngh," Maz managed, that familiar sound returning to her as she experienced what it would have been like to be drawn on a rack by a medieval torturer. She felt every joint in her spine crack and wondered how long before she was torn in two.

Quinton wheeled over as Maz gasped in pain above him. He raised a heavy arm and she realised there was a small gun attached to it. He pointed it towards her and she shut her eyes. It was probably for the best, she thought. Put her out of her misery.

The laser fired and Maz opened one eye. Instead of pain, she felt a loosening. The limb around her waist was falling away, the Yendoi guard who owned it screaming in pain at Quinton's fire.

"Oops," whirred Quinton. He aimed again.

Maz felt her arm become free.

"My mistake," Quinton said. He raised his voice. "I am unused to firing weapons."

If she had had the time to spare, Maz might of thought how lacking in remorse Quinton's excuse sounded. As it was, she was too busy grappling with the inhibitor.

If all else fails, she decided, best just to mash all the buttons. She shut her eyes and pressed everything, and something miraculous happened: the inhibitor lit up red around the rim and Lovely Cheryl's dimmed lights blazed into life, brighter than she'd ever seen them.

The landing legs rose upwards into the craft and Maz felt the engines stir. A tug on her legs told her the others were as excited as she was.

"It's working," Kamello called. "Get your arse back in here now."

"See ya, suckers!" Maz crowed, giving the Yendoi a face-palmed Dross salute as Lovely Cheryl lifted from the hangar floor.

The ship throbbed with a powerful grumbling sound and Maz lurched backwards as it began speeding towards the fast-closing exit.

"OK, pull me up now," she shouted.

She felt another tug on her leg, but her body remained unmoved. Then her other leg was squeezed as someone else grasped her, and she felt more hands trying to haul her in. But the chute held her fast. By now the doors to the hangar were almost entirely closed, which meant Denx would have to manoeuvre them through a very tight gap.

"Pull me up," Maz yelled, panic swelling yet again.

By now the Yendoi were panicking too. Their earlier hesitancy gave way to recklessness as they tried desperately to prevent the Queen of Dross from escaping. They were peppering the air with laser fire now and Maz's body swayed this way and that as Denx swung Lovely Cheryl wildly left and right while also propelling them forwards towards open space.

Her head was going to hit the hanger door, Maz realised. She was going to be decapitated. And if she wasn't decapitated, she was going to be out in space a few seconds after that, freezing her literal tits off.

"Turn on the beam," she screamed, twisting and writhing furiously. "Beam me up, for fudge's sake."

The front of the Lovely Cheryl began emerging from the hanger just as a light glowed all around Maz. It felt like her whole body was being plucked and pinched everywhere all at once.

They had turned on the beam.

It was too late, Maz thought. The beam was so slow and she would be headless any moment now. But, then something surprising happened. With a loud sucking and popping sound, Maz disappeared into Lovely Cheryl's anus just as Denx flew them out of the bay and into the dark vacuum of space.

"Whee!" said Vedna as they were lifted into the air, the ship zipping up and down like a fly evading capture.

Bolts of blue laser fire whizzed by as Roydrick and Vedna helped Maz back up the ramp and into the living quarters.

Denx roared as the ship rocketed out into space at something close to warp speed.

"Good heavens!" said Vedna. "The old girl hasn't sounded like that since we first got her."

"Most odd," said Roydrick.

"Hold tight!" cried Denx, regularly checking his rearview mirrors. The Yendoi cannon were shooting wildly, occasional fire hitting Lovely Cheryl and taking small chunks out of the poor old saucer.

"Steady on there, fella," said Roydrick to Denx. "You'll do Cheryl a mischief if you're not careful."

"What do you want me to do?" said Denx in disbelief.

"I thought they weren't supposed to kill me!" said Maz, her head knocking the ceiling as she clambered into the seat next to him.

"I think that order no longer applies," said Kamello, trying to locate a seatbelt on the sticky banquette.

The tourer was handling like a dream, and Denx was having the time of his life.

"I never knew a craft like this could move so fast," he said.

"Neither did we," said Roydrick, catching an Edward and Sophie commemorative plate as it flew past his face.

"It's got to be that thing Quinton attached," said Maz. "I knew he liked us."

"Robots don't have emotions, I told you," said Denx.

"Ah, whatever," said Maz. "I think he's rooting for us."

"Here we go," said Denx, his attention focused elsewhere. "Prepare for reentry!"

They had a brief moment of triumph when they really believed they might escape. Denx glanced at Maz and they shared a grin of joy. But really what did they think was going to happen? They had nowhere to escape to.

As they dipped downwards and the glowing surface of Dross filled the viewing screen, they felt a rumbling behind them. Denx had just enough time to glimpse a large Yendoi craft coming up behind them when everything glowed red and Lovely Cheryl began to rattle and the atmosphere was breached.

Denx swerved them down to land in a small patch of bog not far from the junkyard.

Everyone not buckled in flumped to the floor. Mostly, that was Smivil. He sat up and began removing a plastic metal-effect participation medal, and a chipped cup that had embedded themselves into his soft flesh.

"That's going to stay with me," he said, tutting at the bits of carpet fuzz flocking his skin.

"Eee! That was quick," said Vedna. "You definitely must have taken a different route to us."

"Yes," agreed Denx. He turned to Maz. "What now?"

The bristly whiskers were now a more manageable scruffy beard, and the warthog face was restored to a slightly rustic handsomeness. He's a bit like Hugh Jackman, Maz found herself thinking.

"I don't know," she said.

"What do you mean you don't know?" said Denx. "Clearly you had some sort of plan? What was that uprising about?"

"Yeah, it might have been nice to have shared that with the group," said Kamello, who had unbuckled herself and moved towards the cockpit.

"Thing is," Maz said, "this wasn't really a plan. It was just a silly last-ditch attempt. I didn't want to get anyone's hopes up. I just needed to stall for time, because Queen Lucan agreed to take in some refugees, and I wanted to give them as long as possible to escape."

"Right," said Denx. "Why didn't you tell us?"

"What would I say? That everything we try is doomed to failure? That I have left my people to be killed by a maniac? I just wanted to save as many as I could. Even if it's nowhere near enough."

"It's something," said Denx.

"These people may even survive to write your story," said Kamello, "to write all our stories. Perhaps one day it will be an entry in the great archive of Dross history. The day we actually fought back."

Maz reached out and pulled the alien into an embrace, ignoring the third eye that stared at her on the top of Kamello's head, and for once, the little alien couldn't think of anything rude to say. She hugged Maz back.

The Yendoi craft appeared behind them and hovered high overhead. Lord Ctan Thunderbeak's voice filled The Lovely Cheryl.

"You've had your fun. Hand yourselves in and we can all get on with our day," he said.

Maz released Kamello and smiled.

"Right," she said. "Let's go and spoil their dinner plans."

CHAPTER 25
THE LAST SUPPER

"IN MANY WAYS, I should thank you," Lord Thunderbeak said.

Someone had placed a throne just inside the Presley Services entrance, and now Ctan Thunderbeak sprawled across it.

"I haven't had this much fun meal-prepping a planet in absolutely forever. You have turned it into a great sport, and for that, I commend you. It is always nice to have felt as though you've earned dinner."

All Maz had to do was step out of the craft to have her brief moment of triumph dampened like a campfire in the rain: it seemed as though the entire Yendoi army had been waiting for them as they alighted. And now she was standing with the rest of the council under the watchful eyes of Thunderbeak's personal guard.

Spread out before them in the parking lot, thousands of Dross citizens stood in queues, one Preparator gleaming for every thousand. Maz felt dejected: even after everything, she had retained some hope that she might win.

But she thought of the Vermies in the tunnels, hiding those refugees. The longer she stalled, the more people she might save.

"Glad to have been of assistance," she said.

Thunderbeak gestured with a tentacle, and a minion passed him a large recipe book, which he started flicking through idly.

"What's the matter?" said Maz. "Can't find a recipe you like?"

"How about a big bowl of stuff it up your bum," muttered Kamello, followed by, "Oi!" when Maz nudged her in the face.

"Oh, I don't know about you," said Ctan, "but I tend to find these batch meals a bit… samey."

"Great," said Kamello. "So you're going to eat us, but you'll be bored doing it. I can't decide if that's better or worse."

"I think it's worse," said Tsin. "I think I'd make for quite a tasty hotpot."

"But that's just it," said Lord Thunderbeak. "It all comes down to meat with some vegetables in a bag."

"I imagine for some people casserole might be boring," said Smivil. "But, I've always favoured a simple diet."

Kamello rolled her eyes at that. "You surprise me."

"Can't say I'm one for adventurous meals either," said Denx.

"All the different cultures living here and you lot would rather just have meat and gravy every night," said Kamello, folding her arms.

"Now that's unfair," said Denx, objecting.

"Oh, really?" said Kamello.

"Dear me," said Lord Ctan Thunderbeak, raising a

tentacle to his body like a swooning southern belle. "The food is bickering. Do stop them."

He gestured to a guard, who pointed a weapon directly at Kamello, the main source of strife.

"Stop!" said Maz.

Thunderbeak turned to her. "How many stay of executions do you think you can get from me? I'm beginning to wonder if you really have any respect for my authority here."

"You know," Maz said, hastily. "I could help you, Lord Thunderbeak."

He hesitated, curious enough to want to hear what she had to say, but reluctant to lose any more control of the situation.

"In what way?" he said.

And Maz knew she had him. "When I was a teenager, I worked in one of my planet's greatest restaurants."

"Do tell," said Thunderbeak.

"It was a wondrous deep fried chicken restaurant," said Maz, "and the food was made using a delicious blend of secret spices – a delicacy on my planet."

Kamello opened her mouth to correct Maz, but Maz put a hand out and covered the curator's face.

"Sounds delicious," said Lord Thunderbeak. "But, no use to me if the spices are a secret."

"Ah, but here's the thing," said Maz, leaning in. "I stole the recipe."

"Clever you," said Thunderbeak. "Give it to my chefs."

"Oh no," said Maz. "I can't do that."

Ctan's flesh darkened a shade and Maz hurried on. "This isn't a batch-cook meal."

"Well then, why are you telling me about it?" Thunderbeak flushed with irritation. "Start the dicing!"

"No listen!" said Maz. "Rather than batch prepping us all, why not allow us here at Dross to treat your people to a feast?"

"Go on," he said, raising a staying tentacle. "But hurry. I'm not stopping the machines again."

Maz spoke quickly. "You're bored of batch-prepared meals, right?"

"I admit, great Lord," said Joubini, stepping forward in a move that was both risky and unnecessary, "we all grow a little weary of the same meals. I admit, too, that many of my frozen meals have lost the labels and so I'm never entirely sure if it will be curry or a pudding when I take it out to defrost."

There was a murmur of agreement from the surrounding Yendoi.

"What do you mean you've lost the labels?" said Ctan Thunderbeak, swivelling left and right to address his people. "Did you not write on the bags with the special pens I told you about?"

There was a guilty murmur as they admitted they hadn't, and the warlord seemed to deflate a little.

"I really do wonder why I bother sometimes."

"I hear that," said Maz. "Leading a planet is not exactly a walk in the park. But here's an idea. Here in our service station we make the best chips in the galaxy – inspired by the King himself. So how about I fry you up some of our Dross in a big vat of oil and treat you to a proper meal? What could be better than breaded Dross and chips? Then you can take away the leftovers and reheat them in your air fryer."

"Air fryer?"

"Don't you have those in space?" said Maz innocently. "Well, if you switch off those machines, I'm sure Denx here can knock you up something similar before you kill and eat him."

"What?" said Denx.

Lord Thunderbeak eyed her warily, then gave a resigned sigh.

"You had better not let me down, Marion. I was looking forward to seeing the Preparators in action, but you have piqued my interest, and I admit I am feeling peckish. Make me this feast, and later I shall chop up those we haven't eaten."

"Sounds great!" said Maz. "Win-win, am I right?"

She turned to Denx. "Denx, have you ever heard of a fondue?"

She turned back to Thunderbeak. "I am gonna throw you the party of your life."

"What the hell are you doing?" said Denx, taking Maz by the arm.

She was giving instructions to some of the service station restaurant workers. "Gather all your herbs and spices," she said, ignoring Denx. He squeezed her elbow a little harder, and she stopped, pulling away.

"Denx, just trust me. I'm buying us a bit more time," she said. "The longer we take to be eaten, the more people can escape through the tunnels."

"He knows about the tunnels, Maz. Or he will do. It's not going to take him long to find everyone."

"And in the meantime," said Maz, "I can do what I can to stop him, and I have a plan. A very loose idea of a plan that may or may not work. So, what I need from you is... Look, are you going to help me or not?"

Denx scowled at her for a few seconds and then looked away.

"Yes, I'll help you," he said.

"OK, here's what I need," she said. "I need a big pan of hot oil. Take as long to build it as you possibly can."

"If you say so."

"We will help the pig man," said the unison of Carabid that had appeared by their side.

"Not you, Taridan," said Maz. "I want you to go and see how Ephew and the Vermies are getting on with the evacuation. Take Matthew and Caroline if you like."

"We will visit the strange dog and the fleshy pupae," agreed Taridan.

"What can I do?" said Kamello.

"Do you know anything at all about spices?" Maz said.

"No, but I do," said a voice.

Maz looked over. It was the chef she had seen in the queue for military sign-up. Tall and slight with incredibly long fingers. Beside her was the pot scrubber with boiled ham hands.

"I can assist," he said.

"Fantastic," Maz said. "Come with me."

An hour later, when Maz returned to check on him, Denx had a working metal saucepan. It was about the size of Belinda's hot tub. The hot tub, Maz realised that Jim and Belinda had spent the night flirting in one evening as Maz put the dishes into Belinda's dishwasher and tried to fend off sloppy advances from Geoff while the kids ran around yelling.

The memory startled her. How far she had come, not

just literally but figuratively, from that person who had been unwilling to recognise what was happening right in front of her nose.

"Happy now?" said Denx as the Dross cooking staff filled the pan with all the oil in the Presley Services. He slouched off before she could answer, still angry about the way the day had gone.

She called after him, but then Smivil approached with a question about the best way to arrange the tables and chairs, and the Carabid had queries about whether the bunting they had hung was too much or not, and Maz found herself caught up in party admin. Organising a feast for your captors in which you were to be the main course was surprisingly complex, logistically speaking. She blew hair from her face and spotted Sammiel approaching.

"Denx is angry with you," she said.

"I think it might be easier," said Maz, "if you just let me know when he's not angry with me."

"Yes," agreed Sammiel, "that probably would be easier. What is it you have done to make him so cross, do you think? Is it your plan to boil all of our compatriots in a large vat of oil? Or is it the fact that you are handing our oppressor the secret herbs and spices recipe?"

"Oh, I don't know," said Maz. "Take your pick. There's plenty to be cross about."

"I believe," said Sammiel, "that things will be OK."

"I'd really like it if you told me that you have some sort of special talent for seeing into the future."

"Sadly, no," laughed Sammiel. "And yet, still, I believe in you."

She reached out and squeezed Maz's arm, and Maz

was struck by how firm her grip was. The fairy alien trotted off just as Kamello appeared by Maz's side.

"I'd love to see how those two have a conversation," said Maz.

"Denx and Sammiel? They don't need to," said Kamello.

"What do you mean?" said Maz.

"They are linked. That's the kind of relationship they have."

"Like psychically?"

Kamello shrugged. "Something like that, I guess."

"Oh, right," said Maz. "I see."

"No," said Kamello, "I'm not sure you do."

Ephew appeared, holding a cup like a lost treasure recently dug from the ground.

"I have great news!" he said, totally oblivious to all the work going on around him.

"You got everyone to safety?" said Maz.

"No!" he replied, still cheerful. "But I did bring you a teaorcoffee."

Maz took this in.

"I don't like to criticise your efforts," she said, "but I believe I asked for that quite some time ago. A pedant might say over twenty-four hours ago. Also, you're meant to be evacuating innocent civilians."

Nevertheless, Maz inspected the drink he handed her.

"What is it?" she said, an eyebrow lifting.

"It's from the Vermies. The slave-drones told me they drink it when they need a little boost."

At this point, Maz decided to ignore the very important lessons she had picked up from years of reading and watching sci-fi about the effects of alien stimulants on *homo sapiens* physiology.

"What harm could it do at this late stage?" she said.

"I could suggest some things," said Smivil.

Maz drank it down like an espresso and gave a little "ah" of satisfaction.

"Pretty tasty," she said.

"They excrete it from their glands," said Ephew.

"Great," said Maz, putting the cup down. "I mean, it's my own fault, really."

"I've had three of them already," said Ephew. "Ooh! Bunting!"

He cantered off to help with the decorations. Or at least, that's how it seemed to Maz, who suddenly felt quite hot.

"Can anyone else taste their tongue?" she said.

The willowy chef arrived clutching the trays of breadcrumbs and began heating the oil.

"It'll be like a retro fondue party," said Maz, rubbing her hands together. "I've always wanted to try one of those. Quite exciting, really."

"She's totally cracked," said Kamello.

Lord Thunderbeak approached the platform and admired Denx's handiwork.

"It really is going to be sad when you have to breadcrumb yourself," he said, turning to Maz. "I wish you could be here to see that."

"Same," agreed Maz. "It would be quite something."

"I believe," said Thunderbeak, "that you have stalled enough now." His huge eyes seemed to pierce her. "I think you have given your people enough time to flee to whichever little hideaway they have found. Rounding them up will take but a moment, but I do applaud you for trying."

"What can I say? These are my people." Maz raised her voice, adding steel to her tone. "And I will always fight for my people."

Silence fell. All eyes on her. Each being stopped and turned to see what the Queen of the Dross would do next. Maz shifted on her feet. She really was feeling quite warm.

"What are you doing, Maz?" murmured Denx.

"Is anyone else sweating?" said Maz. "I'm really sweating."

She raised her voice. "Lord Ctan Thunderbeak," she said, unable to stop herself. "I challenge you to a fight."

If Ctan had eyebrows, he would have raised one.

"You challenge me to a fight?" he repeated.

"Correct," Maz said, feeling her vein throbbing in her neck. "One ruler to the next. You and me. Let's fight this out."

"This is too amusing," said Thunderbeak. "You really are quite a poppet, aren't you? I shall be almost sorry to eat your fried carcass."

"As your adviser," said Smivil. "I don't advise this."

"I'm serious," Maz said, prodding the rubbery Yendoi warlord with an index finger. "I, Marion Star, Queen of Dross, would like to invite you, Lord Curtain Thunderbum, out for a fight."

Somewhere inside, the rational part of Maz's brain told her this childish insult wasn't a good idea. But right now, the rational side of her brain appeared to have been abducted by a younger version of herself. A version who thought nothing of starting a fight she couldn't win.

The octopus alien paused – tentacles still, giant eyes unblinking – and then, slowly, a low chuckle emanated from his beak.

"You want to fight me?" he said.

The rational part of Maz's brain was currently bound and gagged and desperately trying to scooch the metaphorical kidnap chair towards an exit. It was no use: teenage Maz remained in control.

"Sure! Why not?" she said. "Or are you afraid? How do you call someone a chicken on this planet?"

She turned to the members of her council, who were regarding her with varying levels of disbelief, horror and amusement.

"Is there a special scaredy animal?"

"Chicken works," said the marshal.

"We understand the reference to your headless edible birds," said Zono.

"Well, do you want to fight or not?" said Maz. "Or are you too chicken? Buck-caww!"

She made chicken movements with her arms tucked in, elbows out.

"What are you doing?" said Kamello.

"I don't know," said Maz, bouncing like a boxer before a bout, "but it feels good. I can see electricity."

She gave another "Buck-caww!" and started strutting towards Lord Thunderbeak.

"Stop that," he said.

"Here's the deal, Thunderfarts," said Maz. "If I win, you leave and never come back. If you win, I'll breadcrumb everyone myself and fry them for your dinner."

"What did you call me?" said Thunderbeak.

"I'm not sure this is a good idea," said Smivil.

"Well," said Maz, "it's that or this creature's starter, and frankly, I'm rather fed up with being shoved around. I don't know about you, but where I come from, we put bullies like this in their place."

"Where you come from?" said the Yendoi warlord with disdain. "Your puny, pathetic planet."

"No, I'm not talking about my planet," she said. "I'm talking about the Trenchmire estate in Telford. I'm talking about the years I spent in care," she said, "I'm talking about Dross. Because we Dross don't like bullies. Do we?"

She turned around to the captives, who avoided eye contact. There was an awkward silence. Somewhere someone coughed.

"So there!" she finished, determined to be her own hype woman. "Hey Quinton," she called. "You there, mate?"

Quinton wheeled reluctantly out from around the back of a Yendoi warrior.

"There you are!" said Maz. "Quinton, what is the chance I'll win this fight?"

"To win this fight," said Quinton, a tinge of regret in his voice, "would require a set of highly unlikely circumstances."

Maz put out a hand. "See! You're in no danger, Lord Bladderweak."

Thunderbeak glowered at her and Maz felt the buzzing in her brain turn up a few notches, but then he seemed to relax.

"I accept," he said, lifting his beak. "Why not? It's a bit of fun. If you win, we will leave everyone unharmed."

"Everyone unharmed," repeated Maz. "And you'll bog off for good and not return."

"And if I win – which, I'm afraid to tell you, I certainly will – then you will assist in the bread crumbing, and," he added, "you will provide your secret mix of herbs and spices."

"Fine," said Maz, "I was hoping it wouldn't come to that, but fine."

"And my people will revel in our victory and enjoy your flesh for weeks to come!"

"Deal," said Maz.

She headed over to her council.

"It's going well, isn't it?"

The council stared at her in appalled horror.

"Are you a complete idiot?" said Denx.

"Not a complete idiot, I hope," said Maz.

"You can't fight him," said Denx.

"It's true," said Marshal Tsin. "I've seen more muscle on a prawn."

Zono nodded, his armour clanking. "He will crush you to death with his tentacles and then snap off your tiny head with his beak."

"Well, in that case, I won't be able to help him breadcrumb everyone, will I? So in a way, I'll still win," said Maz, which was the smartest retort she could come back with at this particular juncture.

At that moment Taridan appeared with Matthew and Caroline.

"The evacuation continues," they said in unison. "The fleshy beasts herd the big folk into their dark caverns. The Queen has nearly reached the season finale."

Maz turned to the council. "While I'm causing a

distraction, you all escape with as many citizens as you can."

"We're not leaving you," said Marshal Tsin.

"Yes, you are," said Maz. "That's an order." She paused, head tilting. "Can I say that? I feel like I should be able to say that. Gosh, it's hot isn't it?"

She flapped the front panels of her coat, trying to waft in some cooler air and looked expectantly at her council. They weren't moving.

"I'll say it again: that's an order."

Denx turned more pig-headed and shifted angrily on his feet.

"No way I'm going anywhere," said Kamello. "I want to see how this debacle ends."

"I need to keep a tally of your bill so far," said Smivil. "This has been an expensive day for you. That return flight, now this party. The pan alone is going to–"

"Please," said Maz, putting a hand on Smivil's squidgy arm and giving them all an imploring look. "I want you all to get out. Live to see another day."

They stared at her. She was deadly serious now, in spite of the drugs that were coursing through her veins.

"Look, I've never had a family before. I was passed from pillar to post as a kid, never really wanted anywhere, never really belonging anywhere. I went to more schools than I can count on one hand, and I've had a hundred-and-one temp jobs. Wherever I go, whatever I do, I'm the outsider, the rough kid who didn't have a family. I thought I'd found one with Jim and the kids. But it turned out that when Jim promised me the life of my dreams, he meant that recurring one I have where I'm drowning in a sea of dirty underpants in the school gym and the whole class is laughing, and then I realise I'm actually naked and I start crying and then all my teeth fall out."

She blinked.

"What I'm trying to say is, you're the closest thing to a family I've ever had."

"We've known you for like a week," said Kamello.

"And I'd really like you to save yourselves, so that when I get suffocated by a giant squid, I know that at least you all got away – even if they eventually hunt you down like dogs and eat you for tea."

"That speech was probably worse than the last one," said Sammiel, stepping out from behind Marshal Tsin's lobster tail. "But we understood the sentiment, even if we will ignore the request. We will stay with you, Maz Star. Not because you are our Queen, but because you are a person we have spent a week with and quite like."

"That was a compliment this time, right?" said Maz.

"I think that's as good as it gets, soft shell," said Marshal Tsin giving Maz a friendly punch with the big claw and sending her staggering back a few steps.

"I am ambivalent about you as a person," said Zono. "But I will stay because to leave would be cowardly. And also pointless."

He gave Maz a Dross salute, and Maz returned it without mentioning the trickle of emotional snot that was running down from his nose towards his purple lips.

"Your death will cause considerable paperwork," said Smivil. "I will act as witness to save on the cost of a notary."

"I appreciate that," said Maz, giving his soft arm a sisterly nudge.

"We will also stay," announced Taridan along with

the other Carabid. "To witness the spectacle of your demise. And then we shall gather your belongings and keep them with the rest of the Scrap."

"Thanks gang," said Maz. "I'd be honoured."

Ephew said nothing. He was too busy crying, and Maz couldn't help patting him on the head.

"You've been a really good boy," she heard herself say. "Even though I think maybe the drugs you gave me made me offer an octopus out for a fight. But don't be sad, because I've got one more job for you."

He looked at her eagerly.

She nodded towards the area that was being cleared for their fight. "Let Bug stretch her legs over there."

"You got it," Ephew said, darting off.

Maz looked around for Denx but as usual he had gone off somewhere.

"Well," she said, feeling disappointed. "Looks like it's time to have a fistfight with an eight-limbed sea creature.

She did an arm stretch.

"What could possibly go wrong?"

CHAPTER 26
FIGHT

THE SPECTATORS FORMED A RING, and Maz Star, Queen of Dross, and Lord Ctan Thunderbeak, warlord of the Yendoi, stood face to face.

"I look forward to defeating you, puny girl," said the Yendoi warlord.

"Puny girl, eh?" said Maz with a flicker of a smile. "Yeah, you're right. I've always been a puny girl."

She turned to the crowd, once again becoming her own hype woman – the teaorcoffee Vermie gland drink still making her feel like someone had lit all the hems on her clothes.

"But here's something he doesn't know about me. I grew up in care, bouncing from one foster home to the next, in and out of different schools–"

"You have already said this bit," chorused the small voices of the Carabid.

Maz ignored them, determined not to lose her momentum.

"–Always in trouble, always dodging the bullies.

And if there's one thing I know, it's how to fight like a girl, because fighting like a girl is a serious business."

She clapped her hands together like a sumo wrestler preparing for a bout, rolled her neck, and gave Thunderbeak her meanest stare.

"Right, let's do this."

He eyed her with amusement.

"Let us begin," he said, and they moved closer and began circling.

Maz assessed the most obvious targets. The Yendoi leader had rows of gold hoops on what Maz continued to assume were his ear flaps. Really, they could be anything, and she didn't like to ask at this late stage. For all she knew, it was where he kept his testicles – or worse. But whatever they were, she was willing to bet they were delicate, and so the first thing she did was reach out and rip out two of his ear-slash-testicle rings. The second thing she did was slash her fingernails across his face.

Thunderbeak screeched in pain and staggered about, blinded by the nail scratch. Seizing the advantage, Maz reached out and grabbed a fistful of breadcrumbs from the tray, throwing them in his face and Thunderbeak hollered in agony as the secret blend of spices stung his eyes and soft, bleeding skin.

"What are you doing?" he cried.

"Fighting like a girl," she replied.

"How dare you! Stop her."

He shrieked the last instruction in the general direction of his troops but, on a signal from his chief adviser, Joubini, they stayed back. Nearby, Quinton's wheels whirred on the spot, his large arms hanging heavy at his sides, the lights in his visor flashing like little distress signals.

Enraged and in pain, Lord Ctan Thunderbeak underwent an alarming transformation. Where before he had been wide and sprawling, he became tall and slight, his eyes narrowing to slits, his skin darkening to a thunderous black. His limbs flared out into a skirt, and then back into a tight formation, as though someone were shaking the rain from an umbrella. If you asked Maz to draw an octopus dressed as a vampire, the vision before her was what she would have attempted. And now that vision swooped towards her billowing like a furious Victorian woman.

"Oh, fudgecakes," Maz said.

Behind her, she could hear members of the Dross council shouting advice.

"Poke his eyes out," said Kamello.

"Save his earrings for the Scrap," cried the Carabid.

"Try not to do any structural damage to the building," said Smivil.

And then she was aware of another sound. She looked around. It was the people of Dross, the workers in the Presley services, the warriors who had been press-ganged into duty, the civilians who hadn't managed to get away.

They were cheering for her.

All of them, clapping their limbs, or flapping their whatevers, hollering and hooting, cawing and cackling. The cluster of bubbles floated up high overhead, showering down droplets of something that Maz hoped was soap and not a bodily function. Rolypoly Lemonsqueezy was there, waving his crutches. The giant eyeball was flapping his eyelids, and the birdlike aliens, still scorched from the parade, clacked their beaks.

Everywhere were faces she recognised – from the carpet-faced aliens she had met on day one, to Taridan and the shiny-shelled Carabid. Sammiel smiled. Kamello winked one of her eyes. And somehow, it gave Maz courage. Whatever shape or form they took, the Dross were supporting her, however their culture deemed appropriate. Even if that meant some of them were making gestures a human might consider obscene (she didn't want to think about why the insectoid doctor seemed to be opening his white coat to flash her). It was all strangely heartening.

As the Yendoi warlord glided towards her, Maz spotted Bug squatting near a tray of breadcrumbs, and she felt a sudden calm descend. Because, yes, Maz did fight like a girl, and fighting like a girl had taught her something important.

She hadn't met a person alive who didn't squeal like a guinea pig if you pulled their hair.

She reached over and grabbed the short tentacles on Thunderbeak's head, gathering as many as she could between her fingers. Surprise and forward motion lifted his suckers from the ground before he could anchor himself and Maz span, pulling him round in circles as quickly as she could, the teaorcoffee lending her an inhuman strength.

Lord Thunderbeak shrieked. He spread out his long tentacles and tried to wrap them around Maz to pin her arms down, but her momentum was growing and he shrieked again in pain and instead reached up to try to disengage her grip on his small tentacles. That's when Maz let go. Like a hammer at the Olympics, Lord Ctan Thunderbeak, mightiest warlord of the Yendoi, prime planet of the Sinovian Prelode, flew through the air.

Unfortunately, despite Maz's best efforts and the power given to her by the gland excretions of the Vermie slave-drones, it turned out she was still a puny girl. Lord Ctan Thunderbeak landed with a heavy thud just a few metres from where Maz had let him go.

"Is that all you have?" he said.

He lunged out and grasped her with a tentacle, engulfing her like a boa constrictor. Maz tried to take a breath and discovered her lungs had been put out of service. She felt herself going red, as though all the blood from her body had gathered in her head. Soon, she would pop like a pimple, she thought.

"Who needs a Preparator for such a tiny scrap," said Thunderbeak, lifting her off her feet and dunking her in a tray of flour. "I will fry you whole." He dunked her into a dish of beaten eggs. "And alive."

He rolled her in breadcrumbs and brought her close to his face.

"Ngh," Maz said, her breath almost spent.

That's when she saw Bug's mess. The qipoc had done her business in the least sanitary spot next to the breadcrumbs. With painful effort, her veins bulging in her neck, Maz put her feet on the edge of the hot saucepan and put all of her weight into pushing as hard as she could. The movement was enough to free her very slightly from Thunderbeak's grasp and she took the opportunity to gasp a lungful of air before biting down on his tentacle and ripping off a chunk of flesh. She pushed again with her legs.

It wasn't much, but it was enough to send the Yendoi backwards. With a cry of surprise, he lost his balance and landed heavily on Bug's poop.

"Watch out," shouted Ephew. "It's explos–"

There was a bang and Ctan Thunderbeak was propelled into the air, his limbs flailing. Maz flew up with him and saw the waiting funnel of the nearest Preparator yawning below. Thunderbeak let go of her. Maz watched as he landed in the opening and tried to save himself. But as he grasped onto the edges of the chute, the new anti-stick coating prevented him from gaining a purchase.

"Help me!" he squealed. "Quinton!"

Quinton wheeled forwards and turned the machine on. Ctan Thunderbeak slipped downwards and into the machine. With a whirr and a clunk, giant rings of octopus fell from the machine into the tray of breadcrumbs and the blend of secret herbs and spices.

Maz waited for gravity to send her plummeting after him. It took her a second to realise she wasn't falling. She looked up and saw the pointing finger of Elvis Presley holding her long jacket. Far below, the chief adviser Joubini reached out a tentacle and tipped the chopped pieces of his lord into the waiting vat of oil. The room was filled with the scent of salt and pepper squid.

"Now your planet belongs to me," the adviser laughed, growing in stature and assuming control in the blink of an eye. "Guards, begin the slaughter!"

"No!" shouted Maz from her vantage point.

But the Yendoi soldiers had recovered as though nothing had happened.

Maz couldn't believe it. She had won, yet still she had lost. She watched helplessly as the Dross in the building and out in the spaceship parking area were shoved up the ramps towards their certain fate.

Denx looked up at her, turning from feral hog to normal-sized man, hopelessness etched on his face. "It's over," he said.

And then he fell on his bum.

CHAPTER 27
WHOLE LOTTA SHAKIN'

A RUMBLING shot through the Presley Services and out into the parking area as tremors shook the building.

"Woah!" said Ephew as he staggered and fell, the vibrations sending him off balance.

In fact, everyone on legs fell to the ground, even the little Carabid, who rolled and tumbled like dust bunnies.

The tremors grew strong enough to send the King rocking so that Maz found herself swinging precariously, the seams on her jacket straining. And then the ground outside in the parking area seemed to turn to liquid, rolling like a sea before it began to open up.

Within seconds, every Yendoi troop carrier and fighter craft in the carpark had disappeared into a giant sinkhole.

"Haloo!" called a voice.

Once the worst of the swaying was over, Maz found

the source of the sound and smiled. Queen Lucan poked her pale fleshy head out of a hole in floor.

"We decided perhaps we could be Lando after all," said the queen. "The life force expired on your lantern box and we grew bored."

Outside, sinkholes continued to appear, gobbling up each Yendoi ship in turn. And from each came Queen Lucan's grub-people. Maz could hear them even through the acrylic vestibule as the Vermies lumbered onto the Yendoi, flattening the smallest under the weight of their pale blubber and disabling the larger ones with a swipe of their lower bodies.

Back inside, Taridan and the Carabid stepped forward, unsheathing their weapons. No one had thought to frisk such small creatures, and now Joubini, the new chief warlord, was met with a wall of miniature weaponry.

"You will surrender or die unpleasantly," the Carabid said in their choral unison.

"Don't be ridiculous," said the new warlord. "Look at those weapons. I imagine it's like being hit by a pebble."

"This is your last chance," they said.

"I'd do what they say," called Maz.

"Never," said Joubini.

And so, the Carabid shot him."

―――――

"Holy cow!" said Maz.

She was staring at a huge hole in the side of the Presley Services. And in front of that hole was the place where Joubini, the new Yendoi warlord had been.

The cluster of bubbles arrived and absorbed her, bringing her back down to the ground and giving her a quick wash to remove the breadcrumbs at the same time.

"How can guns that tiny do so much damage?" Maz said, stepping from the soapy orbs.

"We made them from the Scrap," the Carabid said proudly. "And no one should underestimate the Scrap."

Maz's gaze slid from the wall to the rest of the service station. All around, Yendoi warriors were surrendering under the gleeful supervision of Zono and Marshal Tsin, raising their limbs and glancing nervously at the platter of crispy calamari that was once their leader.

"What are you going to do with all those breadcrumbs?" said Smivil. "They're going to cost you a fortune."

"That's okay," said Maz. "I'm sure I'll be able to pay for it with the money that we make from fixing up the octopuses' vessels. If they want to leave this planet, they're going to have to pay Denx and the bugs."

"Fairly sure that money will belong to Denx and the Carabid," said Smivil.

"Sure, right," said Maz, nodding. "Well, I guess… add it to my bill. In the meantime, why don't we have a feast?"

The Marshal looked at the octopus rings and turned pale. "I don't eat seafood."

"Doesn't appeal to me now you mention it," agreed Maz. "In fact, you know what? I think I might be a vegetarian now. There's too much risk I might accidentally eat one of my subjects."

"Ho ho, very good," said Smivil. "Because we all

know there aren't any sentient vegetable beings on Dross."

Sammiel stepped forward, and Maz smiled. "You told me it would be alright."

"Yes," agreed Sammiel.

"How did you know?"

"I believed in you," shrugged Sammiel. "Also, what choice did I have at that stage but blind optimism?"

Maz searched the crowd. "No Denx? Don't tell me he's still angry."

"He is prouder of you than he can express," said Sammiel. She gestured to the council. "They all are."

Kamello shifted uncomfortably. "It was pretty badass," she conceded.

"Unwise but effective," said Smivil.

"I thought you were bloody marvellous, soft shell," called Marshal Tsin. "Never seen better."

"Well, it wouldn't be the Goffijn Shove without the shove, would it?" said Maz.

"I really thought you would die," said Ephew, giving her a happy hug. Bug, who was stationed around his neck, licked her face. "I'm glad you didn't."

"Thanks to you and Bug," Maz said, her voice muffled by the cuddle.

"I too was expecting to witness your demise," said Zono, "given your poor levels of fitness and your feeble build."

"Yes," agreed the Carabid. "But you are like the Scrap and shouldn't be underestimated."

"Thanks, gang," said Maz. "It really means a lot to hear that."

She reached out and gathered as many of the Dross as

she could into an embrace. She glanced up and noticed the cluster of bubbles was shedding the breadcrumbs, raining down soapy herbs and spices like confetti. Then she jumped on the base of Elvis, the teaorcoffee still giving her a surfeit of energy, and addressed the Dross.

"Listen up, people," she called. "Spread the word. Dross is no longer a planet to be pushed around. We don't give in to bullies, and we won't surrender any longer."

There was half-hearted applause from some of the Presley catering staff.

"What did she say?" said someone near the exit.

"We will miss you," said Sammiel.

"What do you mean?" said Maz, turning. "Why?"

Sammiel gestured towards the Pollups, who were waiting near the door.

"We're ready to take you back home now," said Vedna.

Roydrick waved. "Now that the Lovely Cheryl's been fixed, we'll get you home in a jiffy – so long as Vedna doesn't get us lost again. Ouch," he said as Vedna elbowed him.

"Oh," said Maz, "right. Good."

She smiled tightly.

"What have you missed most about Telford?" asked Kamello with a level look.

"Er…" began Maz. "Hard to say, really."

"Is it the Scrap?" suggested Taridan. "You mentioned 'the tip'. I would miss that."

"Not particularly," said Maz.

"People will be missing you," said Ephew. "I wish I knew what that was like."

"Yes, they will," said Maz. "I'm sure some of them will."

She tried to think of someone. Inca and Aztec? Would they miss their dad's girlfriend? The woman who had raised them for the past few years? The person they had terrorised in a million tiny childish ways? Maybe. And what about Jim? The man who had promised her the earth and handed her Telford. Belinda? Belinda might miss her, Maz thought. She might miss having someone to listen to her complaining about Geoff. Someone to take in a parcel for her if she was out when the postie arrived. Belinda and Jim might miss having someone to sneak around behind.

She turned and Denx was there, still and silent, watching her.

"OK, you know what?" she said. "I think I'm going to stay a bit longer."

He blinked, looking confused, and Maz grinned.

"So you're not going to return home?" said Ephew, confused.

"Of course," she said. "I can't stay here forever. That would be ridiculous." She made a desperate stab at a casual laugh. "But I haven't had the celebratory feast yet – assuming we can find something safe to fry – and I haven't seen the town yet. Does Dross even have a town?"

"This is excellent news," said Smivil, "because we have a lot of work to do."

"Yes, we do, Smivil," said Maz. "First thing we need to do is start working towards democracy. I'm thinking – ideally – with me as some kind of figurehead. Preferably more like the ones on the Continent, who get to live pretty normal lives and then abdicate at sixty.

Anyway, I'm sure you and the other nerd aliens can iron out the details–"

"No," interrupted Smivil. "It is excellent news because we actually have our next surrender booked in, but after that speech you gave, it might complicate things a little." He waved his ever-present tablet. "I've just had a message from the high commanders of the Tantorian army, and they're not best pleased."

"I can't think why," said Kamello.

"The agreement was that the Yendoi would turn everyone into batch-cook meals and then the Tantorians would be paving over the planet to use as a giant sonoball pitch. They are hosting the Galaxy Cup this time round, and they are keen to have a venue that is truly galaxy-class. If there happened to be any beings left alive, we'd agreed to become slaves and work the turnstiles. Unfortunately, we did give them our word, and in legal terms, your word very much is your bond since we voice stamped it with Gyan T'Fellan binding tape."

"Right, so after all that, we're about to be taken into slavery?" Maz's mind flashed up a gold bikini and neck shackle. "OK, well, I guess we'd better come up with a plan then, hadn't we?" She put an arm around Smivil's cloaked shoulders. "Because I'm the Queen of Dross, and no one messes with my people."

EPILOGUE

QUINTON, standard-issue robot of the Sinovian Prelode, whirred. He had been resting in low-power mode, and now it was time to reload his secondary functions – to regain mastery over his giant limbs and his speedy wheels. He could feel his circuits pulsing with energy, signals sending messages to the things he had put into hibernation in a bid to save as much energy as possible. There was no charging bay here; he would need to be frugal with his battery reserves until he could find something that could be jury-rigged into some kind of power socket.

He felt a strange feeling in his stomach. Except of course he didn't have a stomach. Butterflies again, he wondered? No, not this time. It was something else. And then the memory returned, a detail his power-saving mode had thought unimportant.

Except it wasn't unimportant. The strange feeling in his stomach represented the most important thing to ever happen to Quinton. It was the reason he was here, hiding on this backwards planet with its constant drizzle and its depressing buildings and its strange, chaotic people.

He had hidden in the old ship between their piles of stuff. The owners hadn't noticed him sneak in while they slept off their fried meal. Wedged in between commemorative tat, he might as well have been a lampstand or a pile of fading royal plates. The strange feeling persisted, and Quinton sighed. He supposed he would have to face up to what he had done at some point. And now, what he had done was tapping at the inside of his chassis.

He reached across with his huge hands and opened the door to his stomach compartment.

Tentacles blasted outwards, like innards spilling from a shelled soldier – like an alien erupting from a chest cavity – but the limbs slowed, began feeling around at the edges, blind and searching, tentative, exploring.

"You can come out," whirred Quinton.

And with a sudden plop, she did.

She sat there on the murky floor of the old touring ship, a little dazed from her nap, wide eyes making an inventory of the room. On the sides of her mantle, her little fin-like flaps wafted out rhythmic breezes. Even to a human eye she would be adorable. Quinton had no opinion, save that he knew he wanted to keep her safe. Her mother, Lady Tula, had changed his programming. Empathy had made him understand the danger the little Yendoi was in.

"Princess," he said. "We must find your mother."

But the Yendoi warlord's daughter wasn't listening. She was looking up at something. Quinton followed her gaze and felt the butterflies return. A lizard-like being stood over them.

"Roydrick," said the lizard-like alien. "I think we might have a wee problem."

Thank you for reading the first book in Maz Star's adventures. If you enjoyed it, I'd really appreciate a review, which makes a huge difference to people finding the book.

Book two is coming soon!

ACKNOWLEDGMENTS

This book started as a short story that I wrote a long time ago. Seeking a palate cleanser from writing about dead people (as a crime author under my KJ Lyttleton pen name), I pulled it out of the metaphorical drawer and discovered there was a whole other world waiting for me, much of it drawn from my subconscious thanks to all the funny writers who have gone before. Jane Austen, Douglas Adams, Terry Pratchett, Kurt Vonnegut, Jasper Fforde, Barry J Hutchison (and all those I've no doubt forgotten to mention), thank you for infecting my brain with your brilliance. I hope the outcome doesn't cause any grave turning (for the dead) or dark nights of the soul (for the living).

Also not to blame are my friend and editor, Sophie Lazar; my sister and early reader Caroline Battersby, and Darika Ahrens. My screenwriting crew always keep me fully stocked with love, belief and constructive criticism. Oliver Battersby, Gemma Cartwright, Debs Nock, Elaine Frieman Herbert and Richard Knightwell gave vital and helpful feedback at the early stages.
Thank you.

Susan D Smith constantly patches up all my broken parts and makes me a better human. Thanks Sue.

Big thank you to my lovely newsletter subscribers, who have joined me on the journey and sent me many kind messages along the way. You can be part of the gang over on shinykatie.substack.com if you fancy.

And, of course, my husband Alex Milway, who copy edited and did the cover design and was generally excellent. This book is for you.

Printed in Dunstable, United Kingdom